Culture and Philosophy
in the Age of Plotinus

D1453488

Classical Literature and Society

Series Editors:
Michael Gunningham & David Taylor

CLASSICAL LITERATURE AND SOCIETY

Culture and Philosophy in the Age of Plotinus

Mark Edwards

Duckworth

First published in 2006 by
Gerald Duckworth & Co. Ltd.
90-93 Cowcross Street, London EC1M 6BF
Tel: 020 7490 7300
Fax: 020 7490 0080
inquiries@duckworth-publishers.co.uk
www.ducknet.co.uk

A catalogue record for this book is available
from the British Library

ISBN 0 7156 3563 8
EAN 97807156-3563-6

Typeset by Ray Davies
Printed and bound in Great Britain by
MPG Books Ltd, Bodmin, Cornwall

Contents

For Noël, and other enthusiasts

Acknowledgements

It would have taken much longer to complete this book had I not been granted a year's sabbatical leave in the academic year 2004-5 by my college, Christ Church, and by the Theology Faculty in Oxford. Much of the preliminary research was done in the course of my Junior Research Fellowship at New College, Oxford 1989-92, and in a subsequent year of post-doctoral research funded by the British Academy. In the preparation of the typescript the advice of Mali Purkayastha was indispensable. I owe much to conversation with Mark Allen, Simon Swain and Julia Griffin, though none of them has seen any part of the present typescript, and I am therefore the only one who can be held accountable for its errors.

Christ Church, Oxford   Mark Edwards

Introduction

This is a book about four men who would all have called themselves philosophers; it is not, however, a book about philosophy as that term is now understood in the English-speaking world. Plotinus we can recognise as a philosopher in the strict sense, if only because he cared nothing for history, literature or any other academic discipline. His contemporary Longinus, on the other hand, appears to have read widely in every discipline that could furnish material to the rhetorician, and is of interest to modern classicists, not as a thinker in his own right but as a diligent connoisseur of other men's thoughts. Porphyry, as a pupil of both, agreed with both in according to Plato the first rank among philosophers. It is under Plato's tutelage (as he claims) that he cultivates poetry, religion, rhetoric, even iconography and a vegetarian diet. None of the fields in which the Greek spirit had found employment under Roman sway was now prohibited to philosophers; in Iamblichus, this spirit goes to work abroad, upon rituals, symbols and hermetic doctrines which had not hitherto been thought to admit of logical exposition. Consequently, the word 'culture', which precedes the word 'philosophy' in the title of this volume, should be taken in the most liberal sense permitted by modern usage.

At the same time, I do not intend to leave aside the logic and metaphysics of these writers, or to offer the reader something akin to the popular works of science which, in sparing us the mathematics, are forced to spare us everything except a few anecdotes of personal toil and serendipity. Plotinus is remembered not for his fitful interventions in the public affairs of his time or the eccentricities of his conduct in retirement, but for the rigour and tenacity with which he handled questions that have not been resolved by the progress of the sciences. If we ignore his gladiatorial exercises in logic and his tireless attempts to conquer the obscurities in Plato, there will be nothing left but a handful of lyrical passages to tempt the anthologist of mysticism. No lucid exposition of his philosophy is possible – and none, so far as I know, has been essayed – without the use of terms which are now exotic even in the writings of professional philosophers. Nor – though this experiment has been tried – does it seem to me possible to approach his thought without some knowledge of the history of philosophy before him: his writings prove what Porphyry reports in his biography, that the reasoning of Plotinus generally took the form of a tacit dialogue with his Greek precursors. We must insist upon the word 'Greek' because it was once the fashion to represent his philosophy as an amalgam of the Greek and the oriental.[1] By calling it Neoplatonism historians imply that it was something other than Platonism; in the opening chapter, however, I hope to show that the antecedents of Plotinian thought are wholly Platonic, so long as we mean by Platonism not the raw matter of the Platonic dialogues, but the precipitate of a series of experiments, both synthetic and analytic, spanning half a dozen centuries and the Mediterranean world from Alexandria to Rome.

In Chapter 2 I review what is known of the lives of our four protagonists, though it will be clear that I am not so inclined as many commentators to regard them either as therapists or as casualties of a distempered age. Historians who believe that a great philosophy cannot fail to leave its mark in the public sphere have gone so far as to make Plotinus the court-philosopher to Gallienus, the counterpart of Longinus in Palmyra.[2] Others, for whom the fall of Rome seems to cast a long shadow back into the third century, have accepted Dodds's portrait of this age as one of ubiquitous 'anxiety',[3] when the ills of the body multiplied the diseases of the soul and the philosopher was never at home except within his thoughts. In my second chapter I hope to show that both opinions are fallacious. We must know the political history of the times to interpret Porphyry's account of his master's career, but Plotinus wrote no treatise on politics, may not have been aware of Christianity and did not surprise the Platonists with a treatise in defence of the plastic arts. Longinus, before his last utopian intrigue, had more intercourse with scholars than with Emperors, and if Porphyry or Iamblichus had a public career, we possess no account of either. On the other hand, it is wrong to suppose that the world had become more odious to the Greeks or less hospitable to philosophers. Greek sophists flourished under Roman Emperors and enjoyed the patronage of thriving cities; those who chose the asylum of philosophy did not do so because the world was any less prosperous or secure than it had been for men of their class at other times.

In Chapter 3 I shall try to show why the thinkers whom we call Neoplatonists would have disowned the prefix. Plotinus held – and Porphyry, after some vacillation, agreed – that the true interpreter of Plato is not the philologist but the philosopher, who parses not the mere text but the truths within it. A myth which a shallow critic like Longinus is content to praise for its artistry must be reconciled with the main body of the dialogue, while even what appears to be the plain sense cannot stand if it fails in rigour or coherence. Hence, as I explain in Chapter 3, the discerning reader of the *Timaeus* will see that the creator and the world of forms are one, or, as Plotinus says in *Enneads* 5.5, that the intelligibles are not outside the intellect. It follows that, whatever Plato seems to say, there was no time when the creator was idle, no time when the unchanging forms did not give life and harmony to the realm of generation and decay. Even the fickle substrate which we call matter was to the Neoplatonists not an independent source of evils, but a mirror to the good.

And what is the good? One thing to Plato, many to his pupil Aristotle. We shall see in Chapter 4 that Plotinus vindicates the ontology of Plato by a prolonged assault on the logic of Aristotle, while Porphyry effects a truce by allotting to Aristotle the sphere of language and to Plato that of being. To both men it was a postulate of reason that, since being is not single genus, it cannot be the ground of, or identical with, the unity of the particular, the genus or the species. Thus we ascend from form or essence to that which is beyond essence, from the intelligible manifold to the supranoetic One. Any chapter on this subject is an exercise in unsaying what has been said of the ineffable, so we need add nothing here, except that both Plotinus and Iamblichus attempted to find a way beyond silence through the theory of number, with results that we shall find to be perspicaciously obscure.

Plotinus leaves it to his commentators to draw a line between soul and intellect. If there is one to be drawn, he thinks it permeable, as we shall find in Chapter 5: in his view, while the sensitive and vegetative powers can function only in the embodied state, the higher, or rational element, never falls from the realm of intellect. Our first descent, he argues, is occasioned not by any fault or lapse but by the law which requires that beauty and form should impregnate the lowest plane of being. Descent becomes fall when the soul forgets that her task is to rule the body and instead becomes subject to it. Iamblichus held that the soul descends entire, and neither he nor Porphyry conceives of its return as a deliverance from all corporeality. Perhaps for this reason, both produced works to illustrate the achievement of perfection in the present world, Iamblichus writing the longer of two biographies of Pythagoras, while Porphyry undertook to show in his memoir of Plotinus that, in everything but the texture of his body, a man of his own time could be the equal or superior of the gods.

Another marriage between philosophy and literature is the subject of Chapter 6. It is no surprise to discover that Plotinus thought the artist a more finished piece of workmanship than his art, and that he quoted the poets only to point a moral. For Longinus, on the other hand, philosophy was but another branch of criticism, and in his *Art of Rhetoric* he exposed himself defiantly to all Plato's criticisms of the sophists. The modern world, at least, has taken a higher view of the treatise *On the Sublime* which has sometimes been attributed to him. Some arguments in support of his claim are offered in this chapter, though I am conscious that they fall well short of proof. What is certain is that Porphyry, while his teacher's example of reading a book for the sake of the book alone was not quite lost on him, was less inclined to believe that there could be art without edification. In his essay *On the Cave of the Nymphs* he assumes that the return of a shipwrecked mariner to his own country can mean nothing to us unless it anticipates the soul's escape from the snares and terrors of the world.

In Chapter 7 we see how Platonism in Porphyry's hands became coterminous with Hellenism – though Hellenism was not, for this expatriate of the Roman age, a creed to set against others, but a universal filter for the best that was known and practised among the peoples of the Empire. In antiquity a nation was often identified by its cults, and the traditions that seem most durable, and therefore most veridical, to Porphyry were those that had been encoded in sacred images and oracular divination. His treatises *On Statues*, *On the Regression of the Soul* and *On the Philosophy from Oracles* aimed not so much to make all religions one as to show that all proclaim the unity of the supreme god and his government of the lower world through acolytes whose function is to purge the soul of all that is not divine.

In Chapter 8 I shall argue that the same belief in the natural supremacy of reason informs the great treatise of Iamblichus *On the Mysteries*. This answer to Porphyry's *Letter to Anebo* has been the despair of modern rationalists, who allege that it sounds the tocsin for barbarism and credulity, drowning even the saner accents of Iamblichus in his Pythagorean and Platonic writings. For all that, it is Iamblichus, not Porphyry, who maintains that every sensible representation of divinity is provisional, that beings who deserve the name 'god' are immune to coercion and bribery, and that reason, not inspiration, is the means by which we attain sure knowledge of them. In short, his notion of deity is the one that has been regarded as the most rational, the least superstitious, from Plutarch's day to ours.

What did Christians make of this, or Iamblichus of the Church? The silence of both parties is remarkable, yet we know that the Emperor Julian, an astringent critic of the 'Galilaeans', was a disciple of Iamblichus who brought others to his court. Porphyry was an enemy and a bugbear, yet it is probable that the majority of his readers in the last century have been Christians. It is not my business in the final chapter to determine whether any alliance can hold between the Christian and the Platonist; I mean only to explain, as a fact of history, why the Christian and the Platonist of the Roman world were antagonists, not confederates. In antiquity philosophers asked not whether there was a god, but how many gods there were, whether any was to be identified with the first principle, whether lesser ones should be worshipped, which (if any) had created the visible world and with what design. On all these questions, Christians and Platonists were occasionally united in their premises and generally at odds in their conclusions. Plato made a philosopher of those Christians who wrote to expose his errors and shortcomings, but it was only in the prophets and apostles that they looked for a full disclosure of truths that Plato had glimpsed by the faltering light of reason – such truths as that the Good is the god of Israel and the incarnate one, who created the world in time and chose at another time to undergo a death that redeems the body with the soul.

In a book of this scope, many topics must be handled superficially or elliptically. If space were given to each of the authors according to his deserts, there can be no doubt that the volume and profundity of Plotinus' works would entitle him to a larger share of the volume than the other three combined. But then we should have another introduction to Plotinus, somewhat shorter and far less erudite than a number of works still readily available in English. I have chosen instead to say most about those texts which seemed to me to have been least understood, like the treatise *On the Mysteries*, or to lie open, like the essay *On the Sublime,* to renewed discussion, or to lend themselves to comparison with works of a different provenance, like the *Letter to Marcella*. I have tried throughout to illustrate what was salient, what was new, what was most enduring in each of the many works to which the third-century Platonist turned his hand. If this book has a thesis, it is that Platonism survived the Roman Empire because it was not a reclusive discipline for the intellect, but a mixing-bowl for all the diverse achievements of the Greek spirit. Greek poetry, Greek religion, Greek philosophy, and even the cohesive sense of Greekness that was soon to be dispelled by Christianity, were not quite dead so long as it seemed possible to combine a Platonic faith in the integrity of the rational soul with the Aristotelian[4] dictum that the mind can become all things.

1

The Platonic Tradition

We speak of the school of Plotinus, the school of Plato, even (though not in antiquity) of a Neoplatonic school. The three senses which the term assumes here might be represented by the figures of a circle, a fan and a cone. A circle, though not yet a school, emerges when a group is held together by correspondence or conversation with a single figure whom they agree in admiring and may be disposed to see as an authority or exemplar. Such an association becomes a school when the dominant figure is no longer the self-appointed autocrat of the dinner-table but the recognised teacher of those within his hearing. This is not to say that he teaches with any formality: John Dillon suggests that in the Roman world a man[1] would often found his school by nesting in an alcove of the market-place, where he cried up his wares to passers-by in the hope of securing an audience.[2] The majority of his listeners would be passing strangers; some who thought him worth a second hearing might become regular satellites; only a few would call themselves disciples. Without rooms or desks, without the right of exclusion or the power to exact a fee, it will not always have been possible to distinguish between the master and his pupils – or, for that matter, between a rival and a colleague. Even those who were famous enough to walk the colonnades of a foreign city, like Protagoras,[3] would find that their train included fellow-sophists who considered themselves their equals; for one who preferred, like Socrates, to hold forth as another man's guest at supper, or to accost the city's great men in the forum, it required some force of character and intellect to sustain the didactic role. If the place of assembly was his own house or that of a patron, the lecturer might be at more of an advantage, though he might defer on occasion to those who outranked him in age or wealth. In any case the term school implies a certain freedom of association, and the likelihood of dispersion, or at least division, on the death of the leader. Pythagoreans, united throughout the Greek world by indissoluble bonds of brotherhood, did not form schools but lodges; where a constellation of lodges acknowledges a common law, a common system of government, a common rule of precedence and succession to precedence, we arrive (as the pagans never did) at the notion of a Church.

Platonic allegiances

Succession or *diadokhê* is, however, the presupposition of that usage of the term 'school' in which the circle becomes a line. It is the ordering principle in the *Lives of the Philosophers* by Diogenes Laertius, where Empedocles (for example) is alleged to have been a pupil of Pythagoras and Diogenes follows Antisthenes in the pedigree of the Cynic.[4] Such constructions, so far as they purport to tell us more than that one man influenced another, are now perceived to be artificial, since there cannot be a designated successor unless there is something to succeed to; and, since the notion that the heir is the depositary of the master's secret wisdom is unattested in the classical world, it is difficult to see what could have been inherited except property in a building or the right to a public emolument. Of the latter we hear nothing until four chairs were established in Athens in AD 176;[5] the allegiance required of the pupils was not to the holder of this chair or to its first occupant but to the long-dead founders of the philo- sophies after which they were named. The entailment of a property, on the other hand, was possible in any age, and until the late twentieth century it was generally supposed that the Academy – the line of Plato's true successors – took its name from a private building in which Plato and his lineal successors gave their seminars. Ancient sources profess to know that the site was chosen for its unhealthy air and that a rubric on the door forbade the visitor to proceed if he was unacquainted with geometry. Nevertheless, it now appears that there may have been nothing in Plato's time but a public park in which he maintained his own residence, while a number of his regular companions set up lodg- ings in the same area.[6] There was no provision for the continuation of his teaching, though his nephew Speusippus inherited his mantle in the eyes of some contemporaries. It is only a late and anachronistic tradi- tion which records that Aristotle took offence because he failed to become the next president of the school.[7]

The first heads of the Academy, if we mean by the Academy the surviving friends of Plato, may not have been the holders of any heritable office, but simply those who had won the confidence and esteem of their fellow-students by the fidelity and acumen with which they expounded the doctrines of the master. It was certainly by this canon, and not by scanning lists of real or putative *diadochi*,[8] that those whom we call Neoplatonists identified their precursors. In Athens they had their own seminary, which of course they styled the Academy, but they did not pretend that this had been the site of Plato's lectures, and they did not regard the occupation of it as a sufficient or even a necessary condition of authority. They had only to consult Numenius, one of the pioneers of their own tradition, for an inventory of those whom history recognised as presidents of the Academy, each more sceptical than the last.[9] One gathers from this polemic that the Academy declined because for each successive thinker the point of refer- ence was the opinion of his own teacher, and the arguments of Plato were not always the first to be laid under contribution in his development, qualification or rebuttal of this opinion. By contrast, the Neoplatonist could embrace more than one succession of masters and pupils, but the master of masters – the base of the cone, in our simile – is the inviolable text.

But words survive because they are malleable to interpretation. In our histories of philosophy the term Platonism stands for that equation of being and value that is encapsulated in the theory of Forms. For us the cardinal text is the *Republic*, in which the many imperfect instances of justice are subjected to the Form of the Just, the 'many beautifuls' to ideal beauty, and all that is – all knowledge and the labour for knowledge, all essences and excellences, and perhaps even being itself – to the remote Form of the Good (506b-517b). If there were not one form presiding over the many beautifuls, the word 'beauty' itself would cease to be univocal; if there were not one form of the Good, the Forms themselves would exist without a purpose, or perhaps for a variety of irreconcilable purposes, so that the universe would cease to be intelligible to any mind that asks for reasons rather than blind causes. This is not a theistic position, at least not inevitably so: God, when named at all (597c), slips into the dialogue so casually that it might be thought good scholarship to ignore him; the doctrine of the immortal soul, though inseparable from the sketch of future punishments and rewards in the epilogue, cannot be pressed too hard because the stated aim of Socrates is to demonstrate the utility of justice without regard to its consequences (358a). The Platonists can thus dispense with God, as some believe that Plotinus did; but neither he nor any professed disciple of Plato before the modern age could do without the soul.

Without the belief in a soul which passes from one life to another, it is impossible, according to Plato's *Meno*, to account for our capacity to deduce mathematical theorems from empirical phenomena. The fact that we are better than our actions, and that our reason can on occasions put a harness on our appetites, is explained in both the *Republic* and the *Phaedrus* by the doctrine of a tripartite soul, in which reason, desire and spirit strive for mastery. In the *Phaedrus* we also learn that the soul's capacity to discover beauty and justice in what is only partially beautiful or just is a proof that the first of its future lives was spent in heaven, where it contemplated the archetypes of these qualities.[10] The work most often cited and expounded before Plotinus was the *Timaeus*, an account of the creation in which, although the eternal Forms define the nature of any possible world, the realisation of the present world is ascribed to a personal god, the Demiurge, who appears to work not only in space but in time.[11] Almost as much in vogue, though barely compatible with any of the others, was the *Parmenides*, in which the objections brought against the theory of Forms seem almost insurmountable (130b-135a). The second half of the dialogue propounds a series of paradoxes engendered by the concept of the One and its coexistence with the Many. Aberrant, ludic or desperately abstruse though it seems to many a modern reader, this discussion passed with many Platonists in antiquity for a serious attempt to grasp the ineffable, and thus at once to complete and to supersede the theory of

Forms entertained in the more elementary dialogues.[12] Today our reading of Plato is selective: we know that his mathematics is naïve and the astronomy of the *Timaeus* hypothetical, while if we wish to make sense of the tripartite soul in the *Phaedrus* and the *Republic*, we are more likely to turn to Freud than to the ancients.[13] No doubt we have the right to cut our own path through the ancient wood, discarding as so much lumber almost everything that detained the original readers, but we cannot then expect or wish the Plato of antiquity to be the same man as ours.

'Our Plato' is, of course, a rhetorical figment; it was also true in the ancient world that two intelligent readers might not agree as to whether a passage in the dialogues was ironic or serious, tentative or dogmatic, propaedeutic or definitive. For this reason alone we should hesitate to speak of Middle Platonism as though it were a philosophy. 'Middle Platonist' is a catalogue heading for authors who made sympathetic and knowledgeable use of Plato's writings between his death and the departure of Plotinus from Alexandria; but even had they all been strict philosophers by temperament or profession, six centuries of work by lone individuals in disparate parts of the Mediterranean world would not have produced a common system. In fact they were not even engaged on a common enterprise: Plato was a model of Greek style in the Roman era, and enjoyed the attentions of orators and essayists who were merely repelled by the viscous prose of Hellenistic teachers. Maximus of Tyre, for example, is not so much a philosopher as a philosophical essayist who is celebrated less for what he said than for saying it well. Plutarch of Chaeronea is a priest and polymath, drawn to the *Timaeus* by a combination of antiquarianism, scientific curiosity and a broad zeal for religion; yet he is only an occasional student of the other dialogues, though he imitates and embellishes Plato's myths of the afterlife. Alcinous, in his handbook to Platonism, never declares his own allegiance to the doctrines which he paraphrases for the unlearned reader.[14] Apuleius, who is credited with a Latin version of it, weaves motifs of transmigration and redemption into his novel *The Golden Ass* (or *Metamorphoses*), and may have composed the most sublime of all Platonic myths in the inset tale of Cupid and Psyche; yet the book is fiction, its purpose and the convictions of the author archly dissembled under a scurrilous veneer. Philo of Alexandria accounts for more than half of the literature commonly described as 'Middle Platonic', yet he seldom mentions Plato, and allows his thought to coalesce with that of his Greek detractors in the service of a book which, even after its translation into eccentric Greek, holds out salvation only to those who keep the Jewish law.[15] If a Platonist is one whose speculations characteristically begin from the words of Plato, our canon of Middle Platonists will scarcely be longer than Porphyry's list of authors who left their mark upon Plotinus:

> In his seminars a scholarly discourse was read to him, which might be from Severus or else from Cronius[16] or Numenius or Gaius or Atticus, or the work

of a Peripatetic such as Aspasius, Alexander, Adrastus or any others who came to hand (*Life of Plotinus* 14.10-14).

No want of originality is implied here, since a philosopher who differed in every point from his precursors would be no more likely to hit the truth in antiquity than today. Nor does it seem that Porphyry is exposing any conflict of allegiance, or suggesting that 'eclectic' might be a better term than 'Platonist' to characterise his master, when, in an earlier sentence, he notes his debt to the Stoics and the *Metaphysics* of Aristotle (14.4-7). In the Roman era it would indeed have been an atypical Platonist who refused to admit any tincture of Stoic ethics into his teaching.[17] No doubt there is an invidious note in Porphyry's report that the Christian Origen, having mastered much the same catalogue of Platonists, had forsaken the Greeks for Christianity, borrowing from the Stoics the allegorical devices that enabled him to prune the absurdities of the Jewish scriptures.[18] Since, however, Porphyry was the first Platonist to make copious use of allegory, his sarcasm would appear to be directed not at the method but at its application; at most he may be hinting that the Stoic philosophy lends itself more easily to misuse.

While it is true that recognised philosophers in the Roman world were generally adherents of a named *hairesis* or sect (a school in our second sense), it is also a maxim of controversy – at least of Platonic controversy – that soundness of doctrine is measured by soundness of reasoning, not by faithfulness to a master, a series of masters or even the founder of the school. It was certainly assumed that nothing incongruous with the premisses and customs of 'the Greeks' could deserve the attention of a philosopher; but the Hellenism to which Plotinus adhered included even the truculent Cynics and the godless Epicureans, as well as Peripatetics and Stoics. On the other hand, the tradition that he chose to cultivate – not a tradition of his own devising, to judge by the library of the young Origen – did not subsume all thinkers whom we might now describe as Platonists, while at the same time it accommodated some who professed allegiance to other masters. A Platonist, as we have said, must commence with Plato, but he will not believe that the text suffices to guarantee a good beginning, or that it is a necessary avenue to every kind of truth.

Some scholars have overestimated the ancient fear of novelty, and have assumed that elasticity or diversity among followers of Aristotle or Plato is a corollary of weakness and error rather than of intellectual health. This is not so likely to be alleged of the Stoics, one of whom declares 'we are not under any king', while another reminds his pupils that it is no mark of proficiency in virtue to have memorised the entire 300 volumes of Chrysippus.[19] This great logician, last of the school's three founders, was of course studied and esteemed within the Stoa, but no commentaries are attested and his critics would appear to have been his most assiduous readers. Admirers of Epicurus cherished his works and kept his birthday, but again they produced no commentaries, and it may be for this very reason that his admirers in the Roman world do not test his opinions with the freedom that was permitted to (or at least assumed by) his earliest disciples.[20] Cynics looked to no text, no legislator, but to a series of examples; as these were examples of independence, defiance and contravention of norms, there could hardly be any notion of discipleship. Cynic railed against fellow-Cynic, sparing not even Diogenes of Sinope, the father though not the eponym of the tribe.[21] The Pythagoreans, a conscious fraternity rather than a school, had always professed to honour the authoritative teachings of their founder; but the sayings attributed to him were protean in form except for those that were fixed in verse so cryptic that it seemed malleable to any interpretation. The more lucid works, pseudonymously ascribed to lesser figures, may have served as an inspiration to the Neopythagoreans of late antiquity (of whom more will be said below), but they were not canonical texts.

It is all the more evident, then, from the pains that were taken in editing Aristotle and Plato, that their partisans attached a much higher value to their works. A public that had hitherto known Aristotle only by his 'exoteric' treatises (designed for those who did not attend his lectures in the colonnade or Peripatos) was introduced to the rougher prose and denser thought of his 'esoteric' discourses by Andronicus in the first century AD.[22] Like Porphyry, who took him as a model in his redaction of the *Enneads*, Andronicus appears to have had no object but to bring order to a miscellaneous corpus; the astrologer and philosopher Thrasyllus, on the other hand, thought not only of the convenience of librarians but of the syllabus to be followed in the instruction of the young Platonist when he divided the works of Plato into tetrads.[23] While the plan that governed the compilation and succession of these tetrads remains unclear, there is evidence that the first at least was intended to be the foundation of a system, and we may reasonably surmise that the order of dialogues in the Thrasyllan corpus mirrors the ascent of the soul from elementary truths to those that only one who has grown his wings can master. Politics is, by contrast, the end of philosophy, while logic and metaphysics are merely staging-posts, in the tetralogical syllabus devised by Theon of Smyrna at the turn of the second century.[24] Those dialogues in which no conclusion is reached, or one at odds with the position that we generally take for Plato's in other dialogues, are assigned in both arrangements to the introductory tetrads. The purpose of these is not so much to communicate truth to the novice as to incline him to the study of philosophy, to try his powers of argument, or to bring forth latent knowledge as a midwife delivers a child. These three functions the Platonists dubbed the protreptic (or 'hortatory'), the peirastic (or 'experimental') and the maieutic (or 'obstetric'). Dialogues which convicted the soul of error were called elenctic ('refutatory'), those which purged its stains cathartic ('purificatory'), and those which imparted positive doctrine hyphegetic ('edificatory'). Many works of course admitted of more than one such label: in a short tract by Albinus, an eminent Platonist of the second century, the cathartic and the elenctic function together as overtures to the maieutic works in which the constitution of the universe is examined; then come the hyphegetic works which shape the soul through thought and conduct into the likeness of God, and last the logical texts which render knowledge secure.[25]

Platonists and Pythagoreans

Plotinus, to judge by Porphyry's omission of Theon, Thrasyllus and Albinus from Porphyry's catalogue in the life, did not consult them in his seminars. Porphyry, however, cherished a high esteem not only for the editorial labours of Thrasyllus but for the Pythagorean tradition to which he adhered. Since he includes the Pythagoreans Nicomachus and Moderatus among the mentors of the Christian Origen, while omitting them from his list of authors read in Plotinus' seminars, it is possible that Plotinus had elected to make no use of them. For all that, Plotinus certainly held positions that his contemporaries defined as Pythagorean; to him they were perhaps merely the unwritten tenets that Plato was supposed to have revealed orally to his pupils, and on one occasion to astonished visitors in his lecture *On the Good*.[26] The gist of this secret teaching – not so secret that it might not have been elicited from the extant works of Plato – would appear to have been that the Monad (or One) and the Dyad are the parents of all existent things: the One because all that exists is both one thing and a constituent of one universe, and the Dyad because the particular owes its unity and uniqueness to a synthesis of properties. What is one under some description (in the sensible world at least) is always a multiple under some other description, just as there is always some description under which the many are one. It is, however, the unity, not the manifold – the determinate, not the indefinite – which the mind endeavours to grasp when it forms a concept; unity represents permanence and truth, while multiplicity is a snare to the understanding. The Monad and the One are thus the arithmetical counterparts of the counterpart of the Good. Just as the number one, however, cannot fail to generate the whole series of integers, so the Good cannot remain alone, or there would be nothing that it could endow with a purpose – nothing, in short, for which it would be a good. Thus it engenders the Dyad, which – as Aristotle recognised when he coined the term 'intelligible matter'[27] – accounts not only for multiplicity in the world of matter but also for the plurality of the Forms.

It is this dichotomous metaphysic, rather than the content of the dialogues, that appears to have been taught at first by the recognised heirs of Plato. An excerpt from Speusippus shows that he credited the Pythagoreans, rather than his master, with the thesis that the One is prior to Being and thus (as he seems to have inferred) to the distinction between good and evil. Were it not for this second position, and the fact that he is said to have derived number, soul and magnitude haphazardly from the One without any logical economy,[28] he might be said to foreshadow the Neoplatonic teaching on the ineffability and transcendence of the first principle. Xenocrates, his putative successor, described the Monad as Father and the Dyad as mother, equating the latter with the cosmic soul. He seems to have conceived of the Forms as mathematical quantities,[29] while he characterised the soul as a 'self-moving number'.[30] The *Republic* of Plato lends some authority to the first of these notions, but the definition of soul as number has no antecedent except in the rejected thesis of Simmias and Cebes in the *Phaedo* (85e-88b) that the relation of soul to body resembles that of the harmony to a musical instrument. These friends of Socrates, like the principal speaker in the *Timaeus* for whom the elements of the world are numerical ratios, were considered to be Pythagoreans by many ancient commentators, as by some today.[31]

If the Platonists of the first epoch can be said to have Pythagorised, the Neopythagoreans of the early Roman Empire were no less given to Platonising. Nicomachus of Gerasa, the compiler of one of the first and most seminal lives of Pythagoras, argues that the coupling of the monad with the dyad conveys the truth that Plato expressed when he said of the world-soul in the *Timaeus,* and of all being in the *Sophist*, that it partakes at once of sameness and of otherness. Porphyry and Iamblichus were indebted to Nicomachus as a biographer, and the latter also drew upon his works in his philosophy of number.[32] More striking still, however, as an adumbration of the Plotinian system, is a passage culled by Porphyry from Moderatus of Gades, in which the first One is anterior to being, as in Speusippus, the second is identical with true being and with the realm of forms, while a third (he does not expressly say a third One) participates both in the Forms and in the highest principle.[33] It is not clear whether this third term is the Monad which is styled elsewhere the limit of quantity and the source of number; below it, in any case, lies amorphous matter, which participates in nothing and receives only the bare simulacrum of things above. Porphyry's report, which is unsupported and implies that Moderatus was among the first commentators on the *Parmenides*, is not above suspicion. Yet there was nothing in his own system that would have tempted him to father on Moderatus a second One before the Monad; the Forms he might have smuggled in, but unless the subordination of the intellect to the One is another supposititious feature, the original text contained in embryo all three of the Plotinian hypostases which will be discussed in Chapters 3 and 4.

Aristotle and Plato

If the Pythagoreans represent, or came to represent, one limb of the early Platonic tradition, we must look in the *Metaphysics* of Aristotle for the other. Although he was regarded in antiquity as an apostate, there is no other pupil of Plato's who insists so strongly upon the universality and incorporeality of the form or on its priority to matter. Against Plato himself he denies that the form exists when not instantiated in matter,[34] but he also denies that matter itself is an entity or an object of the senses unless it participates in form. Matter is the mere potentiality for existence, patient of every quality but endowed with none until it combines with form to produce the material particular. This, in the nomenclature of the *Categories*, is the *prôtê ousia*, or primary substance, while the Form is a secondary substance (*deutera ousia*); the primary substance, for all that, is not first in the order of knowledge, since it is only through the union of the mind with the form that the senses grasp the material object in its particularity. Knowledge is possible only because the particular instantiates the Form.

Speusippus had described an evolution of the definite from the indefinite, according at best a perfunctory role to mind among the first principles. Aristotle, by contrast, holds that the actual is prior to the potential in the order of being as well as in the order of knowledge: what could the potential be said to *be* if the thing that it is has not been actualised? Mind, in its strict definition, is pure actuality – though in us that is true only of the *nous poiêtikos* or active reason, which is not the mind of which we are conscious through perception and ratiocination, but the productive and illuminative source – the sun, as it were – of these operations when they are carried out by the lower, or potential, intellect.[35] It is only this lower intellect that assimilates itself to the form of the thing perceived; a mind that is fully actualised will lack the potentiality to assume new forms, and since to become cognisant of anything other than itself would entail coalescence with the form of it, with consequent diminution of its own actuality, perfect mind is the sole and eternal object of its own thinking. This mind, as we learn in the *Metaphysics*, is God, the thought of thoughts and the cause of motion in his inferiors insofar as, to be what they are, they must aspire to actuality. In short, he is not the efficient but the final cause of every cosmic process, moving the starry spheres and all below them in the same sense as the thing desired may be said to move desire.[36]

Even in antiquity, these arguments seemed porous and incomplete. Does the active reason, for example, know the objects which it causes us to perceive, and if it does, does it know them beforehand or in consequence of perception? Again, if we grant that perception is the union of the mind with the form of the object, why should it not be possible for one pure actuality to accommodate another – one that is equally eternal, universal and immutable – without incurring either the dissipation of interest or the experience of succession that would entail imperfection and change? Alexander of Aphrodisias, the first commentator on Aristotle whose work survives, deduced that the active reason, which enables the lower intellect to perceive but does not collude in its perceptions, is indistinguishable from the self-reflexive intellect that is God. At the same time, he does not hold that the perfection or actuality of God would be compromised by the contemplation of the Forms, and he was one of the first philosophers – perhaps the only one among those who were read in the school of Plotinus – who affirmed that the forms are thoughts in the mind of God.[37] No more than Aristotle does he believe that God takes note of events and objects in the phenomenal realm, but for him the operation of final causes is synonymous with the providential government of the universe. If, with the Stoics, we recognise only efficient causes, rational design gives way to mere succession, providence to fate.[38]

This was an Aristotelian philosophy that a Platonist might have embraced; but it either failed to convince, or failed to catch the attention of, the most strident Platonist of the second century. Atticus is known to us chiefly through passages transcribed by the Christian archivist Eusebius, and perhaps it is for this reason that he appears to so little advantage as a philosopher. The tone throughout is satirical and declamatory, the one thesis being that Aristotle differs from Plato only for the sake of innovation. Where there is argument, all of it is on Plato's side, and, weak as it is, it is assumed to admit of no rejoinder from Aristotle. Except for a few notorious tags, the latter's views are represented in paraphrase, often strangely, and he appears to have been confused with the Stoics when his adversary credits him with the opinion that the realm above the moon is governed by fate, the realm below by nature, and human affairs by providence. In short there is no evidence that Atticus had read Aristotle; Plato he knows much better, and some parts of the *Timaeus* extremely well. Atticus may have been the first reader of Plato to identify the doctrine of Forms as the substrate of his entire philosophy: whether or not he was also the first to affirm that the Forms are the thoughts of God,[39] it would seem (making all allowance for the bias of our Christian informant) that the benign creator or Demiurge is for him no longer a mythical conceit but an indispensable presupposition of all the moral and natural sciences. To admit no providence but final causes, to deny that God can intervene to protect the good from wrong or correct injustice, is to preach an atheism indistinguishable from that of Epicurus, who had argued that the gods seek happiness only for themselves.[40] Again, to maintain the eternity of the world, on the unsubstantiated premiss that whatever has a beginning must have an end, is to make necessity the author of a work which Plato ascribes to divine benevolence: the 'friends' who endorse this tenet fail to see that it dethrones providence and annihilates the incentives to virtuous conduct.[41] No less pernicious to virtue is the doctrine that external goods are required to complete our happiness; Atticus protests that, on the contrary, virtue is nothing if it is not everything, since no one, however, just, can be secure from the whims of fortune.[42] The power of doing good or evil lies with the immortal soul, which is also the beneficiary of its own actions. In styling the soul the form of the body, Aristotle makes it inert

16

and gives the lie to our universal perception of its activity, while his impoverished doctrine of immortality artificially separates mind from soul, and once again deprives the latter of its reward.[43] The soul's consciousness of its own unity will of course mean nothing to one who capriciously adds a fifth element to the four of Plato, asserts that the heaviest objects fall to the middle and not to the base of the cosmos, denies that the visible motion of the stars is their proper motion, and ignores the logic of symmetry and fitness that invariably precedes the appeal to observation in Plato's sublime account of the physical world.[44]

Neoplatonists do not quote from Atticus, but their allusions to him confirm that he read Plato through the lens of the *Timaeus,* and that creation was for him the act most characteristic of deity. He himself was aware that other Platonists did not countenance a creation in time or from pre-existent matter; his appeal to the master's text without further gloss suggests that no one had yet proposed that the term *genêton* or *gennêton,* which is used in the *Timaeus* to distinguish the realm of becoming from that of being, might betoken not so much creation in time as the ontological dependence of the contingent on the necessary, of everlasting change on eternal rest. In his own day Atticus may have been representative, for Plutarch also concludes that the world has an origin in time, and goes so far as to posit, not only the pre-existence of matter but the presence in matter of an evil soul which survives to trouble the world even after the intervention of the Demiurge.[45] This notion he corroborates by appeal to the *Laws*; the *Timaeus* is, however, the only dialogue on which he wrote a discursive study, and no more for him than for Atticus is its credibility weakened by the tentative manner in which Timaeus introduces his myth as a 'likely tale' (*Timaeus* 29d). Both, in their indifference to the irony, elasticity and detachment that we now prize in Plato's dialogues, are at one with an age in which the term 'philosophy' connotes a system rather than a method, a practical discipline rather than a disinterested pursuit of the unattainable. Many, it seems, approached Plato not through his writings but through handbooks in which the prooftext supersedes the play of argument, and the summaries of each doctrine are as perfunctory as the reasoning employed in its defence.

The most famous of these tools, the *Didascalicus* of Alcinous, was abridged in Latin, perhaps by Apuleius;[46] even if he is not the translator, and even if (as most scholars now concede[47]) the name Alcinous is not a mistake for Albinus, the author's ignorance of the Neoplatonists is a reason for dating the work to the second century. Were he a seminal thinker, it would be surprising that the Neoplatonists know no more of him, but it seems reasonable to suppose that he is another man who is speaking for his time when he gives the name God to the highest principle, describes the Forms as his thoughts, yet hesitates to say whether he is mind or more than mind. His demiurgic principle is certainly mind and god, but a subaltern to the highest deity; his third transcendent principle is the world-soul, a supine prisoner of matter until activity and form are imparted to it by the Demiurge. There is no residual evil in this soul, as Plutarch imagined, and it is not clear that we are literally to envisage a time when the soul was not informed by intellect. What is clear is that Alcinous, Plutarch and Atticus habitually accord divine predicates to the highest principle, not so much because they are Platonists as because there is no longer any conflict between their philosophical predilection for unity and the polytheism of the civic cults. Even those who were not philosophers in this epoch were accustomed to pay devotions to a single god or to one god who was thought to subsume the many. What Zeus the highest is to one the sun is to another; where one hails Mithras as the only saviour, another maintains that all divinity resides in Isis. That the peoples of a cosmopolitan empire, under the sway of a single despot, should imagine themselves to be subjects of one god is surely intelligible enough: there is little to show that the intellectual figures of this period were consciously thirsting for a new religion, or labouring under a sense of irreversible decline. The sophists to whom we owe most of the literature now surviving from the Antonine era seem to be unaware that the ancient creeds are bankrupt or that even the silver age of Hellenic Culture is on the wane. They can live in the past without being dead to the present and are not less proud to be natives of one city because they have grown to be rich by fanning the pride of others. Plutarch's speculations on the afterlife are unusual, and so is the 'anxiety' of the orotund valetudinarian Aelius Aristides, who in any case sought little from Asclepius beyond worldly fame and physical health, the chief concerns of the leisured plutocrat in any age.

Religious Platonism

Rebels against the laws of nature and man there were, but Platonists (when they noticed them) did not concede them a place among the Greeks. The Ophites, a Christian group in whose cosmography the seven planets served the soul as a ladder in its escape from the 'accursed god', appeared at once eccentric and derivative – typical Christians, bastard Mithraists – to the Platonising rhetorician Celsus.[48] The main premiss of the 'Gnostics', that the cosmos and its demiurge are by-products of a rupture in the godhead, is denounced in a well-known treatise by Plotinus. To him they are errant Platonists, lost friends and Greeks no longer, but in his life of Plotinus Porphyry describes them as Christian heretics whose errors were falsely derived from the 'old philosophy'.[49] To him, as to Celsus and all the Church fathers, Gnostics are a Christian sect; Iamblichus names them once in a synopsis of Platonic views on the fall of the soul,[50] but this is paltry evidence of a Gnostic movement outside Christianity, let alone of a universal disenchantment of which Gnostic Christianity is but a symptom. Nor do the reports of Celsus and Porphyry add any weight to the theory that Gnostic thought is a morbid instance of 'Iranian dualism'. Porphyry satisfied himself that the Book of Zoroaster to which the Gnostics of Rome appealed was a fabrication, while even if Celsus is right to allege that the Ophites stole their ladder of salvation from the Mithraists,[51] the Mithraism of the Roman era is as much the creation of Greek astronomers as of magian priests.

Few Classicists of the last fifty years have endorsed the nineteenth century's view of Neoplatonism itself as a fusion of the Greek and the Oriental. The 'Orient' is no longer imagined as a giant pharmacy in which all the irrational elements extruded by Greek culture were blended anew into cunning palliatives for worldly *ennui* and atrophy of spirit. The cults of Isis, Cybele and Attis flourished in every part of the Roman Empire where their native adherents set up new communities; if their Greek or Roman neighbours toyed with one or two exotic practices, this did not mean that they became disciples or even that they were conscious of any summons to conversion. Philosophy, by contrast, made a claim upon the lives of its practitioners; but to be a philosopher, one must become a Greek. Even those Neoplatonists who might be regarded as Orientals carried little of the east about them. Plotinus, as we know, was raised in Egypt and is labelled an Egyptian by Eunapius; he himself, however, speaks but once of the Egyptians, as a people whose arts, though admirable, are known to him only by hearsay.[52] Both Porphyry's name and his sobriquet Basileus are Greek equivalents, as he tells us, for his Phoenician birth-name Malcus; if he knew any more of that tongue he does not reveal it, and for all we know he read the *Phoenician History* by his compatriot Sanchuniathon in the Greek of Philo of Byblos.[53] As we shall see, he commended the Magi, the Brahmins and the Essenes and embraced the theology of the Chaldean oracles; Iamblichus extends this vicarious championship to the mysteries of the Assyrians, the Chaldaeans and the Egyptians. Yet all that they imbibed from these traditions they believed to be compatible with a philosophy whose chief tenets were the sovereignty of intellect in the universe, the freedom and immortality of the soul and the sufficiency of virtue. As they derived these tenets from Plato, so they maintained that Plato himself derived them by sound reasoning from unassailable premises. No more than the sophists do they exhibit that 'failure of nerve'[54] – the sense of fading vigour and mental deracination – that was once supposed to be characteristic of late antiquity.

Plato is free (though perhaps not free from irony) in his eulogies of Persian and Egyptian science;[55] so far as we know, however, it was not until the later second century AD that a disciple of his convened the nations to underwrite his entire philosophy. Numenius of Apamea is without doubt the most important precursor of Neoplatonism. He left such a mark on Plotinus as to excite the suspicion of plagiarism, though Porphyry maintains that this was exploded by Longinus.[56] Amelius, the outstanding pupil or colleague of Plotinus, is said by Porphyry to have had the works of Numenius by heart, while it was a truism for Proclus that Numenius and Porphyry could not be expected to hold diverse opinions on the same question.[57] Nevertheless, in the first of the excerpts quoted by Eusebius (to whom we owe most of our knowledge of him), he declares that even the testimonies of Plato can be reinforced by the study of corroborative dogmas and rites among Egyptians, Magi, Brahmins and Jews.[58] How he proceeded to demonstrate this Eusebius does not tell us, though he quotes (with circumspection) the saying attributed to Numenius: 'what is Plato but an Atticising Moses?'[59] It is certain that Numenius (and Porphyry after him) identified the motion of the spirit on the waters in Genesis 1.2 with the descent of the soul to matter;[60] while it appears less certain that Numenius adopted the locution 'he who is' (*ho on*) from Exodus 3.14 as an appellative for his own demiurge, he admired the Jews for their notion of a God who was wholly removed from association with his creatures.[61] At the same time he declares that the Egyptian sorcerers Jannes and Jambres had the power to mitigate even the worst of the calamities that Moses brought upon Egypt; and, just as he favours no barbarian race above another, so he subordinates all peoples to the Greeks when he enjoins an *anachorêsis* or ascent to Pythagoras as the only teacher whose authority exceeds even that of Plato.[62]

The longest surviving passages are those in which Numenius labours to vindicate his own doctrine against the 'Academic' tradition which was willing only to destroy with Socrates and not to build with Plato.[63] The defection of the Academy, in his mock-heroic narrative, is a grievous tale of larceny, imposture, secession and mutual emulation, all compounded by the failure of Plato's self-styled heirs to perceive that he, like Socrates, followed Pythagorean methods both in the construction and in the concealment of his doctrines. Numenius thus appears to espouse the Pythagorean interpretation of Plato; at the same time it is Plato's written teaching that preponderates in our fragments of his treatise *On the Good*, where he adapts the terms monad and dyad to a cosmogony that is plainly designed to reconcile the *Timaeus* to other dialogues by assigning separate functions to the Good and to the Demiurge or creator in the economy of the Forms.

As we have observed, in the *Timaeus* it is the Forms that determine the character of the sensible world, the Demiurge who brings it into existence. The paradigm, or realm of Forms, is the object of his contemplation and not, so far as we know, the product of his creative will. Yet Plato speaks of the Demiurge, not the paradigm, as the *nous* or governing intellect of the cosmos (*Timaeus* 47e-48a), and there are passages in his works where the priority of intellect might be taken for a metaphysical axiom. If the Demiurge is the author of the Forms, he assumes the role assigned to the Good in the *Republic*, where it is said to resemble the sun in being at once the source of all things below and the means by which we know them

(509b-c; 516e-517c). Numenius makes explicit what he understands Plato to have said implicitly by making the Good an intellect; it is, however, the higher of two, at once First God and First Mind where the demiurgic intellect is the Second. The latter is the home of the Forms, and in a sense their progenitor, but only by contemplation of the First. From its desire, the yearning of the Beautiful for the Good, the Forms emerge as a manifold of beauty, from which all beauty in the visible realm is derived by participation.[64] At the same time the goodness that we attribute to beauty and intellect belongs to them only by participation in the unqualified unity of the first intelligence, the one Good of all lower entities. The First Mind is the true existent (*to on*) – not one discrete particular among many but the absolute simplicity of being that remains when we strip the particular of its accidental qualities. Since any change would compromise this simplicity, it is not subject to motion or cognisant of other beings; like Aristotle's Prime Mover it initiates motion only by being an object of love to entities that seek their own actuality and perfection.

The contemplative desire which the Second Intellect, or Demiurge, feels for the First would not explain the creation of a material universe, unless there were some countervailing tendency to confer goods on its inferiors. Here Numenius innovates by ascribing the creation not to benevolence but to a fatal double-mindedness which arises when the Demiurge looks away from the Good to fix his gaze on matter. If he is not ensnared, like the Gnostic Sophia, he falls prey to a forgetfulness which in Plato can afflict only the individual soul, not the soul of the world or its author.[65] Two intellects, it appears, become three, the third being so enmeshed in the toils of matter that the world itself, in some accounts, is the third member of the triad. 'Tragically', as his critics protested, he called the two primordial minds the sire and grandsire and the third their grandson.[66] 'Mythically' is the kinder and more Platonic term, and it may be that Numenius adopts this poetic idiom only to demonstrate the coherence of his teachings with the oldest intimations of Greek wisdom. His grandest effort in this vein was a treatise in which he argued that the cave of the nymphs in *Odyssey* XIII, with its doors on opposite sides for mortals and immortals, is an image of the zodiac, and that Capricorn and Cancer are the two openings through which souls are said to descend and reascend in the vision that closes the *Republic*. In support of his exegesis, he appeals not only to Moses but to the representation of the planetary orbits in Mithraic iconography; his allusions to Pherecydes of Syros, one of the first philosophers of the Greek world, seem to have fostered a vogue for the allegories and myths that were attributed to that author.[67]

Numenius may have flourished as early as 150 AD;[68] yet, with the exception of Ammonius, about whom we know so little, he is the last Platonist of note before Plotinus. We may feel inclined to deny the name Platonist to such an eclectic thinker; to his own mind, however, he had shown that it was possible to be at once a true Platonist, a true Pythagorean and a true disciple of Homer. He is the forerunner of Plotinus, but the mentor of both Porphyry and Iamblichus, who shared his desire to amplify Plato's teaching with the testimony of witnesses from diverse lands, in the belief that such a chorus would reveal the universality without impairing the unity of his thought.

Four Philosophers

Books on Plotinus frequently commence with a biographical, sometimes even with a historical introduction; it is possible that he would have disliked the practice. Porphyry informs us that he bore himself like one who 'was ashamed to be in the body'; his own peroration to his earliest treatise begins, 'let us fly to our own dear country', while the last words of the treatise with which Porphyry crowns his arrangement of the *Enneads* are 'alone with the alone'.[1] His work contains the germ of a political philosophy,[2] but it bears no fruit to vie with his logic or his metaphysics. Porphyry himself, if we may judge from his writings, knew the kings and magistrates of his epoch only by hearsay, and Eunapius quotes his own statement that he had never been in receipt of a civic bursary. The travels of Longinus, as he recounts them in his own letters, took him from one enclave of scholarship to another; when at the end of his life he gave political advice, it was not to Rome but to her enemy. Iamblichus knew (or fancied) that the first Pythagoreans were often framers or destroyers of constitutions,[3] yet his own speculations seem to have been confined to matters best pursued in the study, or in secret. Of course to understand the Neoplatonists we must know something of their world, of which they are after all the most famous and enduring representatives. They were not, for all that, its masters, creatures or official spokesmen: they owed their subsequent fame to what they had written in leisured obscurity, and it cannot be proved that they were better known to the general public in antiquity than they are now.

An age of tribulation

Plotinus was born in 205, Longinus (we must suppose) at about the same time. The triumph of Septimius Severus in the civil wars of 193 had already secured twelve years of ironclad peace for the Roman world, and though his statesmanship was to die with him in 212, there was no immediate change in the ruling dynasty or in the fortunes of the Empire. Of the two sons who succeeded him the elder, Caracalla, swiftly disposed of his brother Geta; he enjoyed the fruits of his crime for a mere five years, and the most notable event of his reign was the grant of citizenship to every freeborn man and woman of the Empire by a decree of 215. Citizenship at this date made a man eligible for service as a legionary, but no longer exempted him from fiscal burdens, and would soon cease even to guarantee immunity from torture. Yet even as a purely honorific measure, it may have rendered imperial rule more palatable to the Greeks whom it enfranchised, with the consequence that philosophers – even those who were not, like the four discussed here, citizens born of citizens – would be less inclined to take up the posture of opposition that characterised the Stoics and Cynics of the principate. Their own interests forbade this also, for the women of the Severan dynasty seem to have taken an indiscriminate pride in the cultivation of men of letters. Their circle included not only the sophist Philostratus (biographer of the defiant Apollonius, as well as of the more obsequious Dio) but also their eminent Christian contemporaries Origen, Hippolytus and Julius Africanus. Perhaps they were more eclectic in taste because they had acquired their culture in Syria – as was the egregious Heliogabalus who, on succeeding Caracalla in 217, set out to violate every protocol of the senate and to impose upon the whole Empire the cult of a solar god who was represented in Syria by a black stone. In 222 his assassination brought to the throne Severus Alexander, the last of the dynasty and the only one who was worthy of its founder. If we are to believe the *Augustan History*, he tried his own hand at verses, while in his household pantheon Orpheus and Christ stood side by side with Apollonius the Pythagorean sage.[4] Such was the hybrid culture in which Longinus began to write and Plotinus to study. The rise of the militant Sassanids in Persia, however, forced Alexander to spend more time in the camp than at his court, and in 235 he became the first of three Emperors to fall on the eastern border in the space of twenty-five years.

His successor, perhaps his murderer, was a Thracian of low birth called Maximinus. He lived, the historians tell us, for his vices, which were subsidised by the goods of peaceable citizens, killed without trial. Tyranny and fiscal exactions pricked the dormant senate into its last attempt to dispose of the sovereign power. Their nominees, the two Gordians, never took power because the ship carrying them from Libya foundered almost at the same time as Maximinus received his sentence from his own troops. A third Gordian was now recognised as Emperor, notwithstanding the opposition of two generals whom the senate had raised up against Maximinus. His six-year reign was troubled by insurrections, none of which proved so formidable as the recrudescence of Persian power and greed under the new Sassanian dynasty. Gordian raised an army to defend the eastern border in 244. The Persian King Sapor was later to boast of having killed him on the battlefield,[5] but in Rome it was widely held that he died by the hand of his successor Philip the Arab, or at least as a result of the disaffection which the latter had fomented among the troops. Within five years rebellions had erupted in two provinces; when the leaders died in internecine conflict, Philip sent Decius, an astute and well-born senator, to take command of the Thracian mutineers. He in turn was quickly persuaded to assume the purple; Philip joined battle and perished with his son. The Empire was now racked within by discord, plague and want, while Gothic raids along the Danubian frontier were proving more deleterious even than the encroachments of the Persians in the east. Surmising that the gods had been estranged by neglect, the Emperor issued an edict requiring everyone to pay homage to them in sacrifice.[6] Only the Christians disobeyed, as even a vegetarian philosopher like Plotinus could comply by scattering incense; nevertheless, the woes of the Empire multiplied, and Decius, with his lieutenant Gallus, marched against the Goths in 251.

The battle was all but won when Gallus decided to promote his aspirations to the throne by making a compact with the barbarians. Decius was trapped and slain, the Goths retired across the Danube with their prisoners, and Gallus enjoyed two years of troubled rule. At home he was forced to assassinate the heir of Decius; in the east the Goths returned, and the slaughter was accompanied by a plague which carried off whole populations. The Persians, having sacked Antioch, could have seized the Asian provinces had they not preferred to carry off the booty. When, therefore, a barbarian host was routed by the enterprising general Aemilianus his troops lost no time in saluting him as Emperor. Gallus fell in battle, but was avenged at once by Valerian, the commander of the Celtic and German legions. At the outset of his reign in 253, he named his son Gallienus as his colleague and heir, but neither was able to match Rome's enemies in the field. The Goths despoiled the cities around the Bosphorus, plague depleted the armies sent against them, while the royal exchequer could not raise funds sufficient to bribe the Persian King Sapor. In 260 another inept campaign against this enemy resulted in the capture and enslavement of Valerian. In Rome the senate was forced to raise an army to repel the invading Goths; when Gallienus returned to assume sole power he did nothing to redeem his father, and little to save his Empire from dismemberment by rebellion. His one plan was to raise funds to pay his army by taxation and the debasement of the coinage, but the result was merely to aggravate the poverty of his subjects without cementing the loyalty of his troops. His eight-year reign was remembered as an era of plague and poverty, for it is only in modern accounts that he becomes the architect of a renaissance in arts and letters. By contrast the efflorescence of Greek culture in the city of Palmyra, whose suzerain Odenathus had been an ally to Valerian but rebelled under Gallienus, was vigorously promoted by the usurper and his daughter, the great Zenobia. Gallienus was detained in the west, and in 268 succumbed to one conspiracy while preparing to meet another. His murderer Claudius Gothicus, though the plague of his time (which drove Plotinus from Rome[7]) became a byword, was a soldier and administrator of genius, and from him we may date the revival of Roman fortunes. Although he died in 270 before all the revolts had been suppressed, the recovery of the Empire was completed by Aurelian, who led Zenobia in chains to Rome in 271. After his death in 275, the Empire fell to Probus, another soldier, who not only maintained the integrity of his dominions but fortified the Danubian frontier.

If there was ever a 'crisis of the third century'[8] it was over. Even in the most troubled years the integrity of the realm had not been compromised, the beggared and depopulated borderlands had not ceased to excite the cupidity of Rome's neighbours, and the armies levied in haste against the invaders had on occasion proved superior both in strategy and in numbers. We need not doubt that, as trade declined, individuals had become poorer, and the culture of the provinces more parochial;[9] no doubt it would have required exceptional hardihood and an ample fortune to cross the sea in search of a philosophy. Yet these conditions, toxic as they were to the sophist and the dilettante, could be said to have restored the health of Platonism: students who had no prospect of advancement in the present world were more easily induced to seek their goods in a higher one, and with the help of unworldly masters. The strongest deterrents to study, moreover, vanished under rulers who were strong enough to protect the loyal subject, while they were not disposed to corrupt him with their patronage. At the same time, that philosophy and rhetoric were only superficially the same disciplines that they had been in the classical era; the city was no longer a state, philosophers could not hope to be legislators, and their aim was not so much to change the world as to protect the individual from the changes wrought by others. It is true that this pursuit of invulnerability was open only to men (and women) of the leisured class, and that even the most reclusive Platonist was never far from the seat of power; nevertheless, having no share in that power, they enjoyed less political freedom than a Plato or a Cicero, and were consequently more free to live in accord with their philosophy. In contrast to Plato or Cicero, they may be called professional philosophers because their vocation not only secured them a livelihood but determined their place of abode and choice of friends. Conversely the life of such a man was a measure of his philosophy, and the biographies that his friends composed were an indispensable preface to the study of his thought.

The work of Claudius, Aurelian and Probus was too sound to be undone by their weak successors Numerian, Carus and Carinus. Only two years elapsed between the Probus' death in 282 and the accession of Diocletian, perhaps the most resolute and innovative Emperor since Augustus. He divided the realm and assigned the western half to his colleague Maximian, thus at once diminishing his own burdens and enhancing the efficiency of his government. His early nomination of successors to the eastern and western thrones forestalled rebellion; his wars against foreign nations may have been dilatory, and his attempt to fix the prices of goods for his troops a predictable failure, but there is no doubt that the revenues of the exchequer were augmented by his laws against change of domicile and the rigour with which his officers collected the fiscal dues. His persecution of Christians at the end of his reign may not have been unprovoked and was applauded by philosophers; when he and Maximian abdicated in 305 the Empire was as prosperous and secure as at any time in the hundred years since Plotinus' birth.

Diocletian enforced the observation of Roman customs, and authorised the repression of the Manichees, whom he saw as Persian agitators, even before he promulgated his measures against the Christians. At the same time, he is notorious for his introduction of eastern pomp and flattery into the fashions of the court. But even if his precursors were less sumptuously attired, and the genuflections of their courtiers less supine, it was true from the beginning of the third century that the Empire belonged to no one but the Emperor, and no other public figure commands the interest of historians and biographers in this epoch. The numerous lives of sophists and philosophers – so different in their content from the parallel lives of the noble Greeks and Romans written by Plutarch at the turn of the second century – conferred upon private men a universal and durable fame that it had now become impossible to achieve in political life. It was in the Severan epoch that the maxim *lathe biôsas*, 'live unknown', was first ascribed to Pythagoras rather than Epicurus.[10] The political quiescence of philosophers is illustrated in Porphyry's *Life of Plotinus*, where events are dated not by the names of consuls (as in Roman republican annals) or by Olympiads (as in Greek chronicles and universal histories), but by the year of an Emperor's reign.

The career of Longinus

It was the least seminal of our four philosophers who cut the greatest figure in the world. Longinus, as Eunapius informs us, was renowned as a 'walking library'.[11] The epithet was deserved, for in this age of itinerant scholars there were few, as he himself boasts in a letter, who had encountered such a variety of 'cities and populations' or frequented the schools of so many eminent teachers (Porphyry, *Plotinus* 20.20ff). If the inventory that follows is a record of his own travels, he had lent his ear to Euclides, Democritus and Proclinus in the Troad and to Plotinus and Amelius in Rome; to these five Platonists he adds four Stoics (whom he assigns to no locality) and a single Peripatetic, the Alexandrian Heliodorus. Since, however, he notes as a common and salient characteristic of these thinkers that they committed their thoughts to writing, it is possible that some or all were known to him only through their publications; Porphyry asserts that it was his own reports from Rome, where he had settled after quitting Longinus' school or circle in Athens, that had enabled his former tutor to confute those who maintained that the whole philosophy of Plotinus was derived without acknowledgement from Numenius of Apamea (ibid.19.1-4). It was certainly in Athens, where he appears to have resided in middle age, that Longinus encountered a number of philosophers who did not choose to communicate their opinions to the public. These included the Platonists Theodotus and Eubulus (both recognised 'successors' in the Academy) and the Stoics Musonius and Athenaeus (ibid. 20.39-48); again no seat is assigned to two other reticent Stoics Hermaeus and Lysimachus (the second of whom taught Amelius before the latter came to Rome) or to four other figures – the Platonists Ammonius and Origen and the Peripatetics Ammonius and Ptolemaeus – who all have Egyptian names (ibid. 20.36-7 and 49-50). The first Ammonius is evidently the tutor of Plotinus; Origen,[12] whom Longinus seems to regard as either the colleague or the successor of this Ammonius, is the man whom Porphyry numbers among his master's fellow-pupils in Alexandria. Writing after Porphyry's arrival in Rome in 263, Longinus is acquainted with no work by Origen other than his treatise *On the Daemons* (ibid. 20.41); from this we may deduce that the other treatise known to Porphyry, *That the King is the Only Maker*, was composed, as its dedication to Gallienus implies, in the period when that Emperor ruled alone.[13] It follows that he cannot have been the Christian theologian of the same name, for this copious author died at the latest in the same year (254) which brought Gallienus to the imperial throne as son and junior colleague of Valerian. Porphyry (who had no cause to confuse the two) alleges that the Christian Origen also attended the lectures of an Ammonius who had turned from Christianity to philosophy; if he does not exaggerate the fame of this Ammonius, it would seem that he is speaking not of the tutor of Plotinus, but of Ammonius the Peripatetic, whom Longinus and Philostratus agree in styling the most illustrious scholar of his day.[14]

Not long after Porphyry's defection to Rome, Longinus wrote to Porphyry from Phoenicia, soliciting transcripts of Plotinus' seminars which would enable him to correct the errors in those which Amelius had already brought to him.[15] Amelius was perhaps on the way to Apamea, the city of Numenius, where he took up residence after the disintegration of the Roman school (Porphyry, *Plotinus* 3.48). Longinus too migrated again, this time to the court of Zenobia, the rebel queen of Palmyra. As her tutor in the art of composition, he was thought to have inspired her haughty rejoinder to Aurelian's demand for her submission; the letter had in fact been drafted in Syriac and translated by one Nicomachus, but after the Roman victory in 270 he paid for his putative treason with his life.[16] His literary remains included a commentary on a portion of the *Timaeus* – weighty and durable enough to attract the hostile animadversions of Proclus, almost two centuries later – a treatise *On Impulse*, an *Answer to Amelius*, a discourse *On the End*, another *On First Principles* and a companion to this, entitled *Philarkhaios,* or *Lover of Antiquity*.[17] If these titles play on the double meaning of the Greek noun *arkhê* ('principle' or 'origin') the intended lesson will be that no philosophy can be true if it is not true to ancient masters. The judgment of Plotinus – 'a philologist, no philosopher' (*Life of Plotinus* 14.20) – concedes to Longinus tacitly the praise that others openly accorded to him with the epithet 'most judicious' (*kritikôtatos*).[18] The remnants of his work *On the Art of Rhetoric* – a dozen pages of print in the standard edition – are unlikely to reconcile any modern reader to this estimate; on the other hand, if the treatise *On the*

Sublime, which is attributed by the scribes to 'Dionysius or Longinus', is really his, he possessed abilities which not even his admirers in the Roman world were competent to appraise.[19]

Longinus alludes to his disagreement with the Roman Platonists in a preface to his treatise *Against Plotinus and Gentilianus Amelius on the End*:

> [Plotinus], I believe, has produced a clearer exposition of Platonic and Pythagorean principles than any of his precursors, for there is nothing approaching the accuracy of Plotinus' writings in those of Numenius, Cronius, Moderatus and Thrasyllus on the same matters … . As for the friend that [Amelius and Plotinus] and I have in common, Basileus of Tyre, who has himself made no small effort to imitate Plotinus, and, preferring to take him rather than myself as his mentor, has undertaken to show in a treatise that his opinion about the ideas is better than the one that I embrace, I think that in my answer I have convicted him, though in measured terms, of singing too hasty a palinode (*Life of Plotinus* 20.71-96).

Longinus lets it be known here that he is one of the philosophers who write, that he is conscious of his own learning, that he sets a higher premium on fidelity than on enterprise in the use of ancient sources, and that he values the allegiance of his pupils. How and in what milieu he imparted his views to Porphyry we do not learn, nor how he and his pupil came to differ as to the nature of the ideas. We do not know that the doctrine 'that the intelligibles are not outside the intellect' is one that Plotinus found himself obliged to defend in *Enneads* 5.5 against fellow-Platonists; anyone who tested this position against the superficial (or 'philological') reading of the *Timaeus* would be sure to retort that the paradigm in that dialogue is an object of perception to the Demiurge, and hence would seem to be extrinsic to him. We may reasonably conjecture that the nature of the Good, which is deduced in Plotinus' system from the coincidence of the intellect with its ideas, was another of the subjects in dispute. At the same time it appears, from the importunity with which Longinus sought good transcripts of the Roman seminars – and also from the fact that he did not expect the return of Porphyry even when he supposed him to have recanted his opinion on the ideas – that he concurred in his pupil's estimate of Plotinus as 'the philosopher of our time' (*Life of Plotinus* 1.1). The life prefixed by Porphyry to his edition of the *Enneads*, and indeed the mere decision to write his master's life at all, leave little doubt that it was his qualities as a man that won disciples for Plotinus, and not only his astuteness in the interpretation of texts.

The career of Plotinus

What then do we know of the man Plotinus? More and less than the truth, no doubt, for Porphyry's life is as much a vindication of the pupil as an encomium of the master; the latter was a plagiarist to some, a reclusive visionary to others, while Porphyry was an apostate twice over, having left Plotinus for Sicily five years after his defection from Longinus. Amelius and Eustochius, two older and more durable associates of Plotinus, had put abroad their own versions of his teachings decades before their temporary classmate produced an edition of the *Enneads*.[20] One purpose of the life, then, is to show that it is sympathy, not proximity, that makes the pupil a fit custodian of the master's doctrine. As to the mere phenomena, the public facts of his own career and that of Plotinus, Porphyry is almost always contradicted where he is not the sole witness. The critical reader, noting the many discomfitures of Amelius in the life and the recurrent use of the orotund 'I Porphyry', will not dismiss these other informants merely because they counteract the palpable bias of Porphyry's account.

In what concerns Plotinus himself, omissions and distortions will have arisen from a natural desire to portray the philosopher according to his philosophy. Of course it is more than probable that Plotinus lived as he thought, and that his conduct justified Porphyry's remark on his opening sentence that he 'seemed like one ashamed to be in the body' (*Life* 1.1-2). We may well believe that, as Porphyry adds, he declined to talk of adventitious matters such as his place of birth or his ancestry; on the other hand, the source used by Eunapius had no reason to imagine or invent the information that he was born in a town called Lyco, whether or not this is a short name for Lycopolis.[21] That he was also an Egyptian, as Eunapius asserts, is not improbable – all the less so if we take Egyptian to signify any inhabitant of the hinterland, whether of Greek or of native stock. Porphyry claims to have heard Plotinus say that he was not weaned from his nurse until the age of eight (ibid. 3.2-6); this anecdote can hardly have been the biographer's invention, and suggests, along with his Roman name, that he came from a well-to-do household. How he spent his early years we are not informed, but Alexandria was the city in which he began to pursue philosophy at the age of twenty-eight (3.6-10). His tutor was Ammonius the Platonist, in his own day the less illustrious of the two namesakes; we owe to Theodoret the information that he bore the surname Saccas and that this denotes a carrier of burdens.[22] No other speculation on its meaning is sustained by a shred of evidence from antiquity; most attempts to reconstruct Ammonius' thought are marred by the gratuitous assumption that Plotinus and the Christian Origen both sat at the feet of this Ammonius, and that only his instruction could explain what the two are alleged to hold in common.[23] Where the pagan Origen and Plotinus agree, we can argue with more confidence that they are both rehearsing the lessons of Ammonius; but such cases are few and trivial, and neither of these pupils seems to have formulated a statement on the unconfused commingling of incorporeals which is expressly ascribed by Porphyry to 'Ammonius the teacher of Plotinus'. Porphyry himself reports that after the death of Ammonius in 243 the three members of his inner circle – Origen, Plotinus and one Herennius – struck a pact to keep secret everything that he had taught to them in private (3.24-30). Herennius is said to have been the first transgressor (3.30), but, since Plotinus set up his school in Rome within months of his master's death, it would seem that he was able to teach a great deal without intruding upon these esoteric doctrines. Longinus, who had heard Herennius and read Plotinus, does not characterise the latter as a disciple of Ammonius, and the latter does not appear in Porphyry's catalogue of predecessors whose influence is discernible in the *Enneads*.

Plotinus, according to Porphyry, left Alexandria for ever in 243 in the train of the luckless Emperor Gordian III. When Porphyry opines that he wished to acquaint himself with the wisdom of the Indians and the Chaldaeans, he is crediting his master with his own interests; there is nothing in the *Enneads* to suggest that Plotinus gave a thought to either of these races, and even Porpyhry does not pretend that this campaign enlarged his knowledge of them, since it ended in a calamitous defeat which drove Plotinus first to Antioch, then to Rome.[24] His flight need not be attributed to personal affection for the dead Emperor, and his settling in Rome is sufficient proof that he nursed no animosity to the new Emperor, Philip the Arab, who was widely (though perhaps not justly) held to have been the author of Gordian's death. In Rome he was joined by the Alexandrians Serapion and Eustochius the physician (7.8 and 46). These, we may guess, were members of the circle of Ammonius who regarded him as the master's heir; since, however, we have no record of Origen's departure from Alexandria, it would seem that a larger faction adhered to him. Porphyry records that on one occasion he paid a visit to the school in Rome, but only to hear Plotinus decline to lecture on the plea that there was now one in the audience who knew everything that he was about to say (14.20-5). If Porphyry did not invent this compliment, it may have contained more irony than he divined, and it is certainly no evidence that the two pupils of Ammonius coincided in all their teaching; on the contrary, Proclus demonstrates in his Commentary on the *Timaeus* that they were frequently at odds.

Plotinus' wealth in Rome consisted only of his friends, for he resided at first in the house of two rich women, a mother and daughter, both called Gemina (9.1-2). After this he lived with a certain Chloe, upholding the discipline of the house without encroaching on her 'chaste widowhood' (11.1-3); he administered wills, detected at least one theft and made a disciple of the senator Rogatianus, who embraced the philosophic life on the very day appointed for his installation as consul (7.32-46). To him, as to Plotinus, the pursuit of the good implied the renunciation of the world, and it would be rash indeed to conclude from his defection – or from the friendship between Plotinus and three other members of the senate – that Plotinus was a favourite of that body.[25] Gordian III had owed his elevation to the senate, but it was seldom at peace with subsequent rulers, least of all with the autocratic and bellicose Gallienus – the dedicatee (as we recall) of Origen's treatise *That the King is the Only Maker*. Yet Porphyry (who, like all Greeks, was devoid of republican sentiment) is not ashamed to make Plotinus a friend of Salonina, this Emperor's consort, and to declare that Gallienus would have granted him land and funds for the foundation of a city of philosophers in Campania had he not been turned against the scheme by evil tongues at court (12.1-12). This too we may hesitate to accept as history: it was customary for encomiasts of a philosopher to award him a royal patron, and even so poor an economist as Gallienus must have perceived the futility of a project to found a city on the model of in Plato's *Laws*.

It does not seem that Plotinus inherited any part of his audience from a rival or predecessor in the capital. The school of Gaius,[26] informal and unendowed as such collaborations often were, would not have produced a line of heirs extending to the third century, while 'Numenius the Roman' seems to be either a different man from the great Numenius or the figment of a Byzantine compiler.[27] Whether the classes were held where Plotinus lived or at some other venue, they were plainly not esoteric in intention if, as Porphyry tells us, anyone could attend without test or fee (1.13-14). Amelius took advantage of the crowd (and of the shortsightedness of his teacher) to seat an artist at the back without his knowledge. This intruder was able to execute the portrait without the knowledge of Plotinus who, when asked to sit, had protested that an image of the body would be but the shadow of a shadow (1.1-5). Porphyry makes this anecdote the preface to his own text, the speaking icon, in which his next stroke is to dissolve the body itself with a circumstantial account of the malady that led to Plotinus; death and the dispersion of his friends.[28] The object of what follows is to reveal as much of his soul as can be made tangible, not only by the preservation and polishing of a literary corpus but by a memoir of his characteristic utterances and the regimen that he observed in life and teaching. When he spoke, we are told, he displayed acute powers of analysis, and was easily understood despite a propensity to transpose the consonants of similar terms (13.1-5). It was, however, the radiance of his face that arrested the gaze: it was then that, exuding kindness and affability, it acquired a beauty surpassing even his natural comeliness (13.5-10). He did not forbid interruptions, but on the contrary allowed Porphyry to interrogate him for three days on the manner in which the soul coexists with the body; when a newcomer named Thaumasius objected, he explained that 'if we do not resolve Porphyry's difficulties, there will be nothing that we can put into a text' (13.15-17).

In fact, according to Porphyry, his master required his services as editor, and not only as interlocutor. Not that he declined to write even before he was introduced to his biographer; nor was it beyond his talents to punctuate his concise and astringent style with soaring passages that sprang, as his disciple remembered, from 'the depths of feeling' (14.4). For all that, since he wrote only to express his thoughts, and would not divert those thoughts from the inquiry in hand even when he was in dialogue with others, he had no more time for orthography, calligraphy or even the clear division of the syllables than for eloquence of style. His sight was so poor than even when interrupted he was unwilling to review what he had written, but proceeded to the next topic, often neglecting (as every reader knows) the transitions that would have helped an outsider to catch his train of thought (8.1-12). It was Porphyry's task to amend the punctuation, correct the spelling, and (except in the earliest treatise, where his master had pre-empted him[29]) to affix a heading to each of these meandering compositions. It was also his decision to arrange them in six *Enneads* of nine, an act which may have entailed the division of the longest works, and even in one case the assignation of four segments from the same text to different *Enneads* (24.12-13). This attempt to make an encyclopaedia of the corpus was inspired, as he confesses, by Andronicus' redaction of the esoteric works of Aristotle (24.7-8); in contrast to Andronicus and Thrasyllus, however, he knew the man whose labours he was refining, and was able to draw up a second list of the treatises in the order of composition. Had there been any development in Plotinus' thought in his twenty-five years of teaching, it would therefore have been possible for modern scholars to plot this metamorphosis without recourse to the circular hypotheses which scholars are forced to advance in their endeavours to fix the chronology of Plato's dialogues. Since, however, his teaching commenced at the age of forty, his writing somewhat later, we need not be surprised that critics have for the most part found the corpus homogeneous, and that claims to have detected a crisis, a watershed, a shift of position or even a contradiction of earlier notions in any given text have seldom been sustained. It is not even true that the most inconsequential works are invariably the earliest, or the densest the most mature – and there is little to justify Porphyry's boast that Plotinus reached his acme as a writer during the five years of his own sojourn in the capital.

Plotinus did not speak only from the heart or only from Plato. His seminars would commence with the recitation of some text by an Aristotelian or Platonic commentator. 'Yet nothing that he said', continues Porphyry, 'came straight from these books; on the contrary, he was his own man, independent in his scrutiny and applying the doctrine of Ammonius to the investigations' (14.10-15). When he encountered a text that called for piecemeal refutation, he entrusted the task to pupils. Thus, while he himself composed a sharp harangue against the Gnostics, former associates who denied that Plato had fathomed 'the depths of intelligible being' (16.16.8-9), it is Porphyry who names them, who describes them as Christian heretics and who composed a series of tracts against the book that they paraded under the name of Zoroaster. Amelius devoted forty books to the refutation of its companion, the *Zostrianus*; the Coptic version of this, discovered in 1945, does not seem long enough or profound enough to excite such industry, but it is probable that mutual emulation would have tempted both Amelius and Porphyry to go far beyond the stipulated brief.[30] The two were matched again when Plotinus asked Amelius to answer Porphyry's treatise against his own view that 'the intelligibles are not outside the intellect'. Porphyry at first declined the accept the resolution of his difficulties which Amelius had advanced in 'a book of no mean length', but once he had produced his own reply and seen it answered, he perceived that he had misconstrued the doctrine of Plotinus, and read a 'palinode' before the whole class (18.8-19). This is the one occasion in the life when he comes second to Amelius; he won back his laurels after a rhetorician named Diophanes had extolled the benefits of sexual intercourse between teacher and disciple, and Plotinus, almost too indignant to listen to this travesty of the *Symposium*, 'enjoined me Porphyry to write a response' (15.12). Plotinus, we are told, admired his response, as he admired the sublime and enigmatic piece which he composed for the feast of Plato, waving aside the banter of other pupils with the words 'you have shown yourself to be simultaneously a poet, a philosopher and a lover of sacred truth' (15.4-6).

We do not hear that Plotinus imposed any discipline on his pupils, but we know that he abstained from meat, and would not even suffer remedies derived from the flesh of beasts to be applied to him in his last illness (2.8-11). Porphyry assumes, in his remonstration with Castricius Firmus after the death of Plotinus, that every member of the circle had a duty to follow a vegetarian diet.[31] Plotinus himself was barely a vegetarian, for in order to reduce his hours of sleep and thus avoid any dissipation of his thoughts, he adopted a diet so austere that on many occasions he refused to take even bread. For all that, his unbroken communion with the noetic world, and the perpetual 'reversion of his mind to itself' (8.23) did not prevent him from noticing the ailments of his pupils. When Porphyry conceived a desire to 'expedite his departure from this life', Plotinus visited him in his house and, having persuaded him that this urge was merely the symptom of a 'melancholic illness', advised him to go abroad for his convalescence. It was only for this reason (Porphyry tells us) that he retired to Sicily, staying at the house of a certain Probus near Lilybaeum, and was not in Rome at the time of his master's death (11.11-19).

This death, in the eyes of the larger world, was terrible. He appears to have contracted a form of leprosy, elephantiasis,[32] though some details of the literary epidemic phthiriasis, which had carried away Pythagoras among others,[33] may have found their way into Porphyry's description of the symptoms. His breath became so noisome that his habit of greeting his friends with an embrace became unbearable, and one by one they departed to other quarters (2.13-18). At the same time his servants were either killed or driven away by the most virulent of the plagues which sapped the vigour of the Empire in the third century (2.7-10); having no one to attend him in Rome, Plotinus spent his last days on the estate of Zethus, one of his former pupils, in Campania, where he had hoped to found his city of philosophers (2.17-22). The astrologer Firmicus Maternus, paraphrasing Porphyry's account with malicious increments, holds up this scene as an admonition to Platonists who think themselves superior to the fate that the stars ordain for them;[34] to Porphyry, by contrast, the resolute bearing of his master in his final hours is an illustration of Plato's famous dictum in the *Phaedrus* that philosophy is a preparation for death. Plotinus, he says, was about to draw his last breath when he received a belated visit from Eustochius; his quiet reprimand, 'I am still waiting for you', has perplexed scholars, but must surely mean 'you are fortunate to find me still alive'.[35] The next utterance – syntactically opaque, but clear enough in didactic intent – is either an exhortation to 'reconcile the god in you to the god in the all' or a testimony that he himself had all but attained that goal.[36] The moment of death is said to have been marked by the appearance of a snake which vanished at once through a hole in the wall – not an apposite symbol for the departure of the incorporeal soul, but perhaps a hint that the god Asclepius had been tending him in the absence of his doctor (2.27-8). Nineteen chapters later, it is Phoebus Apollo, father of Asclepius, who celebrates the translation of Plotinus from the turmoil of this 'blood-choked' sphere to the dances of the gods.

The career of Porphyry

Almost all of the information above is drawn from Porphyry's memoir *On the Life of Plotinus and the Arrangement of his Works*. We have seen that the biographer takes numerous opportunities in this work to prove his own loyalty as a pupil, his proficiency as a philosopher and his authority as editor of the *Enneads*. How differently his life appeared to outsiders we discover when we turn to Eunapius' *Lives of the Philosophers*, an anecdotal and garrulous compilation in which the conventional antitheses between magic and philosophy, or philosopher and rhetorician, are almost lost to view. Nevertheless, it is easier to convict the author of folly than of error, and we should not assume that all that he says of Porphyry is worthless when it not corroborated, or that he is the more tendentious of the two when they disagree. In any case, Eunapius at the outset merely confirms and embellishes what was have learned from Porphyry: the Phoenician Malcus, born in Tyre of honourable parents, received his schooling in grammar, rhetoric and philosophy from Longinus, who bestowed on him his conventional name Porphyrios, this being the Greek for purple, the colour of royalty, while the name Malcus signifies 'king'. Longinus, in the letters preserved in the life of Plotinus, oscillates between Malcus and Porphyrios, while Porphyry informs us that the name Basileus, the more literal Greek equivalent for Malcus, was conferred on him by Amelius in Rome. So much then is true, but now Eunapius seems to turn against his subject. Having already acquired some reputation, he says, the young man conceived a desire to see the great city of Rome; on arriving there he attached himself to Plotinus and abjured his former masters. Insatiable in his studies, he at length became so elated by the 'inspired and seminal teachings' of his great mentor that the body and the human condition itself grew odious to him. And so – retracing the journey of Odysseus, but with no eyes for the cities and haunts of men that that hero saw – he departed for Sicily, taking up residence in Lilybaeum, where he shunned both food and human company. Here Plotinus found him, and, as his soul was on the point of quitting the body, reasoned him out of his despair. This, we are told, is Porphyry's own account, not in his biography of Plotinus, but in the treatise or *hypomnêma* in which he recounted his deliverance.[37] Since arguments against suicide which do not appear in the *Enneads* are ascribed in other sources to Plotinus,[38] we need not doubt that such a book was available to Eunapius. That it contradicted the life of Plotinus as flatly as his own account we can hardly believe; on the evidence before us we can say only that the narrative in Eunapius exposes Porphyry to charges of the kind that he appears to be rebutting when he says that it was Plotinus himself who caused him to be absent at his death.

It is not the way of Eunapius to give dates; Porphyry, in his life of Plotinus, tells us that he came to Rome in 263 at about the age of thirty, and departed in 268 for Sicily, some two years before his master's death (*Life of Plotinus* 4.1, 6.1). Of his later career he says nothing in this work, except that at the time of writing it he had passed the age of sixty-seven and tasted that communion with the 'God above all' which Plotinus experienced three or four times in his presence (23.13). Eunapius says that he returned to Rome, where his elegant prose served as a 'Hermaic chain' for doctrines which Plotinus had wrapped up in dark and elliptical meditations.[39] It is Bidez, not Eunapius, who concludes that he was the master of a school,[40] and it is in a tone of friendship, not of authority, that he addressed Castricius Firmus, the Campanian, when the latter had renounced the meatless diet which he and Porphyry had followed under the tutelage of Plotinus.[41] Old ties may have been strengthened by his marriage to one Marcella if she was a relative of the Marcellus who had been his fellow-pupil.[42] It is clear that the pair married late, since in his letter to her he is old enough to be thinking of his last days, and she has seven children by a previous husband. The Christian tradition that she was a Jewess is no more credible than the anecdotes of his having been a Christian who turned against the Church when he was publicly chastised for a heinous sin.[43] An allusion in the *Letter to Marcella* to a work performed on behalf of the 'Greeks' has sometimes been supposed to refer to his writing of a tract against the Christians.[44] Whatever the truth of this, it is likely enough that imperial measures against the Christians would have acted as a stimulus to polemic,[45] and a number of scholars now concur in identifying Porphyry as the philosopher who scandalised Lactantius, the Christian author, by his readiness to inflame the wounds of the Church in 303.[46]

The catalogues of Porphyry's work surviving from antiquity include many works now lost while omitting some that we still possess. A number of the extant books – the treatise *On Abstinence* to Castricius Firmus, the *Letter to Marcella*, the life of Plotinus and a digest of his thought in aphorisms commonly known as the *Aphorisms* – may be regarded as expressions of his mature thought, since they were plainly written after he had completed his studies in Rome. Of the texts that survive, it has sometimes been assumed that those which are more austere and sceptical – like the *Letter to Anebo*, which purports to expose the contradictions of Egyptian priestcraft – are products of experience and reflection, while the more eclectic and credulous – the *Cave of the Nymphs*, the *Philosophy from Oracles*, the *Life of Pythagoras* – must have been composed before he was weaned from his superstitions by Plotinus.[47] The hypothesis fits the prejudices of the modern world; yet anyone who compares the *Laws* of Plato with his *Republic*, or the *Siris* of Bishop Berkeley with his *New Theory of Vision*, will be aware that the evolution of an individual mind does not always duplicate the progress of the sciences. If the *Letter to Anebo* is the palinode of a man who had read his own wisdom into the hieroglyphs in his treatise *On Statues*, why in his work *On Abstinence* does he still speak of the Egyptians as the most rational (*logiôtatoi*) of peoples, and repeat with approval his own account in *On Statues* of rites which the inhabitants of Anubis addressed to a mortal man?[48] It would be logical enough, and true to experience, to imagine that, having slighted the Egyptians in his Hellenised youth, he learned to take pride in his own barbarian ancestry as he grew older, and therefore listened with more attention to Plotinus when he alluded to the mysteries concealed in Egyptian symbols. Again, if his *Philosophy from Oracles* was a juvenile compilation, while the treatise known to Augustine as *On the Regression of the Soul* marks an advance in piety, why are the two so alike that an eminent scholar could pronounce them to be the same work under different titles?[49] Symptoms of development are all the more elusive when an author attempts a variety of topics, as his writing will be informed by a different model in each new venture. When, to the works by Porphyry named above, we add his essays *On the Styx* and *To Gaurum, On the Gestation of the Embryo*, his *Isagoge* or introduction to Aristotle's *Categories*, his commentaries on the same work and those on the *Tetrabiblos* and *Harmonics* of Ptolemy, we see that his not a mind whose growth could be plotted on a simple curve.

The career of Iamblichus

If the *Letter to Anebo* is an ebullition of youthful scepticism, later recanted, it is not so hard to believe that the great refutation, a prolix treatise *On the Mysteries*, was composed by one of his pupils.[50] It is commonly attributed to Iamblichus, who, according to Eunapius, came from Syrian Chalcis, attaching himself to Porphyry after a period of study with one Anatolius who 'held second place to Porphyry', and was perhaps the future

Bishop of Laodicea.[51] We are not told here that either Anatolius or Porphyry was the head of a school, or even that Iamblichus came to Porphyry in Rome. As Dillon remarks,[52] he may have found him still at Lilybaeum; and for that matter, Nicomedia, the eastern capital, cannot be ruled out if Porphyry was the philosopher whom Lactantius accused of fanning Diocletian's persecution.[53] Eunapius certainly indicates that Iamblichus set up his own school, though he does not say where.[54] A letter falsely ascribed to the Emperor Julian seems to locate it in Apamea,[55] where Amelius and Numenius had taught before him; the Byzantine chronographer John Malalas, on the other hand, states that Iamblichus ended his days at Daphne near Antioch, were he had founded a school in the reign of Diocletian's heir Galerius.[56] Most scholars agree that Iamblichus died before 326,[57] while the earliest date assigned to his birth is 242;[58] it would seem, then, that he had time to maintain a school in Apamea between the completion of his studies and his migration to Daphne after 305. Wherever he taught, he gathered about him a 'multitude of disciples', as Eunapius says, the most famous being the rhetoricians Sopater and Aedesius.[59] Anecdotes were told among his pupils of his clairvoyance and his conjuring of spirits; in the first he resembled Socrates and Pythagoras, while in the second he vied with Porphyry, who boasted of having once expelled a daemon from a spring.[60] Nevertheless (Eunapius continues), when Iamblichus heard that some of his pupils professed to have seen him rise ten feet from the ground, he burst into laughter;[61] an ardent rationalist in the study of magic, as in everything else, he evidently concurred with his fellow-Platonists in regarding every gratuitous violation of natural order as the trick of a charlatan rather than a sage.

We need not be surprised that his works included a sober compilation of opinions *On the Soul*, another treatise on its descent (now lost) and commentaries on at least six works of Aristotle, the *Categories*, *On Interpretation*, *Prior Analytics*, *On the Heavens*, *On the Soul* and *Metaphysics*.[62] These were clearly outnumbered by his commentaries on Plato, though only fragments remain of either group. John Dillon has collected his surviving animadversions on the *First Alcibiades, Phaedo, Sophist, Phaedrus, Philebus, Timaeus* and *Parmenides*, and suggests that he will also have handled the *Gorgias, Cratylus, Theaetetus, Statesman* and *Sophist,* as these were the other dialogues on the syllabus which he constructed for his own pupils.[63] His greatest project was a Pythagorean encyclopaedia in ten volumes, the first of which survives as *On the Pythagorean Life*, the second as the *Protrepticus*, the third as *On the Common Discipline of Mathematics*, the fourth as *On the Mathematical Theology of Nicomachus of Gerasa*.[64] His lost works on religious matters included dissertations *On the Gods, On Sacred Images* and *On the Chaldaean Theology*; another (perhaps a section from a longer work) maintained that there could be no migration of souls from humans to beasts or beasts to humans. Dillon, inverting the premises that Bidez applies to Porphyry, declares all these to be late.[65]

Late or early, these works betray no failure of nerve, no loss of faith in reason; on the contrary, as I shall argue below, they presuppose that nothing lies outside the sphere of reason. For Iamblichus there are not two realms of knowledge, the logical and the supralogical, for logic in his view leads us inexorably to the truth beyond logic. Nor is he aware of two intellectual traditions, the Pythagorean and the Aristotelian; in the second book of his Pythagorean enterprise, the *Protrepticus*,[66] excerpts from the Aristotelian work of this name appear to sit cheek by jowl with reminiscences of Plato and exhortations from Pythagorean masters. The table of contents promises to illustrate the utility of philosophy both from common notions and from ancient maxims,[67] to lead the novice through moral and political inquiries to the contemplative life,[68] and to furnish him with a key to the difficult sayings and symbolic figures in which Pythagoras hid this goal from all but the earnest seeker.[69] Typically Aristotelian are the arguments that since we are nobler than beasts we must be ordained for higher ends;[70] that since the soul is either the whole of us or the best of us, this end cannot lie in the appetites or passions of the body;[71] that we can prove this by observing that no human would give up his intelligence even for an unbroken career of pleasure;[72] and that a good which, like intelligence, is desired for itself is logically superior to one that we desire for the sake of another.[73] For all that, it is Anaxagoras who is quoted to show that the end of human life is the contemplation of the heavens.[74] The discipline enjoined in the Golden Verses frees the intellect by ennobling pleasure, extinguishing vice and educating the senses.[75] The three ends of philosophy are virtue, wisdom and happiness; ethics, physics and contemplation are thus the three exercises which the soul must pursue in turn until at last it achieves that 'likeness to god' which consummates the purposes of nature.[76] Elsewhere it becomes apparent that this is the journey which Plato adumbrated in his *First Alcibiades* and completed in his *Parmenides*; it is the same ascent that Porphyry prescribes in his arrangement of the *Enneads*, from the cultivation of virtue to a state above virtue, happiness or finite being, 'alone with the alone'.

These four men, then, nurtured in different provinces of the east, were all Greeks in spirit because they all held that philosophy – the philosophy of Plato – was the one instrument by which the true goods of life could be secured against the perils of war and the injuries of peace. To Longinus, it seems, the dialogues of Plato were texts for academic study; to Porphyry they served both as a canon in their own right and as a companion to Homer and Aristotle; Iamblichus and Plotinus set them before the soul as a ladder from mere perception to the truths surpassing knowledge. The Plato whom they perused with such attention, however, is not the Plato of modern times, or at least not the Plato of English-speaking scholars; the following chapter will try to account for this parting of the ways.

Platonists on Plato

For at least two hundred years it has been the general practice of classicists to handle every dialogue of Plato as a distinct work, to which nothing
may be added from other texts unless it is manifestly demanded by the
argument. Apparent contradictions between two dialogues are assumed to
represent changes in the author's mind, and no attempt is made to
reconcile them by appeal to unstated premises. As change in such a great
mind implies development, it is commonly maintained that the earliest
dialogues are those in which Socrates humbles his interlocutors but
advances no conclusion of his own. Next, on this theory, come the middle
dialogues, in which Socrates assumes the magisterial role, often speaking
to silent parties. In the last phase, he gives way to other protagonists, who
subtly interrogate his own opinions or advance their own with little
circumspection. Statistical investigation of syntax, rhythm and diction
seems to confirm this scheme, though it might be argued that they serve
only to distinguish pedagogic or exoteric works from those designed for
initiates, and that Plato could have had motives at any stage of life for
composing in either manner. If it is the intention, not the date, that defines
the content of the text, we are free to urge, with a minority of scholars, that
every dialogue rests tacitly on the same small body of presuppositions.[1]
These are concealed, it is argued, on the principle that the mind cannot
fully assent to what it has not found out for itself, and maybe also as a
precaution against the cheapening or misconstruction of tenets which it
was easier to publish than to defend. Proponents of this theory are apt to
cite Aristotle's testimony to certain unwritten doctrines, mystical precepts
of geometry and arithmetic, which in fact are not wholly unwritten for
those who uphold the authenticity of Plato's *Seventh Letter*.[2] Adversaries
protest that, if the *Seventh Letter* is genuine, the excursus on first principles is not, and that the unwritten doctrines could easily have been derived
by Plato's followers from his written works.[3] To this last point the unitar-
ian critic can retort that it is only to be expected that the oral and written
doctrines of the same man should coincide.

To Platonists of the third century, it was beyond dispute that the
dialogues formed a system. Proof of its coherence they sought, however,
not in any unwritten doctrine but in an ordering of the corpus which was
designed to lead the student from the experimental or tentative stage, a
mere testing of his wits, to the consummation in which all truth becomes
luminous to the intellect. It was no part of their theory that a whole system

of philosophy is tacitly presupposed in every dialogue; they did contend, however, that Plato himself had such a system before his mind from the beginning. They also believed – and here the gulf between them and the modern exegete is widest – that whatever we conceive to have been the opinion of Plato we should be ready to hold as a philosophic truth.

Philosophy and philology in the interpretation of Plato

Plotinus judged Longinus: 'a philologist, no philosopher at all' (Porphyry, *Plotinus* 14.19-20). We may turn for elucidation to the commentary of Proclus on the *Timaeus*. This author sees some acumen in Longinus' analysis of the opening sentence of the *Timaeus* into three periods (I, 14.7 Diehl); but when he deplores the redundant use of terms denoting youth and age in another sentence, Proclus echoes the sentiment of Plotinus (I, 86.24-5). The *aporia* or uncertainty of Longinus is often the fruit of exegesis without philosophy (I, 51.9-22); after recording his disagreement with Porphyry as to the placing of an adverb, Proclus ostentatiously shifts from words to things before stating his own position (I, 94.10-14). Betraying throughout the interests of a critic rather than of a severe philosopher, Longinus praises Plato's art in composition (I, 59.10-16), inquires whether Homer is one of the ancient poets who are said to imitate best what they know by acquaintance (I, 63.25-6), and asks why the poets should be less fit to teach than others not raised in the city (I, 66.14-20). Philological ingenuity led him to opine that Plato envisaged a martial commonwealth, independent of the one sketched in the *Republic*, to which he alludes at the beginning of the *Timaeus* (I, 31.19-27). While Origen also flirted with this hypothesis, we do not hear that anyone joined Longinus in proposing that the soul in the *Timaeus* is congenital with the seed (I, 51.9-12). His task, as he conceives it throughout, is not to propound a system, but to ascertain what Plato had in mind at the time of writing. Citations from him in Proclus end where the text becomes most interesting to philosophers: his last recorded judgment is that the demiurgic intellect is inferior to the paradigm which it copies, and in this he is contradicted by his own disciple Porphyry, who maintained the superiority of the Demiurge to the forms (I, 322). Both are ranged here against Plotinus, for whom it is an incorrigible maxim that 'the intelligibles are not outside the intellect',[4] and this is the opinion to which, after Porphyry's recantation, every Platonist subscribed.

Plotinus arrived at his views, as Porphyry intimates, by 'paying attention only to the sense' (Porphyry, *Plotinus* 8.4-8). This would be a fair description of his exegesis, which ignores not only points of grammar, canons of style and textual variations, but even the structure of the dialogue and its function in the corpus. He mentions Plato the man only to chide him for an enigmatic style which leads him at times into superficial inconsistencies. The removal of contradiction and the illustration of fundamental principles are his chief concerns: of the dramatic mode that Plato favours he might have said, as he said of the myths within the dialogues, that 'these expressions are used perforce in order to convey some meaning' (*Enneads* 5.8.12.24-5). But how, we may ask, does a man who eschews the study of grammar and rhetoric elicit the 'sense' of a text? From the text itself, he would answer – not from the logic of its surface but from axioms too deep to be retrieved by lexical paraphrase in the manner of Longinus, The philologist will easily remark that the principal subject of the *Parmenides* is the transcendent One, that the Demiurge of the *Timaeus* is a personification of mind, and that the *Phaedrus* and the *Phaedo* are the great dialogues on the soul. But until he discerns the One in the *Timaeus*, mind in the *Phaedrus* and all three of these primordial hypostases in the casuistry of Parmenides, he will fail to grasp the integrity of Plato's thought and misconceive the intention of any dialogue that he proposes to interpret. The paradoxes engendered in the *Enneads* by talk of the One, with the comments of Plotinus on the *Parmenides* and the superfetatory reasoning of Iamblichus on the principle of unity, will be discussed in the following chapter. In this chapter, however, we join Plotinus in approaching the ineffable through the intelligible, through the study of soul and intellect. If he brings more introspection than exegesis to his discussion of the intellect and its relation to the forms, he would have argued that an exegete cannot otherwise steer a course between shallow pedantry and sophistical caprice.

The doctrine that the 'intelligibles are not outside the intellect' is not an immediate datum of exegesis, but (in Plotinus' view) a necessary assumption of the quest for knowledge which Plato's dialogues set before the reader. It is one thing to hold a true belief by accident, another to know, for knowledge must be obtained by means that erase all doubt of the truth of what is known. This certitude never accompanies our perception of things contingent and discrete, because there is nothing in the object, or in our manner of observing it, that precludes our being deceived. Of the object itself indeed no predication is strictly true, for nothing in the material world is identical with the qualities that we predicate of it, and therefore it would be equally true to predicate of it the absence of that quality. Furthermore, while the quality itself may be immortal, the material particular in which it inheres will pass away, or cease to possess that quality; and even if the argument is limited to local and instantaneous perceptions, it is often the case that what is true by one criterion is not true by another, and that what appears so to one observer does not appear so to all. Such terms as 'equal' and 'short' are never absolutes, but are asserted in relation to some standard (*Phaedo* 74b); there is no body that appears beautiful, no action that appears just, to all spectators, and the lover of absolute beauty or absolute justice will therefore not seek goods like these in the sensible world (*Symposium* 210d-211b). Like is known by like, and that which is indefeasibly true must therefore be known through infallible organs (*Republic* 478a-d). It is clear that our senses are fallible, and so is the mind that depends on their reports; it is, however, only through the senses that the mind can make the acquaintance of the phenomenal particular (*Republic* 509d-510b). That the impression which strikes the senses can be translated into knowledge at all is the work of the mind, which embraces the incorporeal form or essence of the particular; but then it is the form, not the particular itself, that the mind subsumes, and hence it is not the particular, but the form, that is truly known.

To Platonists the form (*idea* or *eidos*) is that which is equally present in all particulars of the same kind. Its properties are defined only by the meaning of the word that designates it, not by circumstantial traits of the particular; in contrast to the particular, then, the form is necessarily and eternally what it is. That the form is more than a concept in the mind we may deduce from the existence of the particulars which instantiate it in the phenomenal world. Were there more than one form, the unity of the kind would be unaccounted for; were the form not equally present in all particulars, each of them would instantiate not the kind, but a different part of it. The first premiss entails the transcendence of the form, the second the presence of immanent (or 'enmattered') form in all particulars; Plato had deduced the transcendence, Aristotle the immanence, and in accordance with his usage the word *idea* had come to be reserved for the transcendent form in contradistinction to *eidos*. On Aristotle's view, we come by knowledge of the particular when the everyday mind – the potential intellect, as we might call it, or the matter of intelligence – abstracts the immanent form from the particular and coalesces with it;[5] knowledge of its essence, and the knowledge that we know it, are guaranteed by the active intellect, of which we can learn little from Aristotle except that it renders knowledge possible as light facilitates vision, and that, like his god, it acts upon the embodied world by escaping the limitations of embodiment. For Platonists the work which is assigned to the active reason in Aristotle is performed by the ideas, whether these be conceived as self-subsistent absolutes or thoughts in the mind of God.[6]

For the Platonist it would not suffice to say that knowledge of sensibles is regulated by the transcendent form, for even this would not bring certitude unless we were able to verify that the particular is an instance of the form. It is thus the transcendent form itself, the idea, that is the sole object of infallible cognition, and, as the form, is incorporeal, so that the mind that would unite with it must be wholly free of matter or extension. Before all minds there is mind or *nous* itself, and this is the intellect that Plotinus declares in *Enneads* 5.5 to be the seat of the intelligibles (*noêta*) – that is to say, of transcendent forms. 'If, when the mind knows and knows the intelligibles, it knows them as something other, how would it chance upon them? For it is possible that it would not, as it is also possible for it not to know except when it chances upon them, and then it will not always have knowledge' (5.5.1.19-23). Again, if the objects of the mind were external to it, how would its knowledge differ from that of the senses (5.5.1.48-9)? Truth, which we know to be foreign to the senses, cannot reside in the mind unless the mind itself is as unitary and immutable as truth; and this is possible only if mind and truth are one (5.5.1.42-3, 65-8).

Pure intellect never turns its contemplation from the intelligible, and being subject to no motion from without, is unconscious of time. At the same time it is the seat of life, because life is an inalienable property of the noblest things, and hence (as Plato urged at *Sophist* 248e-249a) one that we cannot fail to predicate of the forms. Intelligence in the biological realm is a function of life, but in the domain of the intelligible life is a function of intellect, since this is the source of motion as of rest (5.5.10.10-15; 6.7.8.25-7). On the one hand there is no entity that does not instantiate a form; on the other, it is only through the medium of life that the form can impress itself on the undulating manifold without giving up the timeless immutability that belongs to it as form.

Nous in Plotinus, then, is not simply one or simply many, but, as he himself expresses it, a 'one-many', corresponding to the Pythagorean Dyad, which, in so far as it is the sole Dyad, is the first exemplification of that unity which it negates by introducing a second principle.[7] Three new questions arise for any Platonist who accepts this paradox. How – to begin at the level of experience – does multiplicity break the seal of unity to extend itself through space and time and produce the manifold contents of our universe? Secondly, does the plurality of the forms impair the unity of intellect, or does each contain the others? Thirdly, if Nous, being one-many rather than one, does not contain in itself the principle of its own unity, whence is that unity derived? The first question concerns the soul, and every Platonist sought the answer in the *Timaeus*. The *Philebus* and the *Sophist* are the dialogues which address the second question, while the third demands recourse to the *Parmenides*. Such is the rich obscurity of the last dialogue, however, that it is possible to derive from it not only the ineffable first principle, the One itself, but the 'one-many' and the 'one and many', which under the names of *nous* and *psukhê* (soul) are the second and third of his three hypostases.

Time, creation, matter: Plotinus on the *Timaeus*

The *Timaeus* of Plato – much the best known of his dialogues in antiquity, serving Platonists (and others) as an encyclopaedic synthesis of theology, natural science and psychology – draws a strong antithesis between two realms. In the realm of being there is no time but the present: we cannot say of anything that it was or will be, but only that it is. In the realm of becoming, by contrast, nothing endures, and where we say 'this is' today we can only say 'this was' tomorrow (27d-28b). The adjective that describes the phenomenal world is spelt indifferently *genêtos* and *gennêtos* in our manuscripts (28c1); in either spelling, the term was understood by a number of critics and disciples to imply that the world has an origin in time. This was a tenable exegesis, but it offered no reply to the philosophical strictures of Aristotle, who argued that before the world all times were as one, and hence there could have been no more reason to bring it into being at one time than at any other.[8] He rejected indeed not only the creation but the creator, Plato's demiurge, who, like a human artisan, succeeds in producing only a blemished copy of the archetype which guides his deliberations because he cannot wholly subdue the recalcitrant forces in the substrate. This substrate – the 'receptacle', 'nurse' or mere 'space' of the dialogue (*Timaeus* 52d3) – is assumed by Aristotle to be identical with the 'great and small' of Plato's oral doctrines and the *Philebus*, and also with *hulê* ('matter') in his own system (*Metaphysics* 1091b-1092a; *Physics* 187a); matter for him, however, is not so much the antonym of form as the potential which the form converts into concrete actuality. Most Platonists appear to have endorsed his interpretation of the receptacle, and to have recognised the force of his objections to Plato's mythical account of the creation. The exegete who wished to redeem the dialogue from his criticisms was therefore required to prove (1) that Plato does not intend to assign an arbitrary beginning to the universe; (2) that he does not compromise the omnipotence or benignity of the Demiurge; and (3) that he does not suppose the evils of the world to be so pervasive and irremediable that it might have been better not to create at all.

1. *Origins*. The belief that the term *genêtos* or *gennêtos* implies an origin in time had been abandoned by all Platonists of whom we have any record before the end of the second century. Atticus is the last exegete who is known to have defended it; Numenius seems to make the world a corollary of the schism which destroys the primordial unity of the intellect, but his language is so poetic as to suggest that he, like Plato in his myths, is employing narrative as a vehicle of metaphysical speculation.[9] Those who maintained the eternity of the world advanced a distinction between the *gennêton*, which is born and hence originates in time, from the *genêton*, which is contingent on the eternal and hence susceptible to change and revolution, but need not have any temporal beginning.[10] Plotinus himself is apt to use these two words and their cognates interchangeably, but in a sense that is compatible with unlimited duration: a succession of instants need not presuppose a first instant, any more than it entails a last.

Time, as Plato had said, was the moving image of eternity (*Timaeus* 37d5). One purpose of *Enneads* 3.7 is to prove the superiority of this formula to other definitions. Time, Plotinus explains, cannot be movement, for whereas movement may be intermittent, time is a continuum (3.7.8-6-8). It is by reference to this continuum that we measure the periodicity of motion; yet time is not this measure, for it submits to measurement even as it 'runs abreast' of the processes to which we assign a temporal duration (3.7.9.20). It cannot be the measure of only one motion, yet if it measured every motion at once, it would run slowly with some and rapidly with others (3.7.8.24). Furthermore, number and quantity are properties of the finite, whereas no beginning or end of time is logically conceivable (3.7.9-75-6). Likewise if time is said to be a succession we may ask, 'a succession of what?'; and if the answer is a succession of temporal instants, we have once again smuggled time into the definition of time (3.7.10.1-8). The vulgar equation of time with astral motions is clearly erroneous, since it is only the soul's intuitive perception of uniformity in these cycles which enables us to use them in reckoning time (3.7.12.25-49). The motion and life of soul, according to Plato, are indefeasible; it has not acquired them through any external cause, and, having possessed them for an infinite time already, has no propensity to lose them by attrition or decay. It is therefore not corporeal (as all body admits of division and is therefore doomed to perish), and is not subject to time in the sense that body is, though it is through the act of the body, circumscribed as these are in time and space, that the presence of soul is recognised. The time that the body experiences arises from, and is therefore not identical with, the unpunctuated motions of the soul that informs it. Just as it is the incorporeal unity of the soul that unites the members of the body, so it is through its simple and changeless motion that it harmonises the manifold and transient operations of the body; the life that is only partially manifested at any instant in the corporeal realm is wholly and simultaneously present to the soul which generates time (3.7.13.44-64).

This concentrated life of the soul, however, is but an image of the eternity which we predicate of the Forms. The Forms are as they are because they could not be otherwise; soul is, as it were, the superabundance of the Forms, the realisation of their benevolent propensity to ennoble every possible level of being. Its being is thus contingent and derived, and the embodied soul, though immortal, is not impassible or impervious to evils. Nor are we obliged to maintain that each particular soul is the parent of time; Plotinus believes, for reasons which will be canvassed more fully later in this chapter, that all souls are in a sense one, and that the most perfect representative of this common soul is the soul of the all, the world soul, which in contrast to the rest inhabits a body that is equally immune to moral and physical corruption. In the *Timaeus* this soul is the first creation of the Demiurge, a composite of the Same and the Other – of changelessness and the propensity to change – which serves as his instrument in harnessing the confused and anarchic motions of the receptacle (35a-37c). Previous interpreters had surmised that this fusion of contraries is a metaphor for the conversion of an evil soul, which they posited – on the premiss that without soul there would be no motion – as the cause of the primitive turbulence in matter.[11] Plotinus, as we shall see, denied that matter, or the evils that infest it, ever subsisted independently of form; for him the narrative merely encodes the metaphysical truth that soul is stable in so far as it participates in intellect, unstable in so far as it is distinct from, and hence inferior to, intellect, as it must be if it is to carry out its task of bringing the sphere of the mutable under immutable norms. In any rational being it is through the soul that knowledge is translated into discursive thought which culminates in action; just as the world is shaped in imitation of the archetype, so any good that the soul effects in the world is an imitation of the good that it perceives in the realm of Forms. To call time the moving image of eternity (3.7.11.20-35) is to say that change, succession and vicissitude in the cosmos are ebullitions of the same principle – the life-principle – which originates in the superabundant unity of the higher realm, and frames a mobile image of the immovable in the changeless revolutions of the stars.

2. *The Divine Creator*. The Demiurge in the *Timaeus* is both intellect and god.[12] The second title indicates power, benevolence and the exercise of providential government (albeit through lesser deities). The first should imply both incorporeality and plenitude of knowledge; we have seen that the majority of Platonists had concluded, against the plain meaning of the text, that the world is eternal, since there was nothing that the Demiurge could have learned which would have disposed him to create at one time rather than another. Plotinus may have been the first, however, to renounce the ontological distinction between the Demiurge and the objects of his thought. For him, as we have seen, this bifurcation is philosophically untenable: if knowledge requires the union of the subject with the object, it will follow that, so long as any object remains external to the intellect, it cannot be fully known. In becoming conscious of anything not identical with itself, the mind assumes the form of the other, and it would therefore be impossible for the Demiurge to be conscious of his own creation without coalescing severally with the contents of the manifold. But as this could never befall the mind in its character as mind – it is only the ensouled or embodied mind that can be dragged into multiplicity by the senses – Plotinus infers that the Demiurge in Plato is a combination of intellect and soul:

> It may be that mind is in one sense the one that divided [pure being among the particulars] and that in another sense mind is not the one that divided. For in so far as the divided entities are from it, mind itself performed the division, but in so far as mind itself remains indivisible, while its products are the ones divided, and these are the souls, it is soul that has performed the division into many souls (*Enneads* 3.9.1.29-34).

Porphyry, then, was at most half wrong if he thought that he was speaking for Plotinus when he identified the Demiurge with the supramundane soul.[13] The passage quoted here from Plotinus, however, is his rider to a comment on *Timaeus* 39e, where, speaking only of contemplation in the supernal intellect, Plato declares that 'mind, when it beholds, in their number and kind, the ideas that are within the living creature [i.e.

paradigm of the living world] knows by meditation that it is necessary for it to possess them in just this number and these kinds'. This text distinguishes three operations – being, seeing, possessing – the first two of which (as Plotinus admits) appear to set the knowing subject against the thing known. The opposition holds, he argues, only in *noêsis* or conception; in reality they are one because the seeing mind is one with the content of its meditation (*to dianoêthen*); the meditative function (*to dianooumenon*), he adds, appears to be tacitly differentiated here (though once again, in concept only) both from the seeing mind and from 'mind at rest in unity and stillness' (*Enneads* 3.9.1.17). His reasoning has now generated a triad, which anticipates the one derived by Amelius[14] from the same passage, in which the three terms are the mind at rest, the mind in possession and the mind beholding. For both the mind in meditation serves itself as a substrate, being at once the subject and the object of the same cognitive act.

Plotinus eschews any literal construction of the myth in which the Demiurge fashions soul by a forcible union of contraries. Any creation of intellect, he argues, must be produced by some necessity, not by fiat or the subjugation of a resistant medium.[15] The necessitating cause of soul he finds in the propensity of life to superabundance: soul is no contingent artefact, but the efflorescence, in the realm of the episodic and particular, of the life which abides eternally and indivisibly in the world of forms. The work of soul, as the *logos* or unfolding deliberation of *nous*, is equally free of labour and contrivance. In its higher phase, it gives laws to the universe in accordance with the beauty and order that it beholds in the paradigm; in its lower phase, as nature, it is creative, yet it works without hands, requires no matter as substrate and brings into being what it already possesses through contemplation.[16] Even in human agents, contemplation is the end, and hence the motive, of every action; in nature, which is soul personified but not yet embodied, end and action coincide. If she could speak, she would liken herself to the mathematicians who draw their diagrams only from inward vision (*Enneads* 3.8.4.8); but nature is too absorbed in her contemplation to speak, and her works too perfect to be drawn.

3. *Evil.* If, then, mind is a demiurge in so far as it creates the possibility of being through the determination of essence, soul too is a demiurge in so far as it frames material representations of the essence in the flux of space and time.[17] But is it responsible only for the enmattered form, or also for the matter which lends concreteness to the form? Reason, and the plain sense of the *Timaeus*, persuaded every pagan scholar before Plotinus that matter is not the offspring but the eternal coefficient of the generative principles, since in every act there is both an agent and a subject of action. Matter, for Aristotelianising Platonists, is the bare potentiality which the agent requires in order to bring about some other state than the one that obtained before his action. But what was such a Platonist to say of the agitation in the receptacle, which could not be reduced to a mere potenti-

ality, and was thought by some interpreters of the *Timaeus* to betoken the presence of an evil soul?[18] To Plotinus an evil soul is inconceivable, yet the otherness which is mingled with the same in the constitution of soul itself cannot fail to engender a diversity which, by compromising the unity of its action, must impair its realisation of the Good.

It is not so much that certain motions are good and others evil as that evil is a concomitant of motions benign in origin and fruitful in effect. Any evolution of plurality from unity is such a motion; even the emergence of mind from the One is not free from *tolma* or audacity,[19] and in the case of the Soul the audacity consists not merely in parting from the intellect but in becoming enamoured of the manifold and binding itself to the passion and change which are born of multiplicity.[20] Soul, in short, is one and many where intellect is one-many. Thinkers before Plotinus might have said that it imbibes the fissiparous tendencies of matter,[21] but on his premisses only soul can be responsible for the turbulence in the manifold. The matter which mars the unity of soul is generated by the same dynamic propensity that caused soul to emerge from intellect; soul itself begets matter as the receptacle of the disseminated forms.[22] Again it is not in the act but in its corollaries that the evil resides: as that which proceeds from unity is always less than unity, so matter is necessarily amorphous, and the centrifugal tendencies in soul are necessarily compounded by the proximity of matter. Soul succumbs to infirmity in its procession from the intellect, in the generation of matter and in the covering of matter; yet it is neither sin nor the punishment of it that motivates the soul's descent, but the principle of plenitude (as it was later known), which decrees that the beauty and order of the transcendent must be manifested in every plane of being.

Otherness in the soul is not a weakness or deformity in itself. When the shortcoming in goodness amounts to a vice and is called *kakia* in Greek, the cause is said to reside in matter (*Enneads* 1.8.14.50). Yet it is only the light of soul itself that makes of matter a 'mirror of Dionysus', into which the individual soul is drawn by a perfidious reflection which induces it to forget its home in intellect (4.3.12). In the soul, then, good is essential, evil an accident – though as these similes of light and reflection are temporal representations of the timeless, it can be said only that evil is essentially foreign to soul, not that there was ever a time when the two were unacquainted. That evil is non-being was a commonplace among Platonists, for whom the 'good' of an object is its reason for existing, hence the end to which it aspires. If the term 'good' is to be univocal, it seems that we ought to be able to speak of one good, by approximation to which an object realised its essence. Matter as the vanishing-point of existence, is devoid of essence and consequently incapable of good. This absence of determinate being may be expressed by adjectives such as 'infinite' or 'immeasurable', with the caveat that these are not conceived as properties of a concrete subject. A quality, says Plotinus, must be predicated either of the whole or of the part, but we cannot speak of an infinite whole, since the very notion of wholeness implies determinate magnitude. Further-more, if magnitude were present in shapeless matter, it would act as an intolerable constraint on the formative principle; it is therefore a property only of matter already informed by soul (2.4.8.19-23). If instead we predi-cate infinity of matter as an accident, that would be to assert that infinity is its logos or definition, and thus to define the indefinable (*Enneads* 2.4.8.15). Matter, which (as Plato said) is known only by bastard reason-ing,[23] is opposed to the determinate 'according to infinity' (*Enneads* 2.4.15.36) but without possessing infinity in the same way as the finite possesses limit. While Aristotle was wrong to identify matter with priva-tion (since privation is the absence of that which otherwise might be present[24]), the Gnostics are equally wrong to regard the evil in matter as anything but a deficiency of good.

The intelligible realm:
Philebus and *Sophist* in Plotinus

For Plotinus, therefore, intellect is identical with being and being with form. None of Plato's dialogues treats the question 'what is being?' with more subtlety and rigour than the *Sophist*. To be, his mouthpiece argues, is to be an entity of a certain kind, and he goes on to distinguish five 'chief genera' (*megista genê*), in which all being – not only indeterminate being, but that of any specific entity – must participate. First comes being itself, with motion and rest. Being cannot be devoid of life and motion, since, as the famous passage cited above declares, that would be to rob it of power, and the power to act is inseparable from the definition of being (*Sophist* 248c-249a). The corollary is not that being participates in motion and rest, for in itself it is evidently in neither state, and in any case there can be neither rest nor motion unless these two participate in being. Motion we perceive to be wholly other than rest but identical with itself, and it is equally true of rest that it is identical with itself but other than motion. Above the categories of rest and motion, then, we must set the same and the other, each of the second pair informing each of the first. As all that endures participates both in motion and in rest, so it participates both in otherness and in sameness: it could not exist unless it were identical with itself, but to be identical with itself is to be other than all that is not identical. All that exists must therefore include a leaven of non-being, from which it follows that when we affirm existence of it we also pronounce it to be other than being. The question which had perplexed the older philosophers, 'How can we think of that which is not?' has thus received an answer: that which is not has neither being nor unity – there is no discrete phenomenon of which non-existence is the essential property – yet the many things that an entity is not are presupposed in the definition of its essence, and consequently (if to be is to be an entity of a certain kind) in the very affirmation that it exists. It follows from this reasoning that those who maintain the incorporeality of being (247c) are in the right if they are referring to the genus, since the first partakers of being – sameness and otherness, motion and rest – are incorporeal. But it is only of the genus itself, and not of the concrete entity, that we predicate rounded fullness, immutability and indivisible unity (245e), for it is only from this primordial and transcendent being that all non-being is logically excluded. That which partakes of being is also a whole, but a conditioned one, whose identity is determined by the negation of almost everything in the unconditioned whole.

Socrates takes up the argument in the *Philebus*, where the question at the outset is: does the Good consist in pleasure? That cannot be, replied Socrates, for pleasure without the perception of pleasure is not desired by anyone, and hence we must allot to *nous* or mind a higher place in the order of goods. To discover what the Good is in itself we must in turn ascertain its place in the order of being: it is revealed by intuition (or by God, in Plato's dialect) that the highest grade of being is the *apeiron*, or unlimited, the abode of the Many, which therefore admits degrees of greatness and smallness, excess and defect (23e-25a). The contents of the second plane, *peras* (or limit), are not crude quantities, but mathematical ratios such as equality and doubleness (25e). Above both, as Socrates intimates, stands the primal one; below is the plane of the mixed, in which the unlimited receives from limit that measure or equilibrium which is exemplified in music, health, the natural year and the life of the philo-sopher (26d). To this category of determinate being the Good is assigned (64c), while for mind there is a fourth level, that of cause, which must be posited to account for the mingling of limit with its contrary (26e). It is the beauty, truth and symmetry in the cause that determine the being of the Good (65a). Which, if any, of these four states of being contains the ideas or forms of Plato's 'middle dialogues' we cannot say with confidence; in Aristotle's strictures on the unwritten doctrines, the copula 'great and small' is treated as one of Plato's synonyms for matter, but the unlimited cannot be matter in the usual sense unless the mixed being commended in the *Philebus* is that of the concrete particular in the sensible manifold.

Plotinus, as we know, posited a 'matter among the intelligibles' (*Enneads* 2.4.5.38). In *Enneads* 2.4.15 he reasons that the unlimited or infinite cannot inhere as an accident in matter, since an accident can inhere only in something other than itself, and the unlimited therefore only in the limited. Matter is itself, therefore, the unlimited; but as this conclusion does not explain the coexistence of finitude and the infinite, he turns to the intelligible realm and declares that there too 'there is matter which is the infinite, and this would seem to have been engendered by the infinitude or the power or the everlastingness of the One, which does not contain but produces the infinitude' (*Enneads* 2.4.15.18-20). The One is therefore here the source of the infinite or unlimited, though at the same time it also functions, in Plotinus' understanding of the *Philebus*, as the limit which imposes measure and discrete identity on each form. The paradox is inevitable, so long as we hold – on premisses derived from the *Parmenides* and studied in the next chapter – that it is only because the One entails the many that anything exists beside the One. It is evident at the same time that it is only by reversion to the One that any other being attains that unity which is a presupposition of discrete identity; thus the One entails the many, and the many find in the One both individual and collective unity. As for the infinity of the One, this signifies not that it lacks any finite property, but rather that it is superior to all finitude. The infinitude of intellectual matter, on the other hand, is compared with that of the matter in which the soul builds, and found to be greater on the grounds that (as was explained above) the infinite inheres only in its opposite, and the forms are more determinate than the contents or creations of the soul.

In the evolution of the many from the One, then, the unlimited takes precedence of the forms, though in logic only and not in time. It is perhaps this, and not the mind itself, that should be regarded as the counterpart of the Pythagorean Dyad. If the motions that accompany the procession of matter to soul in the lower sphere cannot be attributed to this matter of the intellect, it is certain that Plotinus does not consider the mind itself to be inert. Paraphrasing the axiom of *Sophist* 249c that 'absolute being' (*to pantelôs on*) cannot be devoid of life and motion, Plotinus concludes that absolute being embraces all the contents and activities of the intelligible, not only the ideas but the life that they communicate (*Enneads* 6.7.8.25-32). The distinction is once again notional, for in the intellectual realm there is no duality that is not also a unity, and whereas the soul possesses or contains the plenitude of life and intellect (6.7.8.25-49), the life of the intellectual realm is entirely at one with its being – which is to say, it is being itself (3.6.6.10-28; 6.2.7.8-15).

Plotinus has thus explained the paradoxical deduction of both limit and the unlimited from the One in the *Philebus*; he has explained, in elucidation of the *Sophist*, how the timeless life of intellect differs from that which is manifested through succession and plurality by the soul. He has reconciled the prevalent view of matter, that of Aristotle, with one of the most enigmatic theses in the Platonic dialogues, enhancing rather than compromising those features of Plato's thought which are apt to be overlooked in popular accounts of Platonism. He has introduced the terms being, mind and life into his analysis of the unified plurality which proceeds from the One, though (as we shall see) it is only in the work of his successors that this triad assumes a formal character.

Porphyry as Platonist

While Porphyry's *hupomnêma* or dissertation on the *Timaeus* bore the traces of his schooling with Longinus, his tenacity in annotation carried him beyond points of style and grammar into pronouncements on the longevity of daemons, the significance of comets and the seasons of the Nile.[25] Against his tutor he argued that the grandeur of Homer may stir the imagination, but philosophy alone can quell the passions and endow the soul with virtue.[26] Plato, he held, conveys this moral instruction through his representation of friendship in the opening scene (I, 24.12-17), through precepts for the instruction of the young (I, 194.15-17), and through the history of Atlantis, which in Porphyry's view was neither a digression nor a bald tale of the past, but a symbolic representation of the warfare between the soul and adverse daemons, which in turn prefigured the victory of the Demiurge over the forces of dissolution in the cosmogony which occupies the remainder of the dialogue. In Atlantis he saw an image of the sublunar cosmos, its priests corresponding to archangels who act as divine ambassadors, its warriors to daemons who descend into bodies, its shepherds to the daemons who take custody of brutish souls, its hunters to those who enclose the soul in a body, and its farmers to those who are given the charge of crops (I, 147.6-24; 152.12-28). Proclus implies that Porphyry believed himself to be fusing the interpretations of Origen and Numenius, and that he hinted at an analogy between the laceration of the soul and the dismemberment of Osiris or Dionysus (I, 77.3-25). At the same time, he appears to have regarded the malign daemons of his own allegory as personifications of the material forces to which the soul falls prey in the course of its descent (I, 171.19-20).

The cosmogony itself he still takes literally enough to maintain that the Demiurge is distinct from, and inferior to, the paradigm; he rejects the plain sense, however, when he denies that perfect wisdom (*phronêsis*) operates by contrivance and infers from the word *genêton* not that the universe was created in time, but only that it is composite and must therefore depend upon a simple cause.[27] The chaos described by Plato, he argues, represents not what was before creation but what would be if the Demiurge had not clothed matter with form. Such epithets as *agen(n)êtos* ('unoriginated') and *aidios* ('eternal') he reserved for this simpler and loftier order of being. Thus he construed an ambiguous text to mean not that the Demiurge 'always' looks upon that which is self-identical, but rather that he looks upon that which is 'always' self-identical (I, 271.28-31); where others had taken the question at *Timaeus* 27c to be in what sense the world is ingenerate and in what sense it is generated, he and Iamblichus favoured a different reading, in which the question is whether the world is generated or ingenerate (I, 219.20-2). We have seen that he identified the Demiurge as the hypercosmic soul (I, 307.1; 322.1-2); in another passage, the title *patêr* ('father') is understood to mean that the Demiurge is the sole author of the cosmos, but Porphyry infers from the associated term *poiêtês* ('maker') that it was formed from matter that he did not create (I, 300.1-3).

Little remains of Porphyry's observations on the *Philebus*, except his comment that the locution 'great and small' denotes simultaneously the infinitely extensible and the infinitely divisible, and that both spring from the *aoristos duas,* or limitless dyad.[28] This dyad he affirms to be the product of two monads, that of the great and that of the small (Fr. 174.28-9 Smith). The good that is defined in the *Philebus* he believes, in opposition to other readers of the dialogue, to be the composite intellect.[29] He appears to have denied the presence of otherness, and hence perhaps of intellectual matter, among the forms when he maintained that in the *Sophist* non-being is predicated only of the contingent[30] – that is to say, we cannot say of any eternal entity that it is this and not another. Of the Form we can only say 'it is'; matter, on the other hand, is deficient in being, and evil not by virtue of any property but because it 'shuns the good'.[31]

Iamblichus as Platonist

Pupils of Iamblichus were required to master a syllabus of ten dialogues: *First Alcibiades, Gorgias, Phaedo, Cratylus, Theaetetus, Sophist, States-man, Phaedrus, Symposium and Philebus.* Only then were they qualified to study the *Timaeus* and the *Parmenides*, one the physical and one the theological epitome of Platonism, and hence of all philosophy.[32] Like Porphyry, Iamblichus maintains against older critics who ignored the tale of Atlantis, or read it only as a bald narrative of facts, that it prefigures the entire subject of the dialogue. Porphyry's explanation of it, however, he denounced as 'barbarous foppery' as it fails to perceive that the gods, not souls or daemons, are the true protagonists of this allegory. The priests of Atlantis, in his submission, stand for the 'secondary essences' which serve and honour the primary causes; warriors are the powers that administer punishment to the impious, shepherds those who govern life throughout the cosmos, hunters the general powers who direct the motions of the phenomenal universe, farmers those who oversee the ripening of the 'seeds' that descend from heaven to earth.[33] We may note, in anticipation of Chapter 8, that this is quite in the spirit of Iamblichus' treatise *On the Mysteries*, where he urges that the proper business of magic is not the evocation of daemons or phantasmal apparitions but the parting of the veil that hides the true gods from the soul.

To make sense of his observations on the cosmogony in the *Timaeus*, we must understand the first principles of Iamblichus' philosophy. With a rigour not characteristic of Plotinus, he distinguishes three modes in each of the three hypostases. The highest, or 'unparticipated', mode, is that in which the One or Mind or Soul is merely itself in contradistinction to all other subjects. Next comes the participated mode, in which it lends itself as a unifying principle to that which lies below it. In the third mode it acts upon the particular 'by way of participation or relation'.[34] Thus there is no contradiction in maintaining, with Plotinus, that each of the three hypostases can be present in the manifold without forfeiting its unity. At the same time, by divorcing the unparticipated One from the One participated and the One existent, he can give an account of unity in the intelligible world without subscribing to Porphyry's conflation of the One with the highest member of the intelligible triad. The triad itself is pervasive in his system, and the order of terms is fixed, since, as he said in his *Commentary on the First Alcibiades*,[35] being is more germane to us than life and life than intellect, though the influence of all three extends to the manifold and to the matter that it subsumes. The diversity among composite particulars has its origin in the Dyad which is the first offspring of the participated One.[36] Yet even the simple and uncompounded contents of the intellect, the forms, are individuated (as the *Sophist* tells us) by the antithetical genera rest and motion, sameness and otherness: this otherness, which we may take to be identical with intelligible matter in Plotinus, is the only cause of individuation among the Forms, while it co-operates with the Dyad to produce the composite entities that subsist in the realms below. The One or unparticipated monad in the psychic realm,[37] by virtue of which all souls are souls, is the offspring of the simple and the dyadic in the noetic or intelligible[38] realm; the noetic monad itself, perhaps identical with the participated One,[39] is already a hybrid by comparison with the absolute simplicity of the first cause.

Iamblichus censures Porphyry's departures from the teaching of Plotinus;[40] yet in his commentaries he is not afraid to correct or amplify the elder philosopher's speculations. Nowhere is this more evident than in his handling of the three topics set out above – the nature of time, the activity of the demiurge, and the generation of matter:

1. Against Aristotle, who held that time is motion, Iamblichus contends that, whereas motion implies the permanence of the thing moved, time is autonomous, and that whereas motion is nevertheless the antonym of rest or permanence, time is opposed to nothing.[41] Time, he declares, is a measure not in the sense that it is measured by moving objects or that temporal succession can occur only as a concomitant of their motions, but in the sense that it is the cause of the celestial revolutions and the one thing that unites them.[42] From the time which accompanies the procession of life and soul he seems to distinguish an absolute time, an 'ungenerated now' which is not, like the time that we experience, a series of instants vanishing into the past as soon as they drop from the womb of the future.[43] It was not this absolute time – omnipresent and indivisible, immeasurable yet measuring the noetic world – that is styled the 'moving image of eternity' at *Timaeus* 37d15, but its manifestation as the periodicity which measures and comprehends all other motions in the cosmos. Time is amphibious, ranking with eternity yet coming into existence with the cosmos, and aspiring to the likeness of eternity even while it provides the conditions under which change and generation can occur in the 'realm of becoming'.[44] This time derives from being its 'was' and 'will be', from life the process of ageing

or growing younger, and from intellect the determination of future, present and past.[45]

2. Proclus reports that Iamblichus equated the entire noetic cosmos with the Demiurge, in agreement with Plotinus. In fact the passage to which he appeals states only that the Demiurge contains the ensemble of being and the intelligibles[46] and elsewhere he affirms more cautiously that Iamblichus 'united' the Demiurge and the paradigm.[47] In this, he adds, Iamblichus is superior both to Atticus, who put the Demiurge above the paradigm,[48] and to Porphyry, who inverted this conclusion. In a longer citation the cosmos, as the chief among living entities in the visible plane, is said to bear more resemblance to the 'essential living being' than to the Demiurge. To the glory of this it owes its own visibility;[49] by aspiring to intelligible beauty it sustains the form of an everlasting sphere, which, by encompassing the elements and all that is made from them, imitates the comprehensive unity of the paradigm.[50] It remains true that the Demiurge is engaged in the eternal contemplation of the forms within the 'existent living being', and that Numenius was wrong to suppose that his vision could be deflected to the lower world;[51] at the same time, this 'living being', as the totality of genera and species,[52] cannot possess the unity of the noetic monad. It is a triad in which the paradigm represents being and the Demiurge mind; while contemplation unites him to the paradigm, they do not become strictly one.

3. Matter is for Iamblichus a pure otherness which enhances the diversity of the *logoi* or rational principles that it receives from mind by way of soul and nature.[53] The descent is all the more fatal to the unity of the *logoi* because it is only the monadic soul, not the soul at work in the universe, that participates in intellect, and because nature is conceived here as a hypostasis inferior to soul. Whereas Plotinus held that all souls are one, Iamblichus delineates five categories – divine, daemonic, heroic, human and animal – in his treatise *On the Soul*,[54] and of these five it is only the divine whose acts are coterminous with their own being. Between the human soul and its objects stands the ponderous body, and in consequence some portion of its labour is always dissipated in matter. Since no part of the individual soul remains undescended, even the will that is strengthened by philosophy will not escape the coquetry of matter without assistance from the gods. On the other hand, it would not be true to say that matter is evil or in conflict with the divine, for it is not in the soul but in the supernal realm that it has its origin. Hermes, we are told (it is not clear whether this quotation is drawn from the *Commentary on the Timaeus* or the treatise *On the Mysteries*) derives materiality from essentiality[55] – and thus, it would seem, accords to matter the second place in the intelligible triad which is elsewhere assigned by Iamblichus to life. The term 'materiality' (*hulotês*) seems to designate not so much noetic or intel-

ligible matter as an idea of matter, and thus to imply that matter has its own essence; in that case matter can properly be said to exist, and by some necessity other than that which decrees that the chain of being must reach an end. Matter in Iamblichus in never called non-being or the prime evil; it is not the ebb-point of an overflowing plenitude, but a substance with its own place in the determinate economy of being.

The genesis of the forms was examined at greater length in the commentary on the *Philebus*, where the intellect was found to occupy two planes, the noetic and the noeric. These terms are untranslatable, but the first denotes a mode of thought to which everything real is present simultaneously and with no sense of discreteness or succession, while the second denotes the highest mode of thought in which the knowledge of the whole is attained through knowledge of the elements. Since the noetic intellect is a pure monad (corresponding to the First Mind in Numenius and the self-thinking God of Aristotle) it unifies the forms which are differentiated in the noeric intellect. It is in the noeric that the first plurality appears; monadic though the noetic is, however, in relation to all below, it is 'adorned' by three distinguishable, though coalescent, unities – truth, beauty and proportion – which appear in the *Philebus* as the determinants of mixed being.[56] By making these the first monads after the One, Iamblichus shows that he regarded the good or final cause, and not the concrete being of the particular, as the *skopos* or principal subject of the dialogue.[57] We cannot say whether he held, like his admirer Syrianus, that each of the monads is the parent of one member of the intelligible triad (truth of being, beauty of life, proportion of intellect);[58] it is clear at least that his method in exegesis was to juxtapose what others had conflated, on the assumption that the dialogues formed a system in which no two names ever denote the same reality. Lest Plato should appear prolix, the interpreter must be prodigal – a maxim that may help us in the next chapter to follow the reasonings by which Platonists of the third century tried to fathom the multitudinous simplicity of the first cause.

4

Logic, Number and the One

The doctrine of the One in Plotinus is often described as 'mystical', yet there is little of what we now call mysticism in his writings – only one account of a rapture which extinguishes the senses, no prescriptions for inducing this, and no celebration of love except as a disciplined rarefaction of thought and feeling. Like Plato he believed that it is only from the summit of conscious reasoning that we can take a step beyond conscious-ness, that the height is scaled by logic, not by the cultivation of subliminal faculties. The third branch of philosophy after ethics and physics, logic was for a Platonist not merely the science of terms but the analysis of being. The method of collection and division espoused by Plato first divides the field of study into that which is x and that which is not-x, then subjects one half of this dichotomy to the same operation, and so proceeds until it defines a set whose only member is the subject of the inquiry.[1] Since it presumes that to be of a kind is not to be of another kind, this method seems to entail that a thing existing in the world will simultaneously participate in Being and in not-Being; yet how can not-Being exist, as a possible subject of participation, unless it has a share in its antonym, Being? Socrates unties the knot with the help of a Stranger who claims to speak for the venerable Parmenides (*Sophist* 237a): together they conclude that whatever exists in the present world is at once at rest and subject to change, combining a measure of sameness to other things with a measure of difference. Motion or Change, Rest or Stability, Sameness or Identity, Differ-ence or Otherness are the four *megista genê*, or 'greatest kinds' that deter-mine both what the object is and what it is not (254b-255e). Not-Being is perceived to have been a mirage, while Being remains, at the head of these four great kinds, to determine not *what* the object it, but *that* it is – and this, as a number of modern philosophers have agreed, is still the great mystery.

We shall see in this chapter how Plotinus defends this account of being against the logic of Aristotle, which not only entails a different theory of knowledge and existence in the sensible world, but precludes the real existence of anything other than the sensible particular. We shall then see how, still following the Eleatic strain in Plato, he passes beyond the determinants of being to the ineffable conditions of all existence, and how his quest for the ground of unity leads to speculation on number. Finally, we shall see how the younger Neoplatonists turned his ontology into a theology, while embracing numerology not merely as an overture to higher investigations but as a means to the liberation of the soul.

In his *Metaphysics* Aristotle states that that the Greek noun *ousia* ('essence', 'substance') may denote the matter, the genus, the universal or the quiddity ('what it is to be').[2] In his *Categories* he describes the concrete particular alone as the 'prime *ousia*', and the form as a 'second *ousia*' to which existence cannot be properly ascribed (*Categories 2a*). These accounts are sometimes thought to be irreconcilable;[3] what is clear in both, however, is that Aristotle holds, in contrast to Plato, that being ought to be predicated only of the particular, or of the universal as a concomitant of the particular. He admits indeed that to recognise the particular as an object of some kind we must grasp the immanent form – that the mind indeed must become identical with this form[4] – but this does not entail that the form exists where it is not instantiated. Again he acknowledges in the *Metaphysics* that there are beings devoid of matter (1073a30-1073b5), but even these are particulars, not universals. At the same time, all *ousia*, whether particular or universal, is logically the subject of the first and most important of the ten categories or modes of predication. The terms that fall under this category are nouns, and it cannot be enlarged by the reification of adjectives which signify quantity, quality or relation. To speak of the Great, the Good or the Equal is only to speak generically of the entities which lend themselves to these predicates, and the generic, as we have seen, has no existence without the particular. There is no one hegemonic form of the Good, as Plato thought (*Nicomachean Ethics* 1096a-b); and since existence belongs primordially to discrete particulars, while generic or second *ousia* is merely predicated of these, Being cannot be conceived as a single entity which presides immutably among the 'great kinds'.

Porphyry's Aristotelianism

The *Metaphysics* is openly inimical to Plato, or at least to the acknowledged heirs of Plato; the doctrine of the *Categories* too seems incompatible with a theory of Forms or Ideas in which the archetype alone is real and the concrete instance a penumbral copy. Nevertheless the dominant view among Platonists, from the second century onward, was that Aristotle and Plato taught the same philosophy.[5] Before Plotinus Atticus was, so far as we know, the sole dissident; after Plotinus the two Athenian masters were fused inextricably in the teaching and historiography of the Platonic schools. For all his strictures on Aristotle's logic (which I discuss below) Plotinus himself did more than any previous thinker to reconcile the Stagirite with his mentor, as Porphyry notes in his biography. While Porphyry's six-part *Harmony of Plato and Aristotle* is lost,[6] his commentary on the *Categories*, with fragments of a longer one, survives to show that he made use of this text in the instruction of his pupils. The extant commentary takes the form of a catechism defending the structure of Aristotle's treatise and eking out the obscurities and lacunae in his definitions of substance, accident, quality, quantity and other predicates.

More famous – indeed the best-known work of Porphyry from his own time to the renaissance – is his *Isagoge*, or introduction to logic, known in the middle ages as the *Quinque Voces* or 'five words', because its object is to elucidate the terms genus, species, substance, accident and property. Although the *Isagoge* neither follows the order nor distils the content of any Aristotelian treatise, it is avowedly a preface to the *Categories*, the subject of which it pronounces to be not the nature of being but the use of predicative terms.

We predicate a genus or a species in response to the question 'what is it?'; we predicate a difference or an accident in response to the question 'what is it like?' (*Isagoge* 3.15-20). It is by an intrinsic difference which is part of its definition that one species of a genus is distinguished from another; each genus (except the highest) is itself a species of a superior genus; each species (except the lowest) is a genus to lower species (5.1-17). An example of the lowest genus is 'rational animal', 'man' being not a genus but a species whose members are individuated by their accidents (4.29-32). Of these accidents some are inseparable, and it is to these that the individual owes his identity. Socrates, as man, is essentially rational; as Socrates, he is properly the son of Sophroniscus, but he is not essentially healthy, either as Socrates or as man (8.21; 9. 8). Inseparable accidents may characterise a whole class of individuals who do not constitute a species: the black skin of the Ethiopian, for example, is not essential to him as a man, but it is inseparable from him as an Ethiopian, and without it he would cease to be, not only this person, but this kind of person (13.2-6). A typical Ethiopian, then, insofar as he belongs to the species 'animal', will be sentient and mobile; insofar as he belongs to the species 'man' he will be rational and biped; his blackness he will possess as an inseparable accident in common with every other Ethiopian, but a cluster of inseparable accidents will set him apart from all other Ethiopians. At any given time he will also possess other traits which could be subtracted from him without destroying his identity or estranging him from his species. Even his inseparable accidents could be taken away without 'destroying the subject' – that is to say that it would not be self-contradictory to imagine an Ethiopian who is white, though such a being cannot be realised in nature (13.3).

An accident of a species is called a property, and four kinds may be distinguished, all in some sense alienable (12.13-22). Properties of one kind pertain only to members of one species, but not to every member of it (being a doctor, a geometrician, or – as the argument seems to demand – an Ethiopian); another pertains to all members of a species, but not only to that species (bipedality in humans, for example); another pertains to all members of it, and only to them (the greyness of age in humans is the sole instance offered by Porphyry); and another pertains at all times to all members of it and only to them (the stock example is risibility, or the power of laughter in humans). Medical knowledge and greyness are thus sufficient but not necessary conditions of being human; bipedality seems to be a necessary condition, and risibility both a necessary and a sufficient one. The necessity circumscribes the species, not the individual, since (as Porphyry remarks at 12.18) no man is laughing all the time, and (as we have all observed) a man may lose his legs and remain not merely the same individual but a man. The inseparable accident, on the other hand, confers identity on the individual but may at the same be predicable of others, even of individuals in a different species: both ravens and Ethiopians are black (22.7).

The genus is superior to the species insofar as it contains it, while the species surpasses the genus insofar as it has more properties (10.21-11.7). The genus might be said to be the matter of the species and the species the form of the genus. But what is it that truly exists – the genus, the species or the individual? The last alone, according to Aristotle, for whom 'exists' is a word that lends itself to a number of uses, neither synonymous nor casually homonymous. Accidents exist insofar as they are attributed to an existent subject; genera and species exist insofar as there are concrete particulars which instantiate them. Porphyry, in his *Commentary on the Physics*, seems to endorse this Aristotelian distinction between primordial and secondary applications of the verb, and in the *Isagoge* he takes the same position, denying roundly that all things that exist are members of a single genus by virtue of their existence.[7] Does he thereby contradict Plato, who in his *Sophist* places being at the head of the five 'great kinds'? If he does, then he also contradicts Plotinus, who, in one of his most mature and delicate meditations, argues against the Stoics that is not one genus subsuming all the others. In fact there is no inconsistency, as Plato had used the term *genos* in *Sophist* to denote not a class but a reified predicate – thus, of course, exposing himself to the strictures of Aristotle – but not in the *Categories*, where nothing is at issue but the logic of predication. Porphyry himself declares at the outset that the subject of the *Categories* is not ontology but the use of words (1.9-18). Where he seems to think otherwise, it is because the modern commentator foists a Platonic sense on such locutions as 'the common man, who makes all men one',[8] as though it were the same thing to say that all men are men by virtue of one humanity and that all men are men by virtue of participation in a transcendent form.

Plotinus against Aristotle

All this Plotinus vehemently repudiates in the first two treatises of the sixth *Ennead*. He will grant that the term *ousia* is ambiguous in the sensible realm, and that none of its senses here coincides with its meaning in the higher realm (6.1.19-30); nevertheless, he argues, there must be some one determinant by virtue of which whatever exists is said to be. Being, he will conclude, has but one genus in several species (6.2.7.16); the categories which follow substance in Aristotle, while not true genera, are more than names. Quantity, for example, is properly number, and it is because they admit of number that magnitudes, intervals, times and spaces in the present world are real quantities and make up a single class (6.1.4-5). Relations too may not constitute a genus, and in the present world they are predicable only of objects brought into juxtaposition; but there would be no true excess, defect, quality or doubleness if these terms did not have counterparts in the intelligible realm (6.1.6-9). Quality too must exist there – though it might be affirmed that in this higher realm it has the character of a power or form (6.1.10.24-7). Of course there is no intelligible counterpart of negation or deficiency, though these terms are as proper to language as their antonyms, but this is merely to say that beauty and ugliness, good and evil, are not equipollent members of the same genus (6.1.10). Plato has shown in the *Sophist* that to be some one thing is not to be any other, that to partake in sameness is to partake of difference; it is through this optic, not through that of the Aristotelian categories, that we see how a thing can fail to be good or beautiful without participating in their contraries, as we also see how the beautiful or the just can be self-identical yet other than the good.

Aristotle's discussion of the other six predicates is so jejune that Plotinus need do little more than hint that some are duplicates while others make a capricious unity of diverse terms. He devotes the longest critique to action and passion, which (on Aristotle's account) he understands to be complementary and mutually exclusive. Does this mean, he asks, that when the teacher teaches, the student cannot be said to have performed an act in learning (6.1.20.26-9)? If (as he and Aristotle believe) it is the mind that is supremely active, will every unconscious process, such as growth, be a passion, and every unwilled corollary of an act, such as leaving a footprint (6.1.22.29-30)? And what of those acts which require no substrate and have no determinate end, such as the exercise of thought, which Plato and Aristotle both regard as the sovereign good in life (6.1.22.26-9)? Plotinus is less concerned here to be just to Aristotle than to establish his own position that activity and passivity are best understood not as correlates but as indices of motion, one of the four great kinds subordinate to being in the *Sophist*. The final chapters of *Ennead* 6.1 (25-30) dispose of the Stoic view that the four genera of substance, quality, quantity and relation are united by the one genus of matter. This, Plotinus argues, is to give first place to that which is last in the order of existence, a fugitive from unity and being, which cannot be the source of anything that possesses determinate properties, since it is itself empty of properties until it is taken up and shaped into body by the soul.

Enneads 6.2 is a vindication of Plato's doctrine in the *Sophist*. We may agree with Aristotle that being is not a genus, that it is not ascribed univocally to substances and to accidents to intellect, soul and stone. But this serves only to demonstrate that the unity of being does not reside in the individual, in the genus or in the aggregation of genera but in some transcendent principle superior to all being. Whatever exists falls short of this sublime unity, and will thus experience being as plurality. Thus soul, though in a sense one, cannot participate in being without participating also in life or motion, which is not logically identical with being or a species of it (6.2.7.5). Motion partakes of being, and soul partakes of being through motion; at the same time, to say of any subject that it changes or moves is to say that it has a share in rest or stability, since otherwise we could not say what it is that changes or moves (6.2.7.24-30). Rest, being the correlative of motion, has no more right to be identified with being; we have thus arrived at a triad which is none the less apprehended both as trinity and as unity. The unity is more perfect in the intellect, which, as the habitation of self-identical forms divorced from matter, is identical with being and the guarantor of unity and being in all lower entities. Yet even in this realm being, motion and rest are not indiscernible, and we must add the category of otherness or difference (6.2.8.35). Our premiss, however, is that these four constitute one subject; accordingly, just as motion was found to desiderate rest, so now we must posit sameness as the necessary correlative of difference (6.2.8.37). Thus we obtain the five great kinds of the *Sophist*, and the second treatise has built a Platonic ontology on the ground that the first purports to have cleared of Aristotelian logic.

The two sciences are treated as one when he goes on to reject other terms which might be proposed as categories or great kinds. Magnitude and quantity, for example, are but varieties of number, which Plotinus has found not to be a genus (6.2.13). No individual thing is a number, nor does the individual participate in number but in unity. Unity and being are not identical, nor is there any strict ratio between them, since an army is as real as a man but does not possess the same degree of unity (6.2.11.5-6). There is a unity of soul and of intellect (6.2.11.11ff), but even the latter fails to exemplify it perfectly; since nothing is truly one, we should regard unity not as a predicate of anything but as the ultimate goal to which all things aspire.

The *Parmenides* and the One

This elusive character of the One Plotinus believed to have been established in the *Parmenides* – the new testament of third-century Platonism as the *Timaeus* was the old. The rigorous critique of the theory of forms (or an early sketch of it) in the first half of the dialogue has monopolised the attention of modern scholars. Plotinus and his contemporaries, by contrast, looked for a more constructive project, and discovered it in the second half, where Parmenides propounds a series of nine irreconcilable paradoxes, or antinomies, which arise first from the premiss that 'the One is', and then conversely from the premiss that it 'is not'. In antiquity, as in modern times, it was generally agreed that the first three antinomies are not only the longest but the most instructive. No summary can disguise the numerous fallacies in the reasoning, which in any case would not be seen by Platonists as errors, but as examples of the midwifery which Plato employs in drawing out the intelligence of the reader:

1. (*Parmenides* 137c-142a). If the One is, it must be one not many, and will therefore be indivisible. On the other hand, it cannot be a whole because a whole consists of parts. Having no parts, it has no beginning or end, and is therefore infinite. It cannot be contained by another body unless it possesses a circumference; but the corollary that the circumference would touch the containing body at many points is consistent with the hypothesis of its indivisibility. Nor can it contain itself, for then it would be at once the thing containing and the thing contained, and would hence be two, not one. Thus the One is in no place; nor can it be in time, for with duration it would grow older, and thus be at once both older and younger than itself. Having no place it cannot be at rest, but it cannot be in motion either, for this would entail translation part by part from one place to another. Plurality would arise if we were to predicate sameness or being of the One, since 'one' is not synonymous with either term; that it cannot partake of otherness without prejudice to its oneness is self-evident. It follows, then, that if the One exists it lacks the properties of existence, does not inhabit space and time, cannot be defined and does not participate in any of the 'great kinds'.

2. (*Parmenides* 142b-157c). Let us stipulate instead that since the One is, it must partake of being. Since being and the One are not identical, we must now admit the presence of duality, hence of parts. The One is the whole that contains its parts; on the other hand, since the whole is not in the parts it must reside in something else, so that the One will be both the container and the contained. What is contained is finite, but, as the one is the base of all number, it is present in every multiple; since there is no limit to multiplicity, the finite and the infinite are equally predicable of the One. That which is in itself is at rest, while that which is in another is in motion: both, therefore, are true simultaneously of the One. Let us now posit the not-one in opposition to the One; each will be the same as itself and other than the other. Yet this otherness cannot reside in either, since it would then coexist with sameness; and if the One cannot be other than the not-one, and does not stand in the relation of part or whole to it, the two must be the same. Since it at once contains and is contained in the other, the One is greater and less than the other, and consequently greater and less than itself.

3. (*Parmenides* 155e-157b). Finally, since whatever exists exists in time and must therefore age, we cannot evade the paradox that the One is both older and younger than the other, older and younger than itself. Some regard this as a pendant to the second hypothesis, taking the

third to commence at 157b with the argument that, if the One is the same as, yet other than, the not-one, it will partake not only of being but of its contrary, becoming, as it passes from one antithetical state to the other. Furthermore, if the parts of the One are other than the whole, we must conclude that insofar as they are other than the One they partake of indefinite multiplicity, while insofar as they are bounded by the One (as, to exist at all, they must be), they partake of finitude.

The modern critic detects not only humour but equivocation: does the term 'one' denote a single entity or is it meant to stand for anything of which we can predicate onehood? For Plotinus and his contemporaries the question did not arise: Parmenides having been a Pythagorean, and Plato a sound interpreter of Parmenides, it was clear not only that this fugue has one theme, but that it is the grand theme of philosophy – the transcendent source of number from which Speusippus (for one) had traced the descent of all numerable beings.[9] That all things flow from the One was the oral teaching ascribed to Plato, which could not be revealed without subterfuge in his dialogues, since he declines in his second letter to put his own name to any philosophical writing. But why, if his *Parmenides* is broaching a serious argument, does he proceed to juggle with it, dropping in every new hypothesis the balls that the previous one had kept in flight?

The logic of Plotinus, as we have seen, can entertain degrees of unity. Accordingly, he can hold that the three hypotheses present the One under different modifications – first as the absolute, then as incipient multiplicity, and finally as phenomenal multiplicity – which is to say that the unity canvassed in the second hypothesis is that of Intellect, and in the third that of Soul.[10] This was a familiar triad to readers of Moderatus, a Pythagorean whom some adduced as a forerunner to Plotinus.[11] Porphyry reports that he subordinated the One in Soul to the One in Intellect, and both to the unconditioned One; whether he was commenting on the *Parmenides*, as Dodds opines,[12] we cannot now determine, and we should not forget, that most Pythagoreans appealed to sources which professed to be older than Plato. The most celebrated treatises of Plotinus on the One are not addressed, in fact, to those who knew the *Parmenides* or had any prepossession in favour of Plato; the man who called Longinus 'no philosopher but a philologist' was as conscious as Plato's enemies and rivals that fidelity in exegesis is not a test of philosophical truth.

The Necessity of the One

The treatise *On the One, or the Good*, which stands as Plotinus' last word to the reader in the *Enneads*, was the ninth of 54 treatises in order of composition. It is not the loftiest or the most abstruse work in the corpus, but it is the most lucid and cogent demonstration that the first principle is superior to the intellect. The argument begins with an elementary reflection on experience. Whatever we can speak of is both a member of some class and a determinate individual, distinct from other members of its class. It follows that whatever can be spoken of in the singular – an army no less than a body, and a body no less than a point – possesses unity (6.9.1.4-8). If it does not exist as one thing, it does not exist at all, and thus if unity cannot be predicated of it, nothing else is predicable. We may add here what Plotinus takes for granted – that no particular entity in the material realm is identical with its own unity, or unity would be a multiple. Nor can the unity of the individual be grounded in any part of it, or in the sum of parts. Not in the part, because there is no coincidence, but rather an opposition, between the integrity of the whole and that of any one portion of it; not in the whole because it is in the nature of the manifold to be many rather than one.

The source of unity therefore lies outside the discrete particular – perhaps, we might conjecture, in the soul which preserves the form of the individuated body, and enables its various faculties and organs to work as one. Yet soul itself is the seat of diverse faculties (6.9.1.39-42), and we must say of it, as of body, that it is one only insofar as it participates in a oneness to which it approximates by degrees (6.9.1.38). When free of the contingent, soul approaches the condition of mind, in which nothing is adventitious, and all that is predicable is logically implicit in the mere affirmation of being. Is unity then is identical with being itself – the Being that is equated with mind in *Enneads* 6.1-2 and found to be prior to every circumscribed existence, including even the essence that is realised in the immaterial form? If we endorsed this inference, however, we should have to dispense with one of two positions which Plotinus believes himself to have proved elsewhere. Either we must give up the equation of being with mind, pronouncing only the former to be identical with unity; or else, in affirming the unity of mind, we must deny that its creative and contemplative operations take the threefold form which Plotinus represents as a 'noetic triad' of being, life and mind.

If (as Plotinus intimates in *Enneads* 6.9.9.2) we are not to surrender either of these positions, it will follow that the principle of unity is superior to being, hence to mind, and thus inscrutable even to minds that have escaped the limitations of the body. All things by their nature aspire to unity, and, since unity is the premiss of being and being is identical with knowledge, the soul has a duty to seek the knowledge of the first principle (6.9.3.13-27). To this end it must shun the contemplation of all that falls short of the One – this being the name that is bestowed most frequently on the highest principle in the *Enneads*, not because it partakes of unity (like everything else that is said to be one), but because it is only by virtue of it that unity (and hence being) are predicable of any subject of discourse. The One itself, however, is not a subject of discourse except by inference or negation: even the beautiful or beauty itself – the highest object of desire and hence the highest that we are constitutionally disposed to know –

must not be mistaken for the first principle, as it owes its being and unity to the One, like all other objects of cognition.[13] The One is the Good beyond beauty (6.9.4.10), the vanishing-point of aspiration beyond desire; and for that very reason, the attempt to know it without an intermediary must fail, and throws the soul into impotent dread (6.9.3.1-5). To the One and to matter – to these two alone – the term *apeiron* (infinite or indefinite) may be applied – to matter because it has no properties to be apprehended and to the One because it transcends the apprehensible.[14] None of the five great genera distinguished in Plato's *Sophist* can be predicated of it: Sameness and Otherness, Motion and Rest, are all functions of Being, and where this is denied they are also excluded, so that even the denial of one contrary does not entail the presence of the other (6.9.3.46-54). Otherness and Motion are incompatible with the permanence of being, and appear first as concomitants of intelligible matter; Sameness and Rest disappear as we ascend in thought from intellect to the One – though one can scarcely say 'in thought', for the ascent itself precludes any representative or discursive exercise of the mental faculties (6.9.4.1-9). Nor will any conventional appellative find a place in strict philosophical meditation on the first principle: elsewhere Plotinus is happy to use the term *theos* (god) as an honorific title both for the One and for mind, occasionally distinguishing the former as *ho theos* (the god) from its image and offspring, which is merely *theos*.[15] An *Enneads* 6.9.6.12, on the other hand he flatly declares that, as the One is higher than intellect and soul, it is higher than *theos*, neither hinting at any gradation of divinity not implying that the term *theos*, with the addition of the definite article *ho*, might function as a proper name.[16]

Even to say that the One is one is a solecism, at least if the meaning is that it is one among other numerable entities.[17] If the One were numerable, it would be a unit by participation in some other ground of unity. But if it partook of anything else, it would not be the highest principle, and would forfeit its simplicity (6.9.3.48-9), since participation entails that there is a substrate to be distinguished from the participated attribute. To say that it is, to say that it knows or wills, is once again to make it composite by the logic of attribution. The One can possess no attributes because it is not a substance; all being stands in need of it, but it stands in need of nothing, not even itself (6.9.9.6.19-26). For this reason it is inseparable from any comprehensive understanding of the finite, and Plotinus is prepared in other treatises to seek it out in the writings of the ancients. When interpreting the cosmogony of Hesiod and the Orphics, for example, he can substitute the One for Ouranos, Mind for Cronos and Soul for Zeus; in *Enneads* 6.9, however, the deities of myth are of so little account that the soul is said to generate its own Aphrodite and Ares in its ascent to *henôsis* or unity. Frequently this is called an ascent to union with the One, but this again is a misnomer as a true union can occur only between two numerable entities. The soul in Plotinus aspires to unity rather than to union with anything; the closing words of *Enneads* 6.9, which stand in Porphyry's edition as a codicil to Plotinus' whole philosophy, are 'the flight of the alone to the alone', but this is an echo of Numenius, characteristic of the early treatises. Numenius here can be only a verbal touchstone, as he seems to have conceived of the Good, his first god, as sovereign finitude rather than as the intangible horizon of the finite.

Unity, in the strict sense that philosophy requires, is unattainable for any subject other than the One, because in every other instance we can still distinguish the subject from the unity that we ascribe to it. Only the simplicity of the One can escape the dichotomy, and the simplicity of the One is the One itself. To be the One, to lose one's own identity in the ineffable, is not, however, the destiny of the liberated intellect in the *Enneads*. There, he avers, the mind is conscious of its integrity as one mind and of the unity of all mind as a species; individuality is not annulled but clarified by the mutual penetration of thinking monads (*Enneads* 5.8.4). Thanks to the One there is unity in union, but no union with the One.

Some corollaries

Maier observes that *Enneads* 6.9 is the ninth of the treatises in order of composition, and the first in which Plotinus favours 'the One', in contradistinction to 'the Good', as a designation of the first principle.[18] Setting this fact against the weight of scholarly opinion, he argues that the thought of Plotinus continued to mature after he had begun to put it in writing; at the same time, when he finds that 'the Good' is still the preponderant term in later treatises, even those in which the unifying action of the first principle is the chief subject, he infers that the philosopher abandoned his experiment in Pythagorean nomenclature when he saw that he had failed to win the approval of fellow-Platonists. Yet since, on Maier's own reading of the evidence, Plotinus found it possible to build without this capstone in his later years, it is rash to infer from the silence of earlier texts that it did not yet lie to hand. We may concede to Maier that the One does not appear in our meagre fragments of Ammonius Saccas and the pagan Origen; we may even allow him to argue, from the title alone, that Origen denied any higher principle of unity than the intellect in his treatise *That the King is the Only Maker*; but we may still ask why, if Plotinus was not deterred from writing *Enneads* 6.9 by the known opinions of his colleague, he would have been intimidated by the predictable rejoinder. If, as our evidence seems to indicate, Origen composed this work after 263,[19] it cannot explain the shifts in the vocabulary of the *Enneads* which are adduced in Maier's argument. Perhaps, then, it would be safer to maintain that, as Plotinus is always more concerned with the goals than with the origin of existence, he consistently prefers the name that is used of the highest principle in the *Symposium*, *Phaedrus*, *Republic* and *Philebus*, while his reasons for describing it in some places as 'the One' are as circumstantial and (for mere readers) as imponderable as his reasons in other places for adopting the title 'god'.

This position would need to be refined if it could be proved that 'the Good' and 'the One' do not always signify the same object in the *Enneads*;[20] the majority of expositors, however, from Porphyry onward, have found it hard to differentiate them, and, if it had been the intention of Plotinus to subordinate one to the other, one would expect him to have been conscious of innovation and to have let his audience know of it. The inconsistencies brought to light by Maier and Hadot may be taken as indices, not of a measurable growth or oscillation in the opinions of Plotinus, but of the indelibly tentative character of his thought. The permanence and rigour of a scholastic definition would belie the inscrutability of his subject and the suppleness of his intellect. The thesis of Lloyd Gerson that the One is that being whose essence is only conceptually distinct from its existence, for example, is clear and tenable enough if it means only that we can predicate the One but cannot predicate anything of it.[21] The terms of the definition, however, are formally contradicted in the *Enneads*, where being is equated with essence and essence with intellect. The One transcends the mere non-being of matter not by essence or existence but by *energeia*[22] – a term that denotes the characteristic activity of a subject, but in this one case not terminating in any new actuality, since the agent, the actuation and the resultant actuality cannot be discriminated or expressed in other terms. It is possible that mediaeval analysis of the premiss that the divine is *causa sui*, cause of itself,[23] may help to elucidate the logic of this process; yet the language of self-causation implies duality, and is therefore more at home in the Christian doctrine of the Trinity than in the work of a philosopher like Plotinus, whose exclusion of plurality and number from the first principle barely permits him to affirm that it is one.

In popular accounts of Plotinus' system, the word 'emanation' is used to describe the emergence of *nous* or intellect from the One. It is the standard equivalent of the noun *aporrhoia*, but whereas the Latin *e-manatio* signifies a 'flowing out', the prefix *apo-* in the Greek term is best translated, not 'out of' but 'away from'. The Latin has given rise to the common notion that Plotinus was a pantheist who taught that all was initially contained within the one, and that the universe that has evolved from it remains in a sense identical with its origins.[24] This may be good Indian philosophy, but Plotinus, as Armstrong reminds us, never reached India.[25] In his thought the One is present to everything but contained in nothing; being the unconditioned source of unity for all that exists, from the world itself to the smallest and most evanescent particle, it is not a part of the unity that it sustains, and cannot even be said to partake of the unity that it imparts to others. If unity were a predicate of the first principle, duality would supervene, as the principle would be one thing and its unity another. Unity, no less than being, is properly an attribute of *nous*; yet, as we saw in the previous chapter, being in *nous* coexists with 'intelligible matter', the possibility of not-being (or rather of not being x by virtue of being y) that explains the plurality of the forms. Thus the consummate unity of *nous*, which makes it identical with its contents, the *noêta* or ideal forms, paradoxically entails that the unified intellect is many, not in spite of, but by virtue of its contents. At the same time, the unity and plurality are inseparable, and the intellect produces soul, in which unity and plurality coexist and are not identical, without any alienation of its own substance.

Still less, since the One is indivisible even in conception, can it be said to give up any part of itself in the generation of the intellectual manifold. Plotinus could permit himself to compare the 'eternal generation' of *nous* to the procession of a ray from the sun because he believed that the sun is not diminished by radiation;[26] in our time, when we know that an infinitesimal contraction of the sun's mass accompanies every emission, he might have preferred to look for an analogy in Stephen Hawking's account of the apparent radiation of light in the neighbourhood of a black hole. This is the result of the dissociation of complementary particles under a gravitational force which draws in only the negative particles, releasing a stream of photons which appears to issue from the hole itself. Plotinus would have said, of course, that a physical analogy may at best illuminate but cannot explain the action of transcendent causes. We cannot suppose that he would have applauded Hawking's attempt, in his later work, to bring the origin of the universe under the same mathematical laws that governed the evolution and working of the universe thereafter. Except that they posit a temporal beginning, whereas he acknowledged only an ontological priority, he would have sided with those who hold that the frontier of time and space is a 'singularity' where all laws fail and no equation presently in use among cosmologists admits of a real solution.

Plotinus' theory of number

Plotinus toys in *Enneads* 6.9 with a mathematical definition of the One, then turns it aside with the elliptical remark that if the One is a number and number belongs to being, then so does the One.[27] To elucidate this remark we must remember that to Platonists the mathematical sciences had always appeared to promise the disclosure of some natural and indefeasible order in the universe. Harmonics and geometry are the predominant studies in Plato's extant dialogues, but it seemed that in his lecture *On the Good*, which derived all things from the conjunction of the One and the Dyad, limit and the unlimited, he had espoused the Pythagorean claim that number is the foundation of all existence. Numbers exemplify many of the perfections that are ascribed to Forms by Plato: as arithmetical quantities, in contradistinction to all empirical units or pairs, the numbers one and two, with all their necessary properties and functions, are known to the mind by thought alone, and hence with a certitude that cannot be challenged by some new observation or discovery. Like the Form, the number is indivisibly and unchangeably present in all its manifestations; it is the object, but not a creature, of the contemplating intellect and its properties, like those of the Form, would not have been any more variable or any less distinct had it been possible for the intellectual realm to exist without engendering any material world..

Yet paradoxes arise if we assign numbers to the same order of being as Forms. While, for example, each Form is unique, they are all denumerable as Forms. It seems to follow, then, that Form is subordinate to number; if each of the intelligible numbers is a Form, these will be countable both as numbers and as Forms. The consequence now arises that, just as the intelligible numbers act as numerators to objects in the lower world, so these in turn must be subject to some process of numeration. If we are to avoid an infinite regress, this transcendent numerator will not be an incremental series of the kind familiar to the arithmetician. Thus we must posit at least three orders: the numerable in the lower world, the intelligible number and the numerating principle above number. Even this may not suffice to resolve another difficulty: how can the intelligible One be an unrepeatable form if the number two is by definition the sum of one and one? What, furthermore, accounts for the unity of the number two as a discrete form, since this cannot be sought in either of the units which comprise it, or in the addition of those units, or even in the intelligible One if this is assumed to be merely one in a series of intelligible numbers? The Pythagoreans, from whom the Platonists claimed descent, maintained that because the One is the source of number it cannot be reckoned among the numbers; if, however, the premiss that the One is the source of number means only that every subsequent integer is resoluble into units, the One of which this theory speaks is evidently not the cause of unity in the integer, and cannot explain the unity which an arithmetic series has by virtue of being one series. No more than a point gives form to the magnitudes derived from it by extension can the arithmetic unit be more than an element in any higher number. Speusippus, the heir of Plato, failed his teacher if, as Aristotle tells us, he extolled this elemental One as the source of number, magnitude and soul.

Plotinus examines the nature of number in *Enneads* 6.6, the thirty-fourth of his treatises in order of composition. The numerical series, he argues, while it appears to be interminable, cannot be a real infinity, since whatever exists at all partakes of limit; the unlimited is that whose actuality consists in being limited by another (6.6.3.1-18). Number in the intelligible realm is surely determinate, as the Forms cannot be greater or fewer in number than they are (6.6.2.9-12). Number, if not identical with being, is a necessary concomitant of it; it cannot be posterior to being, since whatever exists is a manifold in unity, and hence partakes of the monad and the dyad (6.6.8.20-2). Number, we may conclude, resides potentially in undistributed Being, and is realised first as a unity in the determinate

71

being of intellect, then severally in each particular being (6.6.9.23-34). Number is thus not identical with substance; at the same time it is no accident, since to deprive a thing of unity is to destroy the thing itself. Is it therefore to be identified with quantity? That is so in the realm of becoming, where any set is the sum of its members (6.6.16.1-20); but even here a distinction must be drawn between the unity which a man has as an individual and his status as a unit when we number a decad of men. The first is essential, the second supervenient (6.6.21-30). While phenomenal units may be multiplied, the essential number one is no more amenable to multiplication than any other necessary being. So also the intelligible world contains a triad, a tetrad, a decad, indivisibly present in every group that instantiates these numbers in the lower sphere. This true number (as Plato calls it) is to be distinguished from the number in the soul which is its instrument for the counting of things already in existence (6.6.17.51). Just as we saw, in *Enneads* 3.7, that the time which the soul perceives as a continuum originates in the undivided life which is a function of being, so the numbers which form a linear series in the soul are present as one in the higher domain – an infinity still (6.6.17.1-20), but one which, like the intellectual matter in which the Forms reside, transcends the finite rather by surfeit than by want of being.

But again we must remember that the triad, the tetrad, the decad have their own unity, which is not that of the henad, so that even these paradigmatic numerators must participate in some transcendent unity (6.6.16.53). In all there are four constituents in the philosophical theory of number: (a) the discreteness of the material objects which the soul numbers; (b) the representative units which the soul builds into the integers of an arithmetic series in order to count the discrete particulars; (c) the intelligible number, by virtue of which every unit in the arithmetic series is the same one, and every set of three or four the same triad or tetrad; (d) the absolute number, to which the decad of the intelligibles (for example) owes its quiddity, or peculiar identity, as a decad. It is a cardinal law of Neoplatonic ontology that the higher orders manifest themselves in all lower orders – there would be no material bodies, for instance, if matter and the Forms were wholly estranged – and in this case too the numbering which the soul performs is not the cause of number in the material realm, but betokens the presence of number derived, by way of the intelligible numbers, from absolute number. It is the soul's participation in the intelligible that enables it to remain one while subsuming a multitude of discrete particulars in the process of numeration. And what is it that sustains in turn the integrity of intellect? The fact that not only intelligible numbers but their precursors, the absolute numbers, share in the coinherent unity which all number possesses by virtue of its immediate procession from the One.

Iamblichus on number

What Porphyry and Iamblichus made of the three hypotheses (and indeed of all nine) we now learn only from a skeletal account in Proclus' *Commentary on the Parmenides*.[28] Porphyry, it seems, concurred with his master in allotting the second hypothesis to the intelligible and the third to Soul. For Iamblichus, on the other hand, the second hypothesis illustrates the unity of the noetic or intelligible in tacit contradistinction to the noeric or intellectual;[29] the subject of the third he believed to be not the soul but the realm of heroes and angels, who in his system are the nobler intermediaries between gods and their human adepts. How he defined and numbered the rungs of being we shall see in a later chapter; the difference in aim and temper between Plotinus and the younger Neoplatonists is, however, already apparent in their treatments of the first hypothesis. Porphyry identifies its subject as the primal God, Iamblichus as God and the gods, to which Proclus adds that it characterises not the absolute One alone, but every henad or unifying principle of an ontological series. This may be his own gloss, but we need not doubt that Iamblichus, like Porphyry, had given a theological tenor to speculations which had been only intermittently hospitable to the term *theos* in the *Enneads* of Plotinus. It is in the same spirit that Porphyry, in his life of Plotinus, speaks of his master's union with the god above all and professes not to understand his dictum that 'the gods should come to me, not I to them' (10.35).

Iamblichus seems to have followed Moderatus in postulating a 'One of the soul' as an intermediary between unconditioned unity and the manifold of sensory experience.[30] At the same time he thought Moderatus wrong to identify the soul with harmony, as he also disowned Xenocrates' definition of soul as number and the theory of Speusippus that the soul is a geometrical figure, extended though immaterial.[31] At the same time, he believed that the laws and proportions of the soul are those of geometry, arithmetic and harmony, and that it is through the study of mathematics that the soul is liberated from material perceptions. This exercise, he maintains, will carry the soul at last not only beyond the spheres but beyond the domain of intellect, kindling powers of which we are yet unconscious. It is, however, a maxim of his that every level of understanding has its proper discipline, and in his *Common Science of Mathematics* – a preface to more vertiginous studies, as its title implies – he begins with the Pythagorean commonplace that the point generates the line, the line the plane, and the plane the solid figure. Insofar as this evolution follows the ineluctable rules of geometry, it is both necessary and good; at the same time, each new member of the series exceeds its predecessor in volume, and if the higher stands to the lower as form to matter, or as limit to the unlimited, the disparity between limit and the unlimited increases at every stage (14.18-18.23 Festa). Soul is the unlimited in relation to Intellect, Intellect the unlimited in relation to the One;

consequently, the soul's ascent from the palpable to the ineffable is conceived as a transition from solid to plane, from plane to line, from line to point and at last beyond the point to the monad, which is the form of all existence, as the dyad is its matter.

Mathematical properties inform not only the sensible but the intelligible and intellectual realms. While he deprecates the attempts of charlatans to exploit the putative sympathy between elements in the contingent world, Iamblichus holds that certain numbers are correlated eternally with creatures who function as symbols in the hieratic rituals of deliverance which go by the name of theurgy. In the *Theology of Arithmetic* (sometimes attributed to Iamblichus), three is the number of piety and consummation (p. 17), four of stability (20-2), five of peace (34); four again is the number of the elements, the seasons and the chief parts of the human body (24-6), while five is the number of the planets (excluding the sun and moon) and the genera of animals (33-4). Six, as the sum of its factors, is the number of harmony (43), seven as the sum of three and four the number of concord (55). Seven is the number of ages in a full human life, the number of planets including the sun and moon, and (according to religious lore) the instrument of the creation (55-9). Eight is a cube (72), the number of the heavenly spheres (73), the number of notes in an octave and hence the foundation of all music (75); nine, as the final number before the decad, marks an unsurpassable limit (77-8); the decad stands for completion (79), for wholeness and fate (80-1), and has a number of subtle properties, which Speusippus regards as characters of perfection (81-2).

At the same time, Iamblichus mocked Amelius for supposing that the essence of a thing could be discovered by *gematria*, the substitution of numbers for the letters in its name.[32] Nor can any participated monad be for him the highest principle: the One and the point, for example, are not identical, since the line contains the point, while it has been shown in the first hypothesis of the *Parmenides* that the One is not contained in anything. The absolute One is unparticipated, wholly ineffable, so rapt or 'snatched away' from the world that a second One must be posited as the common source of limit and the unlimited.[33] It is this pair that engenders the One-existent, also styled the intelligible or noetic monad, which we encountered above as the subject of the second hypothesis in the *Parmenides*. From this flows all existence – the intellectual, the psychic and the material – and with this increasing crassitude the increasing possibility of evil.[34] Nevertheless, while matter may be the nursery of evil, it is not that evil or the immediate cause of it; conversely, if there can be no good without limit and no evil but in the unlimited, the ineffable One which fathers both cannot be characterised by either term.[35]

How, if it is unparticipated, is it a cause? Only, it would seem, as the horizon of aspiration to form and unity, which, in this as in other journeys, must lie equally far beyond every destination if every destination is to be attainable. Porphyry, by contrast, is reported to have identified the One with the highest member of the noetic triad, and thus to have brought it within reach of the intellect. For Iamblichus it is the second One that represents the highest attainable unity, but for him this too must lie beyond the noetic. He speaks of a 'flower of intellect' by which that which exceeds the intellect is prehended;[36] to experience the highest good that reason sets before us we must cultivate higher faculties than reason. While Porphyry (like Amelius) may be said to have trimmed the philosophy of Plotinus to fit the popular conception of the gods, there is no accommodation of logic to religion in Iamblichus. Piety (as we shall see in subsequent chapters) is at once the precondition and the terminus of philosophic thought because it is in the nature of ratiocination to be finite and of its object to be infinite. Where there is nothing beyond the frontier it is no frontier.

The Pilgrim Soul

For the majority of philosophers today the existence of the soul is a 'religious' doctrine which is excluded from the outset in any rigorous study of the 'mind-body problem'. In the ancient world, however, it was a truism – not least for those who believed, with Epicurus, that it was a friable concourse of atoms, for the Epicureans acknowledged no reality that was not so constituted. Among those who urged that the animating principle and the subject that it animates must belong to different categories of being, there were some who described the incorporeal soul as the form or harmony of its perishable substrate; yet both the Peripatetics (who used the first term) and the Pythagoreans (who flirted with the second)[1] held a concomitant belief in the existence of some concrete agency – be it only the mind – which moves itself, apprehends the world and survives the destruction of the body. It barely occurred to Platonists after Plato even to canvass the possibility that the passions, thoughts and sentiments which are exhibited through the body might originate in the tissues of the body itself; to them it was not the existence of the soul but its simplicity, impassibility and natural immortality that stood in need of proof. It is not that the existence of the soul was for them an unexamined postulate, but rather that the reasoning of Plato – in which the proof that there is a soul is almost always incidental to the proof of its immortality – was supposed to be so cogent that a Platonist who challenged it declared himself no Platonist after all.

The existence of soul

It is self-evident, for example, that there is motion – scarcely less so that all motion requires a mover. If we trace back every motion through a chain of antecedent motions, an infinite regress ensues unless we posit a self-moved mover at the beginning of the chain. Since no body can move itself, this being which is the seat of its own activity is the soul.[2] The proof suffices for every living organism; it also requires us to grant the world a soul to explain the complex regularity of its motions. And of the world-soul, as of every soul, it follows that, since the source of motion lies within the agent and pertains to its definition, it has no tendency to cease. Should the body of the organism be subject to dissolution – which is the case for every body below the heavens – the soul will outlive it, and will thus be obliged to seek another home. A second argument, both for the existence of a soul and for its passage from body to body, can be derived from our capacity to come at truths which have not yet been revealed to us. If a boy can be induced to find the geometric method of doubling a square before he has undergone any instruction in geometry, that is evidence (at least for the interlocutors in the *Meno*[3]) that the method was shown to him in a previous life, and hence that his soul must have experienced at least one incarnation before the present one. In the *Phaedrus* it is not anecdotal facts but eternal principles which are said to have been acquired before the descent into the body,[4] and here the proof rests on a phenomenon which continues to exercise students of epistemology: how is it that, without having been introduced to every instance of a generic term, we none the less know how to apply that term when we encounter a new exemplification of it? The problem is all the more acute the more weakly or heterogeneously the term is instantiated in particulars: how, if our souls have not caught sight of beauty, wisdom or justice in their pure form above the heavens, could we recognise their disfigured and transient images on earth? And if the shock that jars the soul[5] is out of proportion to the beauty of the object that it encounters in the present world, that again is an indication of its capacity for apprehending objects too sublime to be encompassed by the senses. Hence it appears not only that we have lived before in this world but that our souls belong to another in which the vagaries of time and change are unknown.

An argument in the *Phaedo* – that the soul, being life, cannot play host to death and must retire before its onset – rests on premises that are unlikely to be endorsed by one who does not already subscribe to the conclusion (*Phaedo* 105c-107a). The modern mind will be more disposed to acknowledge the force of one that was not expressly advanced by Plato, but was elicited from his dialogues with the help of Aristotle. If we remember that body, when bereft of soul, contains no living principle of unity and is merely a continuum of extended, and hence divisible, parts, we shall see that no one part is able to exercise the manifold unity of apprehension that is presupposed in our most commonplace acts of sight and hearing. A body might respond to a tactile stimulus; it could not of itself determine the speed of a passing horse, detect a false note in music or discover whether a plant was good to eat. The argument carries us beyond soul to intellect if, with Gerson, we insist not only on unity of perception but upon the self-reflexivity which enables the perceiving mind to know that it perceives. At present we need not go so far: the conclusion is that unless we suppose that unity can arise from mere contiguity, or action from the summation of inert quantities, we are forced by the operations of the body itself to admit a soul – albeit a quotidian, not an immortal, one, since nothing whose existence is entailed by one particular can be proved without further argument to survive the annihilation of that particular. The task of the Neoplatonists was to demonstrate that the soul whose existence is presupposed by the body none the less has the power to exist without a body – or at least without any given, transient body – and at the same time that its presence in the body does not frustrate but fulfils its nature, does not impair but enriches the fabric of the cosmos, and communicates good superior to the ills that it incurs.

The descent of the soul

We have noticed already that Plato held the soul to have been originally the denizen of a supercelestial realm. Sometimes he adduces the Orphic saying '*sôma-sêma*', that is, the body is the grave of the soul, and Porphyry writes of Plotinus with admiration that he lived as one ashamed to be in the body. But if even the soul of the wise man is a prisoner, we must ask whether its detention is a punishment, a providential artifice or a self-inflicted yoke. Plato addresses the question in three famous myths, which appear to be at odds. In the *Phaedrus* it is hinted that there are certain determinate periods at which the soul must descend, and that an interval of 30,000 years must be spent in wandering from body to body before it returns to the 'supercelestial sphere'. At the same time, the collisions which break the wings of the soul are said to have been caused by its reckless striving for an unseen goal, the plane of the Good, in the company of its equally turbulent neighbours. In the *Timaeus*, by contrast, the function of soul is to give order and life to the generated cosmos. Individual souls are dispatched from the stars by the lesser gods to inform and ennoble the bodies allotted to them; when the two are parted again and the soul returns to its star, the gods pass judgment on its conduct in the lower sphere and assign it to a new body in accordance with its deserts. In the *Republic*, however, the soul is permitted to choose its own life, so that, although its vision will always be impaired by the crimes and errors of its previous existence, it can be said with truth that 'the one who makes the choice is to blame; no blame lies with god'. Both the *Timaeus* and the *Republic* envisage the migration of souls from human to animal bodies; in the *Phaedrus*, however, the life that the soul receives as reward or penalty is always another human one, though only souls of exceptional rectitude will become philosophers, while, for those who have sinned most heinously, the career of a sophist or tyrant is ordained.

Plotinus, while he considers the myths of Plato more perspicuous than the utterances of his mentors Heraclitus and Empedocles, admits that he seems to fall into contradiction (*Enneads* 4.8.1.27). But the contradiction lies, he suggests, in the hybrid constitution of the soul, which owes its unity to intellect, but its character as soul to the administrative functions which require it to divert its gaze from intellect to the world below.[6] But for this mobility, the lower plane of being would not be filled, and the soul is guilty of no trespass when it descends to take charge of a body. If, however, this tutelage of inferior things should cause it to lose sight of intellect – and how could anyone hope to keep both in view for ever? – the descent becomes an act of presumption (*tolma*[7]) which estranges the soul from the ground of its being and tempts it to mistake the life of the body for its own.[8] The miseries of embodiment are sufficient expiation of the fall itself (8.3.1-6), but the ignorance and blindness to which the soul succumbs in its prison engender new sins, and it is these that come before the divine tribunal to determine its reward or punishment in a subsequent life. Plotinus holds that the fall is at once inevitable and voluntary – inevitable because any soul that remained indefeasibly wedded to the intelligible world would itself be an intellect,[9] yet voluntary because ancient moralists generally applied that term to whatever springs from the nature of an agent, even if he himself would have wished for a different outcome.

It must be remembered, however, that when we speak of fall and captivity, we are dealing in metaphors. As soul is incorporeal, no soul can be properly said to inhabit a place, let alone a body, or to undergo more than a specious individuation through its encounter with matter: if any soul is a unity, it is by virtue of the unity of all soul, from which it follows that every soul is one with every other, and hence with the soul of the world. Particular souls that know enough to seek their own freedom aspire to the condition of this, the one unfallen soul, which employs no organs of perception, since it contains all things perceptible, and never feels the evils of embodiment, since its body is incorruptible and consequently not subject to imperfection.[10] In the everlasting harmony of the world we see the most perfect realisation of the intelligible that the sensible can accommodate; hence there is no reason why the soul which governs it with unceasing vigilance should be seduced by the mutability of its elements or deflected from its contemplation of the higher realm.

To preserve the homogeneity between earthbound souls and the world soul, and to account for our capacity to behold the Forms, Plotinus conjectures that part of every soul retains its seat in the intelligible realm when the rest descends.[11] He knows this to be an unfashionable position, and it is rejected by Iamblichus, whose teaching that the embodied soul is fallen in its entirety entails a sharp disjunction between the human and the divine.[12] Philosophy for Plotinus, as he murmurs on his deathbed, is the reunion of the god in oneself with the deity in the All; the Iamblichean soul is required, by contrast, to storm or coax its way to the gods through a commissariat of inferior, and sometimes hostile, powers. At the same time, while he holds that the fallen soul is wholly fallen, he does not impute a fall to every soul. Against Plotinus he argues, in his treatise *On the Soul*, that it is a matter of some consequence to distinguish souls who enter this world to embellish it (no doubt he has the sun and moon in mind here) from those have been sent hither for their edification (the usual cause of descent in Porphyry's view), and again from those who are truly fallen, because they have been confined to the body as a punishment for their sins.[13]

Both would have concurred with the definition of the soul in Porphyry's *Aphorisms*: 'a substance without magnitude, immaterial, incorruptible, having its being in life that possesses life in itself' – that is, not so much a living entity as life itself and the source of life in others (*Aphorisms* 17). All three would have agreed that it is only because our speech is grounded in common apprehension of the sensible world that we speak of the soul as occupying the place in which its instrument, the body, resides; in reality the soul is everywhere and nowhere, as we also say of the intellect and god (*Aphorism* 31.1-3); the soul's attachment to the body, though for a time it is ineluctable, does not prevent the soul from acting where it chooses (27.2), and it may be said that, whereas body is bound to soul by nature, the soul has forged its own bond and has the power to loose it (8). We ought not to say that the body contains the soul, but that the soul contains the body – not in the sense that the soul circumscribes the body (for what is greater in bulk is less in power: 35.1), but rather as higher quantities subsume every lower quantity. To this it may be objected that the soul must occupy space because Plato himself, in the *Republic* and *Phaedrus*, divides the soul into three *merê* or parts – the rational, the spirited and the appetitive, and expressly declares that when the soul is subject to contradictory affections, it is because it feels each of them in one part only. To Porphyry the contradiction arises once again from the necessity of depicting the incorporeal through the imagery of the senses: the parts are more properly *dunameis* or faculties, which, even in the embodied state, do not impair the unity or simplicity of the soul.

One conjecture of Porphyry's, that the world is a gymnasium for the soul, is mentioned briefly by Augustine and rebutted with heavy satire by Arnobius[14] in the name of Christianity. Not all Christians thought this thesis absurd, for it may be confidently ascribed to Irenaeus, and with more hesitation to Origen.[15] Perhaps we should be surprised that it did not commend itself to every Platonist who believed that the proper function of soul is to animate a body,[16] for this would surely require him to show in his theodicy that the soul descends, not only for the good of the lower world, but for its own.

The reversion of the soul

The soul must be taught to yearn for 'its own dear country' – to quote Plotinus' exhortation near the end of his first publication, the treatise *On Beauty*, perhaps the only one to which he gives his own title. As this title intimates, a reminiscence of supernal beauty, quickened by some encounter with beauty in the visible realm, is one of the common incentives to embarkation; in the tract *On the Virtues*, which Porphyry places second in the corpus, the goal of the voyage is characterised – again by appeal to the faculty of vision – as 'likeness to god'. This likeness is achieved through the practice of virtue, the matter of which is present in every soul, though inert until it takes the form of the four 'political virtues', courage, justice, wisdom and temperance. From these the soul derives only a partial, and largely delusive, resemblance to its archetype, for the virtues of the political man are exercised against perils and temptations which do not exist for beings exempt from matter, time and change. Those virtues which we exhibit in the embodied state are feeble and prosthetic imitations of that virtue which is native to the gods. The soul begins to realise those virtues that pertain to it independently of the body when the soul undergoes purification or catharsis, which, by detaching the soul from the body, assuages suffering, mollifies anger, banishes fear and weans the soul from venereal pleasures. The virtues thus acquired – though in themselves they are merely refinements of the natural capacities that we all possess – foreshadow the higher qualities which the soul begins to exhibit when it resumes her seat in the higher world by turning from body to intellect. Here the noetic functions supersede all lower activities, and the soul's virtues are of a timeless and hermetic cast; they permeate and inform the political virtues which continue to guide our conduct in the lower realm, but the casuistry of our daily lives does not concern the soul, any more than the world soul is aware of every link in the chain of causes that depends on the revolution of the heavens. The analogy is not exact, for the soul of the world never quits its body and consequently experiences neither loss nor sublimation of its functions; it could not be true of this soul – as it seems to be true of the human soul in the *Enneads* – that it stands in a mercurial relation to the self.

That Plotinus was among the first to canvass the relation of self to soul is widely agreed, and it is also agreed that if we simply pluck statements from his works we shall arrive at a diversity of answers. Plato, or at least the *First Alcibiades,* had concluded that a human being is properly a soul making use of a body (129e-130a), and there are passages in the *Enneads* in which the pronoun 'we' seems to designate nothing but the soul. On the other hand experiences of perception which demand the co-operation of soul and body are repeatedly described as 'ours' – 'we' being in this case evidently the composite, since the body alone is incapable of forming an image or recognising a sound until the stimulus has been referred to a unitary centre of perception.[17] Nevertheless the characteristic activities of the soul are those performed without the assistance of the body, and Plotinus on occasions says emphatically that we are properly identical with the seat of our intellectual operations – that we are, in short, pure minds.[18] We may postulate two selves – the endowed and the ideal, to borrow Gerson's terminology[19] – but as Gerson and Plotinus both concede, there must be some principle of identity which disposes each of these selves to take an interest in the other. This principle is not, as in much modern theory, continuity of memory, since the agent who belongs purely to the noetic sphere will have shed all recollection of the contingent, and will be aware only of timeless and simple objects. A new concept of identity seems to be tentatively advanced in the early treatise *On Whether there are Forms of Particulars*, in which Plotinus surmises that the Socrates or

Pythagoras of history instantiates the eternal form of Socrates or Pythagoras, and thus appears to countermand the unanimous view of Platonists before him that there are no forms of particulars (*Enneads* 5.7.1). Texts have been adduced in which he is said to deny that any individual has his own essence, but it has been persuasively argued that he means only to discriminate between the timeless form and its ephemeral manifestation in the material realm.[20] Certainly he believes that the soul is simple, which is to say that neither matter nor any adventitious property enters into its definition; it is identical with its own properties, and shares the immutability and imperishability of the universal. It is true that the individuation of souls is itself a topic of some obscurity – if there is no matter to discriminate them, how is any particular soul distinct from soul itself? – yet both the discreteness and the incorporeality of the human soul are preserved in the repeated formulation that each is a *logos* or expression of *nous*, containing within itself the whole noetic cosmos, but under conditions peculiar to itself as a thinking subject. On such a view the soul is one thing and all things simultaneously – a universe if not a universal. Its simplicity is a guarantee of identity, but what is most obscure in Plotinus' theory is his readiness to identify the soul with a named individual, when his theory of transmigration entails that the soul of Socrates has been embodied in men of other names before and after him. The difficulties cannot be resolved here, but there is reason to think that Plotinus was not the first to countenance forms of individuals, as he had written nothing when the Christian Origen[21] proposed that not only genera and species but all particulars had existed for ever in the mind of God (*First Principles* 1.4.5).

In the longest of his *Aphorisms*,[22] Porphyry distinguishes four stages of merit, each entailing a new taxonomy of the four cardinal virtues. The political virtues are characterised by 'moderation in passion' (*metriopatheia*) and the cultivation of rational decorum in one's activities. Porphyry follows Plotinus in assigning wisdom uniquely to the intellect and courage to the spirited portion, defining the task of temperance as the harmonisation of appetite with intellect, and equating justice with the proper division of labour (*oikeiopragia*[23]) between the three faculties. The second order of virtues, the theoretical, are also called purificatory or cathartic, because they consist in detachment from the goods of the present world. Worldly attachments, evil in themselves, are compounded by the evil of passion; the political virtues deliver us from the second, the theoretical from both. For a soul that has advanced so far, wisdom consists in functioning alone, without subscribing to the delusions of the body; temperance is the repression of sympathy with the body's passions; courage is the fearless contemplation of separation from the body; justice is the subordination of every other faculty to reason, and the elimination of all countervailing impulses. Once purified, the soul begins to revert to its source, without the knowledge of which it cannot truly know its own properties. It now operates 'noerically'[24] – in accordance with the intellect – and exercises virtues of the third order. Wisdom is meditation on 'things which the mind possesses' (that is to say, ideal objects and eternal truths); temperance is an inward turning towards the intellect, courage the impassibility which is acquired by association with the impassible, and justice the performance by each faculty of its own function in attendance on the mind. These virtues of the soul merely prefigure those of the fourth or paradigmatic order, which are peculiar to the intellect. Wisdom for the intellect is knowledge, temperance self-reflection, courage steadfastness, and justice (if Psellus' gloss is to be trusted) nothing else than the performance of its own function.

Thus we may say that the paradigmatic virtues belong to intellect, the noeric to the enlightened soul, the cathartic to the detached soul and the political to the administrative soul. The exponent of this lowest order of virtue is described as *spoudaios* (upright); *daimonios* is the epithet for those who display the cathartic virtues (they may even be styled good daemons), while the noeric virtues make one a god (*theos*) and the paradigmatic virtues a father of gods (*patêr theôn*). This last designation is authorised by a passage in *Enneads* 6.9, where Plotinus describes the fecundity that accompanies the intellect's reversion to its source: 'True life is here. For at present, in the absence of god, there is a print, an imitation, of life, but to live there is an activity of intellect. And activity generates gods in silence by contact with [the One], and it also generates beauty, it generates justice, it generates virtue' (*Enneads* 6.9.9.15-19). Both Porphyry and Plotinus hold that even in the present life one can enjoy a fleeting sense of being 'alone with the alone'. Nevertheless, the higher virtues cannot be sustained amid the turmoil of embodiment, and in Porphyry's view[25] the most that the sage can hope to do in this world is to perfect the cathartic virtues, thus disposing his soul to moral progress after its departure from the body. The first requirement is that he should perceive the soul as his true self and the body as its prison; the second is that the soul should be divorced, so far as is possible, from corporeal perception, and from the pleasures and pains engendered by perception. Only where pain is an obstacle, or pleasure a friend, to virtue should they enter into our counsels. Anger and grief should be banished, so far as lies within the will – and that is enough, for what lies outside the will is weak and paltry. Fear can be wholly repressed, as can desire for 'trifles'; the wise man will not feel his hunger or thirst to be truly a part of him, and will not permit himself any amours outside the imagination. While Platonists were accustomed to mock the Stoic pursuit of *apatheia* or passionlessness in the present life, this is certainly (in Porphyry's view) the state to which the metriopathic life should tend, and one that can be achieved after physical death.

While it was an unshakable tenet of Platonism that souls are incorporeal and therefore cannot occupy place, an august tradition taught that on quitting the body the soul descends to the lower regions of the earth. Homer introduces a different term when – in a passage that Plotinus appears to have cherished – he describes the relic of Heracles in the underworld as his 'shade' (*eidôlon*), contrasting it with the 'self' who has been admitted to the company of the gods.[26] Porphyry opines that every soul which forsakes a body is accompanied by an *eidôlon*, which he defines in the *Aphorisms* as a concretion of the *pneuma* or spirit which souls draw from the spheres when they come to earth.[27] It is the *eidôlon*, then, that descends to Hades; the soul is said to dwell there by a metonymy like that which allows us to speak of the soul inhabiting the body in the present world. The purer the soul, the more tenuous its pneumatic envelope. Closest of all to immateriality is the ethereal *pneuma*; this is a concomitant of the soul from the beginning, for if reason in the *Phaedrus* is personified as the driver of a chariot whose steeds are temper and appetite, what can the chariot itself be but an attenuated body?[28] Philosophy corroborates exegesis when one asks what else but a body would serve to guarantee the permanent distinctness of the soul, or the continuing exercise of its natural functions after it quits its gross integument. All Platonists held that the task of the soul is to animate a body, and at the same time that its higher and more natural operations are encumbered by the presence of a body; the two can be reconciled if we equip it with a body so rarefied that it no longer blinds the eye of the soul with light or deafens the intellect by hearing. So long as her sole activity is ratiocination, the soul will not be detained in any meaner lodging; but when she exchanges reason for *phantasia* – when, that is, it starts to entertain images of perceptible objects, the *pneuma* is of a grosser, 'sunlike' texture. When passion invades the soul, it becomes effeminate, renouncing sunlike for moonlike *pneuma*; when the soul sinks into an earthly body, its *pneuma* is made up of humid exhalations. The first stage in deliverance is the shedding of this integument; the 'dry effulgence' of the ethereal *pneuma* attests the state of perfect dehydration and release.[29]

Can the debauched soul pass into animal bodies? Plato said so, Plotinus appears to have thought so; Porphyry, in a fragment which may belong to his work *On the Styx*, reckons incarnation as a beast among the dangers which the unclouded reason teaches souls to avoid. Yet when, a few lines later, the tenacious desires and pleasures of her past life draw her back to earth, she is not said to become the soul of a beast but to espouse the life of one.[30] The treatise blends philosophical nomenclature with a parabolic reading of the seduction of Odysseus' crew by Circe in the *Odyssey* – a reading that may have been inspired by the dialogue between Odysseus and one of Circe's pigs in Plutarch's *Gryllus*. In late antiquity allegorical criticism is frequently the superimposition of a philosophic on a poetic metaphor: there is nothing in *On the Styx* which should induce us to reject the clear and iterated testimony of Augustine that the pupil of Plotinus admitted only migration from human to human, never from human to brute.[31] The teaching of Iamblichus on this subject is obscure, but what can be gleaned from later authors suggests that he did not regard the experiences of the present life as increments to the vehicle but as 'projections' of the soul which will accompany it, as a concrete medley of images, when it relinquishes the body. Porphyry appears to have taught, by contrast, that the impressions gained in life, though they do not perish, are detached from the soul by stages and dispersed among the elements. Beneath this difference lies a profound discrepancy in doctrines of salvation, for Iamblichus maintains that, as the soul descends entire, so it is redeemable in its entirety, while Porphyry, as a disciple of Plotinus, holds that only the rational soul is proof against death.

How can the philosophy ease the weight of his earthly body? The longest work of exhortation is Porphyry's treatise *On Abstinence* in four books, which purports to show that the vegetarian diet is the most natural, the most ancient, and the one most calculated to purge the appetites, thereby robbing them of their power to corrupt the soul. The most vivid and cogent vehicle of instruction was, however, the biography, which not only fortified precept by example but confuted those who argued that no mortal had the strength to obey the precept. The analysis of Porphyry's treatise *On Abstinence* in this chapter is therefore followed by a cursory review of three biographies, one of which bears a title that might as well have been that of the treatise – *On the Pythagorean Life*.

Porphyry on abstinence

The allusion to 'our teacher' in the first paragraph of the treatise *On Abstinence* hints that it was commenced soon after Plotinus died in 270, at a house not far from that of his affluent friend Castricius Firmus. In the absence of his mentor, it seems, Castricius found it impossible to sustain a meatless diet, and Porphyry's task is therefore to persuade him once again of the merits of abstinence.[32] The use of beasts for food, he says, originated either as an indulgence of the appetites or as a remedy against perils that are now obsolete. To the vulgar it may remain a pleasure, and in certain occupations a necessity, but in the philosopher's life it can be neither. While he concedes that Heraclides Ponticus had represented Pythagoras as a trainer who prescribed this diet for athletes,[33] Porphyry can argue that it always the way of those who legislate for the common weal to make allowance for human frailty.[34] Philosophers must accept more rigorous precepts which forbid them to kill in the service of the belly. Those whose aim and duty it is to mortify the passions will refrain even from self-murder: the teaching of an anonymous Egyptian corroborates Plato's belief that souls who attempt to free themselves by suicide are forced to linger after their separation in the vicinity of the corpse.[35] While the mind is at its station, the senses are its coadjutors, not its jailers; the true ascetic no more tries to escape them prematurely than he will give them up, with the Gnostics, to a lower, mortal soul over which the rational soul can exercise no dominion.[36] Asceticisim is not, as its bourgeois critics pretend, inimical to the body; it is inimical to the hedonism which, under pretence of honouring the body, denies that its privations can be conducive to the discipline or welfare of the soul.

It is a fallacy again – and again a self-serving one – to imagine that the Pythagorean reluctance to kill arose from a superstitious fear that the animal might harbour a human soul. Whether Porphyry endorsed this premiss or not, he was aware that it could be used to support the opposite conclusion, for a soul that knew itself to be human might regard the slaughter of the beast as a liberation. He did, however, remark that the Greeks abstain from the flesh of horses, dogs and asses, because they share in human labours.[37] Thus it is our own instinct that condemns us when we devour the flesh of domestic beasts without the excuse of either war or famine.[38] The universal affinity between humans and the brute creation is demonstrable, in Porphyry's view, from observation alone without appeal to any doctrine of transmigration. The affinity once granted, we can hardly deny the cogency of the argument – which Porphyry ascribes to the Pythagoreans – that there is no moral sanction permitting us to kill our fellow-beasts which will not also permit us to kill our fellow-humans. Book 3 of the work disposes of the reasons commonly urged against the ascription of intelligence to animals. To argue that it is a salient characteristic of human beings to be rational, and hence that other beings cannot be rational because they are not human, would be to prove the gods devoid of rationality.[39] To maintain that no intelligence is shown in the instinctive pursuit of rational ends is again to deny intelligence to the gods, for it is they, not the beasts, who do everything by nature without the intervention of learning; in animals, as in humans, mistakes are rife in youth, and thus the instincts which conduce to the survival of the organism cannot all be inherited.[40] If it were true that animals are incapable of virtue, that would no more be a proof that they lack reason than the absence of virtue in humans; in any case, the docility with which they submit to humans might be imitated with profit in our own civil organisations.[41] Virtue is exhibited in the care of the young – they are said indeed to have suckled gods and mortals[42] – and many beasts have discernment enough to identify noxious herbs.[43] And if there are beasts who employ their wits primarily in the ambushing of other beasts, they kill for food whereas humans kill for pleasure, and do not think themselves less rational for that.[44]

Many of these arguments come from Plutarch's collection of anecdotes attesting the intelligence of animals, the purpose of which is not so much to deter the reader from eating them as to ascertain whether those of the land or those of the sea display the greater acumen.[45] Porphyry also summons a variety of witnesses to prove that human beings in their primitive state were as innocent of sacrifice as of warfare, that their diet consisted only of vegetation and that they offered only the fruits of agriculture to the gods.[46] He does not deny that at times the preservation of society has necessitated the killing of beasts.[47] He admits that sacrifices have been enjoined by divine authority, though he opines that when a victim is a beast the beneficiary is a daemon;[48] he does not profess to know whether divination from the entrails of a sacrificed beast is the work of daemons, gods or a psychic faculty.[49] Nevertheless, he contends that there is no logic which requires us to eat the carcase,[50] and unlocks a whole fund of anecdotes in his second book to show that the gods reserve their approbation for the man who offers frugally and without bloodshed.[51] It is from him that we learn of the ceremony in Athens at which, the ox having been dispatched, the culprits passed the blame by rote from one to another, until it fell upon the axe, which they flung away.

The absence of animal sacrifice among certain nations proves it to be unnatural;[52] the revulsion felt by Greeks at the rites observed by other nations, and the frequency with which such rites are applied to human victims, even in Greece, suffice to show that no such abuse is tolerable.[53] In the fourth book he demonstrates that vegetarianism is not the foible of one group only, as it is practised by two Indian sects, and – with even greater parity between sexes than among the Pythagoreans – by a community of Jews.[54] The pure and austere morality of all these groups confirms that their diet is governed by philosophy; at the same time, the ubiquity of the abstinent life refutes those who maintain that the eating of meat is enjoined by nature. Porphyry does not conflate barbarians with Greeks, any more than he overthrows his own axiom that, while beasts have memory (*mnêmê*), only humans possess recollection (*anamnêsis*) of the eternal and ideal;[55] he does, however, hint that we are more human when we are conscious of our kinship with the animals, and better Greeks when our acts conform to the standards of perfection held elsewhere.

Pythagorean lives

The majority of the ancient books that carry the title *bios* in the manuscripts are serial accounts of the subject's life, observing a loose chronological scheme from birth to death, but punctuated by sayings and anecdotes which, because they illustrate permanent traits of character, seldom follow any temporal arrangement. The tone, as the author chooses, may be laudatory or critical: Plutarch renders a judgment after most of his *Parallel Lives*, while Suetonius and his imitators merely juxtapose calumny and praise. Whereas historiography is sparing of documents but abounds in speeches, the typical *bios* makes little use of either: word-for-word transcription is common only in Diogenes Laertius, and it may be of some consequence that his life of Epicurus, which supplies the richest archive in his *Lives of the Philosophers*, is the only one in which he defends his subject against detraction. The citation of written testimony – avoided in formal prose because it compromised the dignity and unity of the style – was a recognised tool of advocacy in Athenian trials, and apologetic motives may be reasonably imputed to any author who allows such texts to stand in his work unedited. In cases in which the conduct of the litigant himself is under scrutiny so that he feels obliged to offer some account of his own career, we see the germ of autobiography. The literary canons hold, however, in the first extant work of this kind that is not designed for the courtroom: if Josephus had any documents at hand, he must have thought that they were less likely to sway the judgment of the reader than his own set-pieces of eloquence. More openly tendentious, and more likely to be intended for the study than for a judicial or deliberative assembly, the panegyric often has for title nothing more than a the subject's name with a preposition or in the dative; if he is dead, the name alone in the nominative case (*Busiris, Hiero, Demonax*) may be deemed sufficient.

There is, however, another class of works which, while they are not described as *bioi* in the manuscripts, approximate more closely in length and form to the modern biography. Having no other generic name, they are generally called 'lives' in English scholarship, but it is not nomenclature alone that distinguishes them from *bioi* in the classical tradition. They are generally longer than any one life by Plutarch, Suetonius or Diogenes Laertius; for the most part they are untypical efforts of writers who were prolific in other forms, and attest a peculiarly intimate, or peculiarly sympathetic, relation between the biographer and his subject. Xenophon's four books of 'memoirs' (*Apomnêmoneumata*) of Socrates were unparalleled in classical antiquity, but an early Christian gave the same designation to texts that cannot have been very unlike our gospels. The eight vivid books 'relating to' or 'in honour of' Apollonius of Tyana by Philostratus profess to be based on the memoirs of one Damis, a fellow-traveller of the sage; Eusebius of Caesarea used the same prepositional title for his hagiographic account of the reign of Constantine, corroborating his portrait of the elusive king with documents and personal recollections. In the fifth century Proclus was commemorated by his pupil Marinus in a eulogy which he entitled simply *Proclus*; Porphyry, by contrast, when at the end of his life he penned the one work that he meant to stand alone as a biography, called it neither Plotinus nor (as we now customarily style it) the *Life of Plotinus*, but *On the Life of Plotinus and the Arrangement of his Works*. Since it was the biographer himself who devised the 'arrangement of his works', this title is clearly self-regarding, even if no other version of Plotinus' seminars was current. Iamblichus, for his part, wrote no life of a contemporary: his aim was not so much apologetic as hortatory, and he claimed for himself not so much a confidential as a profound and intuitive knowledge of his subject, when he digested the conventional biographies of Pythagoras into a treatise *On the Pythagorean Life*.

While Plato had presented the life of Socrates through dialogues, almost all named after the principal interlocutor, the prototype of narrative biography was Aristotle's compilation of acts and sayings attributed to Pythagoras. Episodic in structure and conceived without manifest bias, it undertook not only to preserve tradition but to interpret the cryptic utterances (*akousmata*) of the founder, and to explain the bifurcation of his followers into obsequious *akousmatikoi* (or 'hearers') and the more inquiring *mathêmatikoi* (or dogmaticians). The two streams, if they had ever parted, no doubt met again in the lost biographies of the Roman age by the philosophers Apollonius of Tyana and Nicomachus of Gerasa.[56] Porphyry avows a debt to both in life of Pythagoras – which is in fact not a work apart, but only the longest fragment surviving from his history of philosophy – but if either of them succeeded in drawing Pythagoras in his own image, Porphyry chose to undo his work. In keeping with his purpose as a historian of philosophy, he appends a laconic commentary on the *akousmata* to his narrative, and it is therefore all the more striking that this narrative should be so diffuse and eclectic as to represent a Pythagoras who, in many respects, is no Pythagorean. Porphyry admits that he was the first to make meat an indispensable part of the athlete's regimen (24.14ff Nauck), and adds that he himself, by adopting this diet, was able to vanquish stronger but vegetarian rivals. In his youth, we are told, Pythagoras had mastered the arts of sacrifice in Egypt (21.8); his other teachers were numerous enough to include the unfashionable Phoenicians and Hebrews (20.2, 22.22), yet no mention is made of a visit to the Brahmins, though Apuleius had already coupled his name with that of this esurient caste more than a century before (*Florida* 15). Nor does this Pythagoras prohibit killing any more than eating: he sets the worst of examples when, distressed and isolated by the ruin of the Pythagorean lodge in Metapontum, he deprives himself of life (49.14-15).

Neither the vindication of the main character nor the portrayal of an exemplary life is an object of such moment in this work as the pursuit of Greek philosophy to its sources, and the demonstration that all thought, whether barbarian or Greek, descends from the same high reservoir of truth. In reckoning the Egyptians, the Chaldaeans and the magi among the teachers of Pythagoras, he is following a source (perhaps Nicomachus) who was also known to Diogenes Laertius;[57] the latter concurs with Porphyry's report that the sage acquainted himself in Crete with the mysteries of the Idaean Dactyls, while Iamblichus (who is apt to follow Apollonius rather than Nicomachus) confirms and augments the allusion to Phoenicia as another place of study. It may have been Porphyry's own decision, however, to put Pythagoras to school among the Hebrews and the Arabs (23.7); it is Porphyry alone who names his tutor among the Chaldaeans as Zaratas (a variant of Zoroaster), and who adds that the magi likened the body of the creator to light and his soul to truth.[58] This doctrine serves him again in his treatise *On Statues*, and it appears to have mattered more to him that a doctrine should be true than that it should have been correctly attributed. He is careful to note the provenance of associates such as Zamolxis of Thrace (23.22) and Pherecydes of Syrus (17.15, 24.12), and his hero is so promiscuous in his courtship of Apollo's shrines that he even becomes an ambassador for the teachings of a woman, the seeress Aristocleia of Delphi (38.19). These facts are not reported elsewhere; they do not imply, as one might suppose, that Porphyry held the door of philosophy open to every visitor. On the contrary, they suggest that the true philosophy is derived from such a variety of sources that it cannot be imparted to those who rest in one tradition. Porphyry, who says something of his own travels in his life of Plotinus, shows off the resultant knowledge here, though he reminds us that such peregrinations are useless if they are not improved by mental exercise. The division of the school into acousmatics and *mathêmatikoi*[59] betokens for him the separation of those to whom the master's words were riddles from the elect who had been permitted to hear his teaching without reserve.

The Pythagorean theories of number reviewed in Chapters 1 and 4 above encapsulate the teachings of the *mathêmatikoi*. Porphyry, as one instructed by them through Moderatus, possesses a knowledge which, though its sources may not be unitary, is universally valid, and thus is able to take a short way with the *akousmata*. We are told, for example, to abstain in sacrifice from the loins, from twins, from the genitals, from the marrow, the feet and the head. And so no doubt the vulgar will do; the philosopher (who in other works is not permitted to sacrifice) will perceive that here the loins represent conjecture, twins and genitals the process of becoming, the marrow increase, the feet a beginning, the head an end. This translation enables the adept to keep the precept even when he is not engaged in sacrifice; if we knew that Porphyry was already vowed to abstinence from meat when he wrote the life, we might surmise that he is urging the disciple to shun the altar, and thus to outdo his master in purity. The protreptic intent is therefore more apparent in the commentary on the maxims of Pythagoras than in the foregoing record of his life.

Iamblichus makes it his project to describe an exemplary figure, since his great work *On the Pythagorean Life* (not, we should note, a mere biography of Pythagoras) was conceived as the first book of ten in a philosophical encyclopaedia.[60] Pythagoras in this work is the perfect sage, who will not consent to lay his offerings on an altar defiled by blood (35.108). Stories of his commending the carnal diet to athletes can only be referred to a disciple of the same name (chapter 25). In the tradition Pythagoras was said to have killed a poisonous snake with a fatal bite of his own; rather than sanction even retributive murder, Iamblichus deftly transforms 'the snake whom he killed by biting' into 'the snake who killed by biting', and the subtle assassin is dismissed with an admonition (142). After making a convert of the priest Abaris by displaying his golden thigh (92), Pythagoras schools him not in the protocols of bloodletting at the altar, but in the use of mathematics to free the soul from all things carnal.

When he prescribes that certain deities should receive offerings on certain days, he appears to be thinking only of libations (153). The story that he perished by his own hand after the ruin of Metapontum cannot be ignored, but is not confirmed (249); a rubric announces a chapter on his death (265), but the manner of it is not related and his fourth successor Gartydas of Croton is said to have been the only head of the school to have died of vexation before his time.

Nevertheless, it is not the biographer's aim to depict a superhuman figure. He is not so willing as Porphyry to countenance the legend that the father of Pythagoras was Apollo, though he concedes that his mother's pregnancy was first announced at Delphi. Nor, in his epitome of the Pythagorean sciences, does he attribute to the sect any great advance upon the wisdom that its founder inherited from his barbarian teachers. The theurgy of numbers which he imparted to Abaris is said, for example, to have been derived from Orpheus (147), whose style he customarily imitated (151). From Egypt he borrowed the theorems of geometry, from Phoenicia the lore of numbers, from Egypt and Chaldaea his observations of the stars (158). While the vow of secrecy, and the fidelity with which it was preserved, are highly extolled, the distinction between acousmatics and *mathêmatikoi* is said to arise from demographic accident, not from the teacher's desire to maintain a privileged circle. When Pythagoras made his home in southern Italy, we are told, he found that the older men were buried in public affairs and had no leisure for the investigation of sciences; content to have mastered certain rules of conduct,[61] they became the ancestors of the acousmatics, while the earliest *mathêmatikoi* were younger men, who had no other business to deflect them from the pursuit of learning (88). The Pythagoras of this treatise is primarily a dispenser, not a discoverer, of truths, and would have neither the right nor the power to enforce the concealment of doctrines which had already been taught for centuries in one country or another, and without any such embargo.

If the Greek sage excels in anything, it is in holiness and austerity – virtues all the more remarkable the more strictly he inculcates them in his followers. The biography begins with an act of worship, and that is also the regular custom of the brotherhood whose foundation it describes. The typical day is one in which leisure follows labour: waking and sleeping, the votaries are dressed in clean white linen like initiates to the mysteries, forgathering only in sacred haunts and garnishing their sparse meals with libations and instruction from sacred texts (98-100). It seems clear that they are designed to resemble the Essenes of Josephus, who also wear white linen, pass daily from labour to refreshment, and sanctify this occasion by the reading and exposition of the Word. It is not in Porphyry's *History of Philosophy* but in his treatise *On Abstinence* that the Essenes are represented as Pythagorean saints; taking Josephus once again as his source, he reports that the community was sustained by the fruits of its own toil in the fields, that breakfast was distributed and consumed in reverent silence, and that, having concluded their eating with a prayer, all present swore that they would engage in no injustice throughout the day. Porphyry does not pretend that these customs were derived from or adopted by Pythagoras, and they do not appear in his *History of Philosophy*. Iamblichus credits the Greek sage with the invention of a discipline that Porphyry had adduced merely as a laudable instance of the abstemious life. Yet even in plagiarism he is at pains not to be utopian: in contrast to the Essenes the Pythagoreans are served with the flesh of sacrificed beasts (98), though the prohibition of sacrifice and the vow not to kill any animal that presents no danger to humans are repeated at the same meal (107, 99). From a commentary on the *akousmata* in chapter 85 we learn that certain creatures are 'eligible for sacrifice', though we are not told which they are or whether some body of acolytes had the duty of slaughtering them on behalf of the more fastidious elect.

Porphyry on Plotinus

Legend colours history even in Porphyry's life of Plotinus. It is above all in the third and seventh chapters, which describe his translation to Rome from Alexandria, that the image of Plotinus coalesces with his pupil's earlier study of Pythagoras. We are told that his tutor Ammonius imparted certain doctrines only to adepts, and that Plotinus was one of three who after his death took an oath to make these doctrines public. This Pythagorean bond of secrecy, Porphyry adds, was breached by Origen, who later visited Rome, reducing Plotinus to embarrassment on the grounds that Origen knew already all that he had to say. We are left to imagine what it was that Plotinus taught while the pact was still in force, and what it was that Porphyry learned from him in Rome that he has not laid bare to the world in his edition of the *Enneads*. Equally lame is Porphyry's explanation of his hero's attachment to Gordian III, whom he accompanied to Persia on campaign until the calamitous engagement in which Gordian fell and his army was dispersed. Since he fled to Rome, which was also Gordian's destination when he levied his troops in Africa, it seems reasonable to judge of his intentions by the outcome. Porphyry, however, declares that his object in departing from Alexandria was to acquaint himself with the practices of the Chaldaeans and the Indians; this we can believe only if it can be explained how military service would conduce to philosophical intercourse with other nations, one of which was not even under Persian rule. Plotinus in the *Enneads* professes only a second-hand knowledge even of the Egyptian hieroglyphics which he could surely have perused at any stage of his Alexandrian novitiate. Of Indians and Chaldaeans he says nothing (in contrast to Porphyry, whose writings teem with allusions to both); and most scholars now agree that there is little in his philosophy that is not prefigured in one at least of the numerous Greek authors (Platonists, Stoics and Peripatetics) who are said to have furnished matter for his seminars (14.4-14). The same motives that led Porphyry to enlarge the list of eastern nations visited by Pythagoras have led him here to substitute curiosity for ambition in his account of his master's travels (3.13-17). Once Plotinus has set up school in Rome, no further itineraries need be plotted for him, as his students are of such diverse nationalities. Serapion comes from Alexandria, Zethus from Arabia, Amelius from Tuscany (7.8-28), while Porphyry is a newcomer from Tyre, whose Phoenician name is not forgotten even when it has been supplanted by a Greek calque (17.6-10). Plotinus and Pythagoras may both have reserved their teachings for an elite, but it was for both a cosmopolitan elite.

Above all else, the life is an embodiment of the ideal philosopher, richer than any portrait,[62] though still meagre in comparison with the living simulacrum of his mind that survives in the *Enneads*. Porphyry congratulates himself on his division of these writings into six blocks of nine – a process that appears to have entailed the separation of texts designed to be read consecutively, if not as a single book. The arrangement leads the reader from ethics through physics to the analysis of soul and mind, and then, after a long excursus on genera and species, to the logic of the inscrutable, which governs all discourse about the One. The perfection of philosophy, and the detachment from the body that it entails, can be discerned in the reluctance of Plotinus to reveal his date and place of birth (2.37-43) – and also in the refusal of his biographer to cull this information from other sources, as his successors claim to have done. Porphyry testifies that Plotinus spent his life in constant meditation, often neglecting food and sleep for the vision of eternity (8.22-3). On four occasions he was caught up from this sublime abstraction into the presence of the One – a beatitude that his biographer knows, not only from proximity, but from personal experience of the same rapture (23.7-14). The *Life,* escorting its readers through the foothills of philosophy, brings into view the peaks to be scaled in the *Enneads*, though without tempering the steepness of the climb.

6

Literature and Dogma

The first half of this book has been dominated by Plotinus, because, alone of the four philosophers considered here, he was never anything other – never anything less, as he might have said – than a philosopher. He cared for no tradition but the Greek, yet seldom quotes a writer from this tradition except to corroborate doctrines that had never been held by more than a small minority of Greeks. For Longinus, on the other hand, philosophy was but one of the many disciplines that could occupy a learned pen – the highest perhaps, to judge by his bee-like flitting from one seminar to another, but not one to be cultivated without close parsing of idiom and literary ornament. Among the remains of his sometime student Porphyry are fragments of exegetic works which made no attempt to force a strict philosophy upon the canonical text. Yet both, in their writing on Homer and other poets, reveal the same intellectual vigour, and the same catholic Hellenism, that they brought to the study of Plato; and the results, if they would not have struck Plotinus as deep philosophy, are among our most astute and original specimens of ancient criticism.

The quarrel between philosophers and poets

Plato denounces the tragedies of the Golden Age, not only because they falsely impute wrongdoing to the gods, but because they lend an alluring beauty to the vices of human characters (*Republic* 386a-391e). The consequence is that, while the mind is taught to blame fate for the suffering and embarrassment that befall it through its own wickedness (380a etc.), the soul becomes accustomed to applaud, to imitate, even to glorify weak and dissolute conduct. Such poetry has no place in a school of virtue, and even a relaxation of the ban to admit the praises of just men and hymns to the gods would not open the city to the tragedians again, any more than to Homer (607a-b). Both suffer from the incorrigible defect that they are mimetic – that the verse requires the poet or his mouthpiece to affect an identity that is not his own and to counterfeit what he does not feel. If this is a change for the better, then the poet is not a just man; if he is just already, the change is for the worse, and must be prohibited for fear of imitation (380c-383c). Equally delusive is the technique of the painter, who puzzles the eye with simulacra of things that are themselves copies, and is no more a creator than a man who rotates a mirror beneath the heavens (596a-598a). Gaudy imitation is the stock-in-trade of the orator too, for he knows that he will prosper if he dazzles his audience with its own conceits. The object of his sorceries, as Plato had protested in his *Phaedrus*, is to make the soul a tool for his own advantage (271d): the paradigmatic case is a speech by Lysias in which a man pleads for the favours of a youth whom he does not pretend to love (230e-233c). The lover who is acquainted with supernal beauty addresses his beloved in a higher strain (244a-257b), but one that a philosopher must sing alone in a world where he is almost wholly eclipsed by sophists. Their trade is quackery dressed as art: its products, like those of cookery, yield only a brief and meretricious pleasure, and, like cookery again, it may be turned with equal skill to good or to deleterious ends (*Gorgias* 464c-466a).

The *Poetics* of Aristotle – not so often or so reverently perused in late antiquity as it is now – offers only a partial refutation of these strictures. He denies that tragedy masks the responsibility of the agent, since in his view the finest tragedies are those in which the hero brings misfortune on himself by some *hamartia* – a term which, in justice to Oedipus, we must surely translate as 'error', not 'crime' or 'failing' (1453a9). The spectacle of such a fall, he adds, will lead the audience through 'scenes of pity and terror' to a catharsis or purgation (1449b28); but, while this seems to be the cause of the innocent pleasure that we take in the play, we are not told whether any emotions are purged apart from those that have been aroused by the play itself. Among the six ingredients of tragedy he includes music, dress and scenery, though he does not say so much about any of these as he says about plot and character. As a metic or resident alien, he was after all excluded from the chief dramatic festival of Athens. For the same reason he would not have been a witness to the feats of manipulation and cold mendacity by which orators swayed the popular assembly; although in his *Gryllus*[1] and *Rhetoric* he maintained that there is both art and profit in oratory, and although his most profound analyses of human passion occur in the *Rhetoric*, he assumes that the proper study of philosophy is not merely what persuades, but what deserves to induce persuasion.

In the Roman era most Platonists showed a similar disdain for the histrionic. Plutarch – one of the few who was not himself a stranger in Athens – holds that a cultivated man may visit the theatre, but only to be edified by Menander, not to laugh with Aristophanes. Porphyry records his own attendance at a play about Prometheus only because it seemed to him to have staged a convincing representation of the soul's entry into the body (*To Gaurus*, p. 48 Kalbfleisch). Elsewhere the epithet 'tragic' is most often used by Platonists of philosophies which appeared to them either fatalistic in tendency or gaudy in expression. Socrates set the precedent in the *Republic*, when he confessed to speaking 'tragically' because his noble lie concealed the true origin of the classes in society. In similar vein, Plotinus accused the Gnostics of staging a 'tragedy of fears' (*Enneads* 2.9.13.7) because they traced our evil destinies to the stars. Two maverick Platonists of the second century, Numenius and Valentinus,[2] were accused of speaking tragically when they argued that the present world arose, without benign or rational purpose, from a schism in the divine. Sophists of the period, by contrast, affected postures from epic and tragedy and devote speeches to the comparison of tragedies which they know from performance rather than through reading. In drama, as in literature, their tastes are devoutly classical; the only new productions that they admit to having witnessed in the theatre are competitions of skill between men of their own profession. In this pursuit it was now no longer possible to win fame as a writer alone, like Lysias or Isocrates; the most distinguished sophists were those who, like Herodes Atticus or Aelius Aristides, were able to act their part, not only on stage, but at home or on the road.

Longinus as critic

But for his own pretensions in his letters, it would be evident that Longinus' *Art of Rhetoric* is the work of a sophist rather than a philosopher, of one who is more concerned to teach us how to exert persuasion than to show us any art by which we might lead ourselves or others to the truth. His subject, like that of Aristotle's *Rhetoric*, is the means of persuasion, *to pithanon*,[3] but he makes no use of Aristotle's distinction between what ought to persuade and what happens to be persuasive. In the same way he takes the word 'enthymeme', which in Aristotle denotes an elliptical argument, and applies it to such tricks of style as irony and histrionic silence, which enable a speaker to gain his point without argument at all (567 Walzer). If he deserves, by virtue of his assiduous cultivation of philosophers, to be regarded as a philosopher himself, he was perhaps the only member of this guild to take an undissembled pleasure in both the diction of tragedy and its performance. Let the orator observe, he says, how the actor in a tragedy or a comedy can engage or repel the audience, how he simulates the high tone and fluent delivery of the impassioned man, or the deferential meekness of the politician taking up his post (568.12-19).

In Aristotle's *Categories* ten modes of predication are distinguished as a prerequisite to the logical analysis of being; these categories serve Longinus, however, merely as rubrics for his own inventory of devices by which orators win attention and goodwill. The category of time supplies such arguments as 'the thing should not be done now' (552), while that of habit or state enables us to make reference to the weapons and advantages of the opponent (553). Arguments from position ('could I have seen that, lying on my back?') admit of illustration in gesture as well as in word (553). To the category of agency belong our attempts to determine whether an act was performed voluntarily, under duress or for mere aggrandisement (553); that of affection yields a list of injuries by which pity may be excited in the audience (553). Since the earlier part of his work has perished, we do not know what conceits Longinus marshalled under the first five categories.

Longinus borrows Plato's similes but inverts the logic. You will never seduce the soul, he writes (embracing another term that Plato had always used disdainfully), unless you cast a spell on it through grace and pleasing diction (560): musical intonation, rhythm and harmony are among the wiles by which one enchants the hearer without producing moral conviction or a reasoned estimation of the facts (558-9). To change the metaphor, one must feed the listening judge with sweet and beguiling dainties (562); rare idioms, assiduous variation and refinements of the commonplace will always please, and, if one avoids presumptuous idiosyncrasy, may be tolerated even in excess.

An example is allegory, which 'embellishes the discourse by changing the terms and saying the same thing in another, more novel mode' (562). Allegory is here a constructive trope, although philosophers were accustomed to use the term in its complementary sense, which signifies the detection of this trope in another man's writing. All such efforts to palliate the errors of myth and the folly of the poets seemed barren to Plato, since they could never be substantiated and led the soul into mazes which could only retard self-knowledge. Nor could such a hermetic reading justify the retention of the myth itself, as the ignorant would continue to be misled by the coarse veneer. Up to Longinus' day, most Platonists held to this position. Plutarch, for example, though he is willing to apply an allegorical key to Egyptian myth, accuses the Stoics of 'violence' when they redeem the putative blemishes of the *Iliad* by fathering their own physics and psychology on the poet. At the same time it is clear that he, like a number of Platonists after him, found a charter for constructive allegory in the didactic myths of the *Phaedrus*, the *Symposium* and the *Timaeus*. The parable of the birth of love from poverty and plenty explains itself, while in the narratives of the soul's fall and the origins of the universe there is much that, taken literally, cannot be reconciled with Plato's thought in other dialogues. Such precedents compelled admirers of Plato to defend the use of fiction in philosophy, and even to excuse the occasional detour into obscenity. From this, as we shall see in the present chapter, it was but a step to remedial allegory in the exegesis of Homer; a subsequent chapter will show that similar principles could be applied to make the licensed indecorum of the mysteries appear not merely innocuous but profound.

For all that, it is improbable that Longinus would have sought any warrant for allegory in Plato. At the end of his treatise he names seven models of style, some five of whom – Isocrates, Demosthenes, Aeschines, Lysias and Herodotus – he considers unimpeachable. Thucydides, however, he finds turgid and laboured; Plato, in his judgment, has encumbered the prose of his dialogues with poetic figures while showing little artistry in the combination of rhetorical tropes. This judgment, though unusual in a Platonist, would have seemed trite enough to critics who were not professed adherents of that school. What is surprising in Longinus is that he carries it over even into commentary on Plato, where (to judge by what is reported) doctrine and argument were subordinated to matters that he robbed of gravity by his own treatment of them. If what we know from Proclus of his *Commentary on the Timaeus* is representative, the paradox lies not so much in his handling of the text as in his choosing to handle only that portion of it which commemorates the grandeur and decline of a mythical city. The story of Atlantis had been neglected by other critics because it appeared to be more an ornament to than an element in the dialogue: this fact made it amenable to a purely aesthetic critique, in which the precepts of Longinus' *Art of Rhetoric* are so deftly illustrated as to leave no doubt that he meant it to be a handbook of good style and not (as one might have hoped) a satire on the false canons of the age.

Kritikos, with its superlative *kritikôtatos*, was to become the conventional epithet of Longinus, and the evidence of Proclus shows that he earned it by his exquisite analyses of Plato's syntax. In the first three *cola* or units of the *Timaeus* – Plato's solicitude in such details being notorious – he observed the arresting clarity of the exordium, the orotund modulation of the thought in the succeeding clause, and finally the majestic amplitude of the peroration, which completed the introduction of the chief characters to the reader (Proclus, *In Tim.* 14.7 on *Timaeus* 17a). Yet in Proclus' view his criticism is barren because he regularly fails to see anything but cosmetic elegance and a design upon the reader's soul (*psukhagôgia*) which Plato himself would clearly have disowned (ibid. 59.31 on *Timaeus* 19b). The same gratuitous variation of terms which he commends in his *Art of Rhetoric* is attributed to Plato at *Timaeus* 21a, where he commences the tale of Atlantis (ibid. 86.17ff). Yet he fails to grasp the point of the grand beginning, just as he fails to perceive why Plato describes the defeat of Atlantis as one of the greatest feats achieved by Athens, because the legend of Atlantis is for him an extrinsic feature of the dialogue.[4] Distinguishing three polities – the natural, the martial, the intellectual – on the model of the three classes in the *Republic*, he decides that Atlantis represents a city of the second kind (ibid. 31.23); accordingly, it seems, he proposed the deletion of the whole narrative in order that the cosmogony (which he took to be the chief subject of the *Timaeus*) could proceed without interruption (ibid. 204.11). Thus he took leave of such precursors as Numenius, who had argued that the war between Atlantis and Athens lent a historical dress to the perpetual strife between good and evil daemons; he does not seem to have noticed any allusion to the great conflict between the Greeks and the Persian Empire (or perhaps he thought it impolitic to mention this in an age of Persian victories; he regularly disappoints Proclus by failing to read the tale as an adumbration of the cosmogony which is to occupy the remainder of the dialogue. While he flatters Plato as an excellent critic of poets (ibid. 90.21), he appears to think that all poetry is technique, and therefore cannot understand that a poet of common education would be unable to imagine Plato's city, since his mind would not be imbued with the requisite knowledge of the Forms (ibid. 66.14-32 on *Timaeus* 19c). Once we transcend the somatic or bodily reading of the text which Longinus offers (ibid. 156.32), the digressions and incongruities which he thought that he had surprised in it are sure to disappear. We may say that Proclus is speaking here, not Plato, that he is blind to the ludic elements in the dialogues and interprets them with a uniform austerity that would not be attempted in any modern study. There is little doubt, however, that he knew what Plotinus meant when he called Longinus 'no philosopher, but a philologist', and that, even had Longinus held a 'Neoplatonic' doctrine of the intellect, the principled irreverence with which he handled Plato's texts would have kept him at a distance from that school.

The sublime

Flippant and superficial as his uncontested works may be, Longinus has been credited with the authorship of an exquisite dissertation *On the Grand Style*, or *On the Sublime*. This book owes its celebrity to its recognition of genius as an inimitable quality which may coexist with glaring faults and cannot be captured, let alone transmitted, by an anatomy of technical devices. Among previous critics, only Aristotle had explored the effects of rhetoric and poetry with comparable tact. The author is said in our manuscripts to be 'either Dionysius or Longinus': the former is Dionysius of Halicarnassus, who wrote in the age of Augustus, and it has been generally agreed in the twentieth century that the writing, although not his, is of his time. Rather than attribute it to Cassius Longinus, some have chosen to postulate an unattested namesake with the praenomen Dionysius; students of Neoplatonism have none the less continued to take a sly pleasure in hinting at the possibility, and the weakness of the case against it has now been exposed by Malcolm Heath,[5] a classicist who cannot be suspected of partiality. Having recapitulated his arguments here, I shall offer supplementary observations which I hope will make it appear not merely conceivable but probable that Porphyry's tutor wrote at least one meritorious book.

As Heath remarks, many classicists may have had no better reason for denying the text to Longinus than a reluctance to believe that the mid-third century could have given birth to such a masterpiece. Such prejudice can be rebutted merely by naming his contemporary Plotinus – the greatest philosopher, just as the author of *On the Sublime* was the greatest critic, since Aristotle. Nor can it be inferred from his allusion to a current state of peace (44.6) that the author of *On the Sublime* could not have been a witness to the 'crisis of the third century'. The comment is addressed only to the Greeks, whose present subjection to the Romans he regards as a deliverance from the internecine warfare of the classical age, when every Greek was free to destroy his own city. Weaker still is the argument that a connoisseur of the sublime in the early third or late second century could

99

not have failed to mention the greatest orator of the past generation, Aelius Aristides. Classicising principles forbade writers of the sophistic era to mention their contemporaries, even when they did not think them as frigid, effete and idly pleonastic as Aelius Aristides now appears to most readers. Both the *Art of Rhetoric* and the treatise *On the Sublime* draw most of their instances from authors who were long dead and beyond the reach of envy. It has indeed been urged, against the theory of common authorship, that the two treatises do not invoke the same touchstones; yet this too is a captious objection, which denies the critic the right to change his opinions or to match his authorities to his current purpose. Only an incorrigible discrepancy in their estimates of the same figure would provide grounds for assigning the works to different hands.

In fact they barely differ in their judgments. Neither, for example, has any quarrel with Demosthenes, whose well-timed artifices are contrasted in *On the Sublime* with the 'wilful' juggling of the syntax in Thucydides (22.3-4); Longinus, we remember, deplored the viscosity of this author's prose in his *Art of Rhetoric*. It is true, on the other hand, that the *Art of Rhetoric* acknowledges no flaw in the style of Isocrates, whereas the treatise *On the Sublime* finds affectation in the opening sentence of the *Panegyricus* (38.2); but one work is concerned with his utility as a model of composition, while the other notes a particular infelicity which is not said to be pervasive, and is chargeable to the vanity of Isocrates rather than any defect of style. Again, when we read that an otherwise noble passage in Herodotus has been cheapened by a poor choice of vocabulary (31.2), we must not forget that the critic is speaking only of this one passage; elsewhere in his treatise he cites Herodotus liberally and with no hint of censure (22.1-2; 34.1; 36.2). Of Plato both texts speak with tempered esteem. The *Art of Rhetoric* taxes him, as we have seen, with inconsistency of idiom, but this criticism does not subvert the praise that is implied by the mere inclusion of his name in a pleiad of classical exemplars. The author of *On the Sublime* declares, in similar vein, that Plato furnishes instances of grandeur, but is frequently injudicious in his use of rhetorical figures (32.7). Where the *Art of Rhetoric* pronounces him too poetic for a writer of prose, his partiality for Homeric diction is observed without reproach in *On the Sublime*. It is not, however, unusual for a teacher to admire an idiosyncrasy which he would not recommend to his pupils for imitation: *On the Sublime* is an essay in appreciation, not (like the *Art of Rhetoric*) a manual for novices in the business of public speaking. Only its judgment on Lysias would have been wholly out of place in the *Art of Rhetoric*, for it roundly declares, against those who think it better to be faultless than sublime, that even on this criterion Lysias is inferior to Plato, since his failings are more numerous, his merits inconsequential and jejune (32.8; 34.2). This is an animadversion on the style of Lysias, not on its aberrations, and it clearly implies a lower view of Lysias than Longinus held when he wrote the *Art of Rhetoric*. This fact alone, however, does not preclude his being the author of both treatises, any more than Nietzsche's strictures on Richard Wagner in his later works cast doubt on the authenticity of his earlier panegyric on the composer in *The Birth of Tragedy*.

But what, except that no one has yet disproved it, can be said in favour of crediting this second-rate man with a first-rate book that is not securely ascribed to him in the manuscripts? The coincidences in vocabulary to which Heath appeals are, to my mind, not quite frequent enough or striking enough to demonstrate common authorship, or even a common date. For this reason I am inclined to put more weight on two other features of the essay *On the Sublime* which are barely congruent with a dating to the first century, but would not have been so anomalous in the third:

1. At chapter 9.9 the author admires the lapidary manner in which the 'lawgiver of the Jews' recounts the creation of light by the simple fiat of God. The knowledge of the Septuagint which this passage reveals is not so profound as to warrant any charge of interpolation; yet no other pagan writer would appear to have known even so much before the mid-second century, when Numenius of Apamea cites the previous verse in an exposition of Plato's myth of Er. Galen, his younger contemporary, cites the Mosaic account of creation by fiat, though only to scoff at it; this we may take as evidence that Longinus, the 'walking library', would have known the text, though not that he would have read it with Galen's eyes.[6] Longinus wrote with authority on Numenius, corresponded with his partisans Amelius and Porphyry,[7] and resided for a time in his native city of Apamea. Even if he would not have joined him in labelling Plato an 'Atticising Moses', he shared the hesitant Platonism, the curious learning and the eclectic sympathies which had predisposed Numenius to find wisdom in this poor specimen of Greek.

2. At 15.1 the author transposes a term from the visual arts, recommending 'phantasy' (*phantasia*) as a device productive of 'gravity, magnificence and vigour'. It was not uncommon in literary criticism to urge that a poet should emulate the *enargeia* or brilliance of the great painters, but to characterise this quality as *phantasia* was an innovation, whatever the date of the treatise *On the Sublime*. *Phantasia* was Plato's term for the treacherous, if inevitable, propensity of the mind to form images of things not present; Aristotle distinguishes it from perception, and denies that it involves an exertion of power. Stoics, on the other hand, argued that the phantasm is a prerequisite of all thought about the future and that neither an abstract concept nor a scientific hypothesis could be formed if there were no such wax at the intellect's disposal. It is, however, only in Philostratus, the helmsman of the sophistic movement during the adolescence of Longinus, that it comes

to signify the creative faculty, superior to *mimêsis* or imitation, which enables the artist to represent an idea that is not already a datum of perception. Porphyry, two generations later, praised the *phantasiai* or compelling tints of life which the painter Carterius was able to bestow on his stealthy portrait of Plotinus.[8] It is clear, then, that the term belonged to the lexicon of aesthetics in the third century; had a critic of the first century employed it to describe the transcendent power of imagination, this would have been a neologism, and stillborn.

Poetry, philosophy and myth

We have spoken above of allegory as an author's trope; we have still to speak of critical allegory – which in English we might prefer to call allegorising – as a hermeneutic tool. Platonists up to Plutarch's time had generally declined to follow the Stoics in the allegorical interpretation of Homer and Greek myth. In the second century those who espoused the practice were initially not philosophers but sophists – a name of good repute in their time as in Plato's, and denoting in both periods a polymath with high pretensions to eloquence and none to originality. To orators who depended for their livelihood on the munificence of Philhellenic Emperors, or else on their capacity to devise a new panegyric on the Greek culture of every city that entertained them, it was necessary only that a phrase or thought should be of good pedigree, not that it should be true or edifying. Maximus of Tyre holds intellectual positions that are plainly (and consciously) derived from Plato; at the same time, a spokesman of Greek culture in this age could not afford to imitate Plato in his censorship of less edifying authors. When he raises the question whether philosophers or poets have spoken better about the gods, he resorts to allegory to show that, since all poets were philosophers, it was fruitless to inquire which had spoken better about the gods; as he did not belong to a milieu in which all claims must be proved from Plato, or indeed by strict philosophy of any kind, his argument is glib, sententious and frequently indebted to the Stoics. It was left to the most eclectic, and the most trenchant, Platonist of the second century, Numenius of Syrian Apamea, to discern in Plato a key to the philosophy of Homer and in Homer an illustration of the harmony between Plato's mind and that of his fellow-Greeks.

The etymology of the term *allêgoria* implies that it yields 'another' sense – another, that is, than the one that would emerge if every word in the text were construed in the way that first suggests itself to a competent reader. In contrast to the recognition of metaphor – which, even when it countermands what is commonly termed the literal sense, need not tax the intelligence of the reader – the allegorical reading is always felt to be an artificial exercise, and one that may betray as much idiosyncrasy in the critic as in the author whom he professes to interpret. The authority of the text guarantees that an allegory is possible; the presence of otherwise irredeemable blemishes, inconsistencies and absurdities proves that the method has not been wantonly applied; and the result is judged to be sound when it confirms the philosophical position that the author already holds. For interpreters of Plato (or the Bible) this position is most commonly derived from other passages in the same text which are deemed to be self-explanatory; for the Stoics, however, the clue to Homer is not to be found in the text itself but in the world. Phenomenon is interpreted by phenomenon, the unpalatable history by known and natural laws of human conduct or cosmology. Athena, pulling the mutinous Achilles by the hair, enacts the victory of reason over passion; the 'moly' given by Hermes to Odysseus represents a natural quickening of the intellect; the shape-shifting of Proteus does not compromise the dignity of the gods because he symbolises the formless elasticity of matter.[9] All this is innocuous enough, we might say, but why should the poet employ such dangerous intrigues to conceal facts which it is neither inconvenient nor difficult to express in the plainest terms? A reading which not merely saved but ennobled the text would urge that the hidden referent is of a kind that could not be unveiled by common speech, that there is nothing in this world that is more than an icon of the truth that it strives to adumbrate, that if the critic's gloss is clearer than the original, this is because it is saying less. The Platonist undeniably has the advantage of the Stoic, because he believes that the sensible world is ruled by principles which are essentially, not artificially, hidden from the senses, and that in the future life the soul's experiences will be of a different kind from those vouchsafed to embodied beings. If the *Odyssey* were, as Numenius held, a *roman-à-clef* of the soul's return to its supercelestial home, we could not demand that the narrative be rendered more perspicuous. If, as he also seems to have held,[10] the apertures through which gods and mortals pass in Homer's cave of the nymphs are the gates of Cancer and Capricorn through which souls come and go in Plato's myth of Er, then we cannot say that the subject has been arbitrarily handled in either text, or that the Platonic myth is more transparent than Homer's, though its hermeneutic value lies in the fact that it is transparently a myth.

Plotinus feels no duty to redeem the lay classics or to elicit the same truths from philosophy and from poetry. For demonstration philosophy suffices, though a snatch of verse may serve now and then to rouse attention or concentrate desire. Both ends are most likely to be achieved when the verse is openly didactic, and his quotations do not suggest that he saw any difference in poetic quality between Homer and Empedocles. Echoes of Empedocles and of Homer meet again in Porphyry's oracle on Plotinus, where the depiction of Plotinus as a swimmer in turbid seas, half-drowned, half-blinded, yet still labouring without fear through spray and rapids to the shore where the gods await him, is plainly modelled on the shipwreck of Odysseus.[11] This episode had already furnished Maximus and Numenius with images of philosophic zeal;[12] yet neither matched the audacity with which Plotinus eased the whole of Homer's narrative into a single paragraph, a tentative finale to his earliest work, which would also appear to have been the only one that he refined for publication:

> He who cleaves to the beauty of bodies and will not resign it descends, not in body but in soul, to shadows and depths unpleasing to the intellect; then he will remain sightless in Hades, a companion of shades in this life and the next. Rather, as one might more rightly urge, let us fly to our own country! [*Iliad* 2.140]. What then is the flight, and by what means? We shall go forth, he says, as Odysseus did from the sorceress Circe or Calypso – this I take to be his enigmatic meaning – not content to remain, for all the pleasures before his eyes and the company of so much that is beautiful to the senses. No, our fatherland from which we set out is there [in the higher world], and so too is our father. What then is the conveyance and the flight? It is not to be achieved on foot, for our feet carry us hither-thither from one land to another. Nor should you prepare yourself a horse-drawn chariot or a maritime vessel; no, all these you must resign and not even keep them in view. Rather, as it were, you must seal your vision, exchanging it for another kind and arousing the faculty that all possess but few employ (*Enneads* 1.6.8.12-27).

'He says' – but is this really exegesis? Plotinus ignores the context of the injunction 'let us fly to our own dear country', which in the *Iliad* is a counsel of pusillanimity, offered and properly repudiated before the Greeks had finished their work at Troy. His account of Odysseus' peregrinations begins in Hades, the centrepiece of Homer's epic; observing the narrative sequence, not the order of events, he returns through Circe to Calypso, no distinction being made between the enchantments of the two women or the reasons for Odysseus' dalliance with them. The hackneyed jest that greets Odysseus everywhere in Ithaca – 'I do not suppose that you travelled here by foot' – implies for Homer 'you must go by sea'; in Plotinus it means 'go nowhere'. The mist that conceals his homeland from Odysseus when he makes landfall there is treated as a symbol of the same false vision that binds the soul to Hades. The phantoms are dispelled not by Athena – Plotinian man is self-reliant, whatever the oracle told Amelius[13] – but by a voluntary occlusion of the senses. The reader who completes the simile is now brought full circle, for in Hades too it is only the blind Teiresias who can see.

The argument is not derived from the poem; it is read into the parentheses of an anecdotal summary. It is Homer who provides the exhortation, but the treatise reaches its climax in the next chapter (*Enneads* 1.6.9) with a meditation on *Phaedrus* 252, where the lover is said to 'perfect his own statue' in the beloved. As this is an embedded metaphor rather than an allegory, the interpretation is clear enough, at least when we shift the reference from the object of love to the soul of the lover himself. According to Plotinus' gloss, the text enjoins us to look into the depths again – not of Hades, but of the soul, in which all is pleasing; the journey is introduced by the same verb *anagein* which is used in the previous chapter of the voyages of Odysseus, but where Homer merely enumerates the wayside stations, Plato shows us the object of the quest. In order to do what is asked of us, we must first become what is shown to us; and here Plotinus touches upon the most famous of Plato's similes (*Republic* 508-9), in which the Good, like the sun, is said to be visible only to faculties trained by exercise, though at the same time everything else is visible only by its light. It is only the reader who apprehends Plato's meaning here who can fully grasp the antecedent parable of the cave, and through this parable the whole plan and intent of the *Republic*. And in the same way it is only (Plotinus says) by becoming sunlike that we can gaze upon the sun, and only when it perceives the meaning of this simile that the soul will know what it is to mould its own statue,[14] and only through its progress in this enterprise that it will see the light concealed by Homer's shadows. One who is no philosopher cannot be a true lover of poetry, since, as Plotinus says in the final sentence of this treatise, even the Beautiful owes its beauty to the Good (1.6.9.42).

As Plato was a known contriver of allegories, it is from his works that Plotinus draws his canons of exegesis. Perhaps the most salient principle – established in the simile of the line which stands between the cave and the sun in the *Republic* – is that the concepts of reality which the soul forms in the present world, unless they arise from direct contemplation of the Forms, are only images of true knowledge: to be more precise, conjecture is an image of perception and perception of discursive thought, but even this, the highest cognitive process that most souls can attain, is only an approximation to knowledge, the icon of an unseen original. Both our reasoning and the rational thoughts that it engenders are embedded in time, itself the moving image of eternity, as *Timaeus* says in the dialogue named after him (37d5). The soul lives, as a tale unfolds, in a temporal continuum: it is only when we release the myth from its narrative envelope, breaking the seal of time, that the perennial characters of truth appear.[15]

Plotinus himself, as Porphyry says in his *Life* (8.1-5), attended not so much to the words of Plato's text as to the *noêmata*, the intellectual truths, for which the words were a pliable substrate. In the *Symposium* (203b-d), Diotima tells Socrates that Eros was conceived when the inebriated Poros or Wealth was surprised by the lady Poverty in Aphrodite's garden. Christians at least had mocked the lewdness of this fable,[16] and the absurdity of supposing that a male god could beget a child without waking. Plotinus waves these criticisms aside with the observation that 'myths, if myths they are to be, will necessarily parcel out what they say in times, and separate from one another many of the things that exist as one but are distinct in rank or potency (*Enneads* 3.5.9.24-7). Poros, he argues, stands for Mind, which diffuses shaping principles to the lower realm, but cannot communicate the noetic vision and is therefore said to sleep. Aphrodite stands for the soul, and Poverty for restless indeterminacy, the 'intellectual matter', which conspires with form to generate a sensible universe for the soul to govern. Eros is the yearning of the lower for the higher, hence the link between the soul and the divine, but for which the soul would lose all recollection of its origins and hence become a stranger to itself.

Platonists accepted the paradoxical corollary that we cannot learn what we do not already know;[17] and since the same mystery threatens to befuddle every act of interpretation – since we cannot construe a sign without some knowledge of the thing signified, or grasp the idea of love except by an exercise of love – Plotinus' exegesis is of the 'self-reflexive' kind which simultaneously deciphers the text and accounts for our capacity to decipher it. If a text describes the progress of knowledge from conjecture to perception, then to discursive thought and at last to intuition, the text itself will be legible only to those who can recapitulate this progress in their own perusal of it. Just as there are two kinds of love – the pandemic and the uranian, one looking downward, one looking heavenward – so there are two kinds of exegesis, one of which is content to parse the words while the other guides us to the truth that words conceal.

Beauty and its temptations

A second canon of exegesis is that the soul is a mirror to the cosmos. We recall that, in juxtaposing Plato and Homer, Plotinus warns us not to allow the soul to linger on the deformities of the world but to turn its eye to the beauty within. From his principle that the lower is apprehended in the higher, it follows (as he explains elsewhere) that the soul can find itself only by looking upward as well as inward, seeking not to project an image of its own beauty but to embrace the beauty of soul itself in the intellectual realm. Each descending soul contains the undescended soul, within which abide the unfallen principles of being; its fall, like the sleep of Wealth in the *Symposium*, is said at *Enneads* 5.8.10 to consist in a forfeiture of noetic insight, which grasps everything as one. It is by the recovery of this inward vision that the soul comprehends such an 'outward spectacle' as the pageant of the gods in Plato's *Phaedrus*: it is because 'the souls see all' that the reader is able to discard the linear narrative, perceiving that it is only to accommodate our fractured and timebound ways of thought that the gods, who 'see all things singly yet as one' are assigned in the myth to different chariots, each with his own train and pursuing his own ideal. In Zeus, the first and eldest of Plato's gods, who embodies all the manifest beauty of the divine, the philosopher sees the Zeus of Hesiod's *Theogony*,[18] though one might ask what philosophy there could be in a catalogue of divine infanticides avenged by deposition and mutilation. Plotinus replies that the temporal generation of the gods is metaphorical, that Uranus, Cronus and Zeus personify stages in the transition from absolute unity to the intelligible manifold, that the castration of Uranus and the fetters of Cronus signify respectively the transcendence of the One and the immutable stability of reason.[19] Zeus is still the eldest of the gods because it is in him that the ineffable assumes the form of intelligible beauty (5.8.10.22-31). Thus the gods are at peace and the poet's concatenation of atrocities is unified by the panoramic vision of the *Phaedrus*, which at once evokes and presupposes a unity of vision in the soul.

To contemplate oneself in a higher principle is to approach, but not to reach, union with that principle, since full union would annihilate the difference between the seeing and the thing seen (5.8.10.33-5). If, on the other hand, instead of assimilating the soul to this higher beauty, one translates it into a plastic and external form, the resulting work of art will be intrinsically of less worth than the vision that inspired it. Plotinus is sometimes said to have upheld the dignity of the visual arts against the strictures of Plato: that is true insofar as he credits the artist with perceptions resembling those of the philosopher, but it is not true that he attaches any self-subsistent value to the artefact itself:

> Now it must be seen that the stone thus brought under the artist's hand to the beauty of forms is beautiful not as stone – for so the crude block would be as pleasant – but in virtue of the form or idea introduced by the art. This form is not in the material; it is in the designer before ever it enters the stone; and the artificer holds it not by his equipment of eyes and hands but by his participation in his art. The beauty, therefore, exists in a far higher state in the art; for it does not come over integrally into the work. The original beauty is not transferred; what comes over is a derivative and a minor one, and even that shows itself in the statue not integrally and with entire realisation of intention but only insofar as it has subdued the resistance of the material (*Enneads* 5.8.1).

Art itself is beautiful, but in creating the artefact it subjects this beauty to the restless principle of otherness, imposing form on the indeterminate only by sapping the unity of form. One could hardly expect a higher view of statuary or painting from a thinker who did not even think it worth his while to master the arts of writing. Plotinus, Porphyry tells us, was reluctant to put the seal of ink on his meditations, loth to read them again and careless of spelling or of the purity of his Greek. It is because there is so little of the rhetorician about him, so little consciousness of an audience, that his treatises meander so unaccountably from one half-quoted text in Plato's dialogues to another. The man to whom he entrusted the correction of his manuscripts was, by contrast, a prolific writer of catholic tastes, and schooled in his adolescence by Longinus, whose devotion to art for art's sake has already been illustrated in this chapter. Under the guidance of these two great masters – one the philologist, one the philosopher of his age – he learned to reach for truth beneath the Homeric narrative with one hand, while with the other he combed obscurities from the surface of the text.

Porphyry on literature

Did he ever make a choice between Longinus and Plotinus? Perhaps not if – as he himself says, adapting a standard metaphor – the word and thought in a text are complementary, like the body and soul of a human organism:

> It seems that in discourse there is a soul and a body: that which may be rightly considered the soul is the invention of the concepts, while the body[20] is the expression (*hermêneia*).[21]

The word *hermêneia* connotes nothing so abstruse as the activity that we now call hermeneutics. In music it is a technical term for 'expression', and often appears to mean no more in literature; in a fragment of Longinus the orotundity of a well-constructed sentence is described as its *hermêneia*,[22] while in his *Art of Rhetoric* (558) the rare cognate *hermêneusis* is used of the periodic rhythm which can work on the ear 'independently of the sense' (*aneu dianoias*). A comment in the epitome of the same work, that '*kallilogia* (elegance of style) is the light of *noêmata* (intellectual content)'[23] seems to put a higher value on the words than Porphyry's simile.

Porphyry also put together a book of *Questions Relating to Homer*, all of which appear from what remains to have been philological or historical. The scholia report that he supplied two names for Priam's mother (Fr. 384 Smith), that he noted an alternative tradition which made Hector the child of Apollo, not of Priam (385), and that he gave the name Archialas to the shepherd who brought up Paris as an infant (386). Eustathius – less concerned to know what the poet might have said than to have a reason for what he does say – discovered in Porphyry's *Homeric Questions* that the term 'hero' is formed from *aêr* ('air'), that Achilles and Ajax the greater were fellow-scions of Aeacus (though Homer does not say so), that eighteen of the twenty-eight captains of Troy's allies fall in the *Iliad*, and that the dead inhabit fields of asphodel because this plant grows close to tombs and has a name reminiscent of the Greek for 'ashes'.[24]

The treatise *On the Styx* was written not so much to explain the inner logic of the narrative as to make it answerable to the higher logic of philosophy. Why is it that a soul not destined for punishment crosses Acheron as soon as the corpse receives a decent funeral, while the soul of the malefactor must receive its due before it makes this passage (Fr. 377.29-33)? Porphyry, thinking more of Plato's Lethe than of Homer's infernal streams, replies that to enter the groves and meadows of Persephone one must renounce all thoughts that pertain to human life; since the soul learns nothing if she expiates a deed that she no longer feels to be hers, any retribution that is intended to prompt remorse must be inflicted before the extinction of her memories. The *phantasiai* or impressions of wrongdoing in her former life adhere to the soul, and her consciousness of sin ensures that the penalties are felt to be apportioned to her crimes (Fr. 377.27-35). As evidence that Homer was acquainted with the tenacity of the phantasm and its role in the perpetuation of the finite memory, Porphyry instances the use of blood in *Odyssey* 11 to summon the ghosts of witless shades; since Homer cannot write his own gloss, Empedocles is cited to confirm that the cognitive faculty is located in the blood.[25] As in Plotinus, the epic is on all fours with the didactic, and no heed is taken of Aristotle's dictum that to be a poet one must do more than argue in hexameters. Empedocles speaks for Homer and both bear testimony for Plato; had Porphyry himself felt the need of a sponsor for his teaching on *phantasia*, it would not have been Longinus or Plotinus, but Numenius of Apamea, who (as Porphyry himself reports) interpreted the whole epic as a *eikôn* or adumbration of the soul's pilgrimage to the next world.[26]

Porphyry's longest essay on exegesis is the one now entitled *On the Cave of the Nymphs*, which in its original form may have been identical with the work called *On the Philosophy of Homer* in the *Suda*. The extant torso commences with a quotation from the thirteenth book of the *Odyssey*, but the argument of the next thirty pages returns only intermittently to this text, after visiting Plato's myth of Er and the Roman philosophy of Mithraism in its long digressions.[27] The combination of themes may not be original, since Porphyry's own allusions to Numenius make it possible to construct an archetype; but, for all we know, it was in Porphyry's hands that the egress from the Cave became not only a symbol of the soul's ascent from the lower world, but an acted parable of the interpretative scrutiny which a reader must bring to any text that professes to enshrine an ancient truth. The method is allegorical[28] – Odysseus stands for the soul on pilgrimage, rock for matter, the portals of the cave for Cancer and Capricorn, the olive for divine wisdom (71.16-17) – but it is not at war with history. Porphyry can entertain the question whether the Cave itself existed as an artefact in Sicily; indeed, he is unwilling to suppose that it is a mere *plasma* or fabrication of the poet (57.24-58.24). His invention lay primarily in imbuing it with a lofty symbolism; at the same time, just as he did nothing in vain, so neither did those whose anonymous masonry he celebrates. Porphyry had no more doubt that these ancients would have adorned the cave with images that they knew to be significant than he would have denied the plain meaning of the astronomical diagrams that adorned the rock-hewn cellars of the Mithraists in his own day (73.2-11).

Plato in the *Republic* represents men who are not philosophers as prisoners chained in a Cave, with no more evidence of the world than the play of shadows cast by images behind them.[29] In Porphyry too the ornaments of the cave may be delusive, for its hardness or *antitupia* is that of congelated matter, which receives only weak and fugitive impressions of more durable entities (59.12-18; 62.15-17). Nevertheless, it is from the vestiges of form in matter that we ascend to form itself; it is from the darkness of the Cave to the light of Athena's beacon, the laurel, that

Odysseus climbs in Homer, so that Athena herself, in due course, may unseal his clouded eyes (78.6-79.20; cf. 57.21). This is a homecoming, at first in ignorance, just as the soul may recognise the beauty in material things before she is able to transcend this copy and recover an intuition of the immaterial beauty that she pursued before her fall. By distinguishing the matter of the text itself from the meaning,[30] by assuming throughout that the hero makes his escape by perusing the images that surround him, and by borrowing the verb *plassein* from architecture to describe the composition of a text,[31] the philosopher hints at an analogy between the practice of reading and the mariner's journey: the former is a means, the latter a symbol of deliverance from the unexamined life.

Why, we may ask, if this is Homer's message, did he choose to put it in cipher? One answer may be, to teach us that all enlightenment is achieved by labour and cautious peregrination. Near the end of the treatise, Porphyry warns us that it is not possible to dissipate our ignorance at a single stroke, or free the soul by a premature departure from the body.[32] Only by a pedestrian advance in knowledge and virtue, by the gradual and circumspect appeasement of the deities set to guard us in the present world, can the soul dissolve the fetters of mortality. As the symbols of the cave are inscribed in rock, so it is from the flux of the material world that the intellect derives its feeble auguries of a higher one; the path to full knowledge lies through partial knowledge, just as truth is often found beneath the surface of a text.

Philosophy from Oracles

In the heyday of the Greek city-state, an affair of any magnitude would commence with the consultation of an oracle, most frequently the oracle at Delphi, where a female priestess, the Pythia or Sibyl, was supposed to speak ecstatically at the prompting of Apollo. Her utterances were notoriously ambiguous, and so never falsified; so too the oracle never lost the sanctity which had led to the creation of a league of neighbouring cities to secure its independence; and, even when this Amphictyonic league was weak, its credit survived because no state won an ascendancy which brought this obscure and mountainous locale within its sphere of influence. After Alexander the mainland ceased to be the centre of the Greek world, while his heirs in the east began to cultivate native gods or assume divine prerogatives to which no classical statesman had aspired. Consequently the oracle was less often consulted on matters of state; to Platonists this neglect ensured that Apollo would never commend the wisdom of any other man as he commended that of Socrates,[1] and that, if a new philosophical inquiry were submitted to him, his answer would not be warped by any temporal or political concerns.

The Romans too were addicted to divination, though they relied much less on prophecy than on the inferences of soothsayers from the flight of birds, the diet of sacred chickens and the blemishes of sacrificial victims. Once again such omens carried less weight in imperial times, when the ruler was more likely to seek the counsel of an astrologer in private than to lay his projects openly before an unpredictable tribunal. On the other hand, the three volumes which were supposed to have been purchased from the Sibyl by Tarquinius Superbus in the sixth century BC survived the fall of the Republic, and were opened in times of danger to the city. Nor were the soothsayers wholly defunct in Porphyry's time, for the failure of a sacrifice was the pretext for Diocletian's purge of Christians from his household, some four years before he issued his general edicts against the Church. These events perhaps betoken not so much the tenacity of Roman institutions as a calculated reanimation of old forms under a Romanising Emperor. But, whatever the cause, it certainly appears that in the Platonism of the late third century, divination assumed a practical significance that it had not hitherto possessed – although the alliance of the seer with the philosopher, foreshadowed in Plato's *Phaedrus* (244b-e), had been partially cemented in Plutarch's Delphi dialogues.

The treatise *On the Mysteries* by Iamblichus concurs with other sources in this account of the rites of prophecy at Apollo's Asiatic shrine of Claros. We may therefore assume that he accurately reports the rites at Didyma near Miletus in his third book, where he transmits and amplifies Porphyry's allusions in his *Letter to Anebo*, using the present tense throughout. How he conceived the prophecies to arise and what he thought of their human conduits we shall see in the following chapter. This chapter, after a brief excursus on the superannuation of the spoken word in prophecy, will consider the written oracles, characteristic of the third century, of which Porphyry seems to have been the most assiduous collector. It will be apparent that, even when they proceed from the ancient sanctuaries, his texts are more verbose and more expository than those of the classical era, while at the same time he is not afraid to put them to the test of his own philosophy. In short, we shall be able to say of him, as of Iamblichus in the next chapter, that his researches are not superstitious or merely empirical, but bring order and reason to matters that had been handled anecdotally, if at all, by their philosophical precursors. In their rationalism they are true heirs of Plotinus, though he was one to whom the oracles were dumb.

The decline of the oracles

Apollo flourished in Asia, but the poor gleanings from his oracle at Delphi in the Hellenistic era – one chapter of nine, nine pages out of 194 in the collection of Parke and Wormell – confirm the report of Plutarch that at the turn of the second century the Sibyl at this shrine no longer gave her responses in verse.[2] It might be said indeed that she never had, for it had always been the function of the male priests at her shrine to reduce her utterances to hexameters. On the other hand, it could not be said (in Plutarch's view at least) that there was more of the divine in the first afflatus than in its metrical epilogue: after all, as a speaker in one of his dialogues avers, the god is not speaking through the Sibyl as a dramatist speaks to us through the performer's mask. Vaticination is always the result of three forces. There is first the native prescience that all souls possess by virtue of their affinity to the gods, though, as a merely passive faculty, this is more receptive in woman than in man. Next (since it is not beneath the dignity of the gods to use intermediaries) there are the natural means by which the human vessel is filled; of these none is more familiar than the subterranean fumes which moisten the soul of the expectant prophetess on the tripod at Delphi. Finally, there is the power to comprehend and to express what has been communicated: this demands the exercise of intelligence, the common patrimony of gods and humans, which among the latter tends to be at its purest and most active in the male. Since the thoughts of gods are perspicuous, coherent and untrammelled by deceit, it follows that any obscurity in the transmission of them must be imputed to the faults of the human medium.

Such recalcitrant organs will be used only where, because a low standard of education prevails, there are none more docile; it is because the Greeks are now a more serene, a more prosperous and a more cultured people that the gods admonish them not through obese hexameters but through the measured prose of science and philosophy. Nor, as the same interlocutors agree in their dialogue on the decline of the oracles in Greece itself, should one suppose that the gods are any less intimate with mortals because one maiden at Delphi now performs the work that was once allotted to three; the suppliants are fewer than in the classical age, not only because the population has dwindled, but because votaries are less inclined to be impressed by a bodily paroxysm than by the quiet fermentation of divine wisdom in the intellect. Visitors to Apollo's shrine, we learn, were enjoined to pursue this inward vision by the inscription 'know thyself' above the door; next to this motto, which Socrates had taken as his own, stood the letter *epsilon*, which the speakers in Plutarch suppose to be either an emblem of the five senses and the five elements (epsilon being the fifth letter of the alphabet) or a variant of the Greek verb *ei*, 'thou art'.[3] This exclamation, whether addressed to the deity or to his worshippers, serves in Plutarch's view to remind the soul that her true home lies in a realm of eternal being, where there is no past and no future, no mundane saturnalia of sense and change.

No doubt it is because allegory – the purposeful encryption of meaning – stimulates and does not suppress inquiry that Plutarch credits it with a timeless power to edify, even after the Sibyl's ravings have been silenced by the progress of education. Authors of the Roman age, however, depict a more knowledgeable, if more reluctant, Sibyl, dwelling at Cumae or Erythrae rather than Delphi, who experiences no loss of understanding when she prophesies, though she feels Apollo's presence as a renewal of his first assault upon her maidenhood. The Sibyl of Cumae, needing no interpreter, became her own scribe, and the books that she is said to have deposited with Tarquinius Superbus, King of Rome, were consulted in times of jeopardy up to 312, when the last pagan Emperor died in battle outside the walls. In the meantime, the Sibyl had become a prolific mouthpiece of involuntary revelation in Christian literature. Exempt, both as a woman and as a barbarian, from the prejudices that blinded the Greek philosophers, she was none the less a reluctant, hence an unimpeachable, witness, because she was not a convert to the truth that she proclaimed. In the second century Christian advocates cited her work more liberally than Homer's; those of the third evinced a more classical taste, but in the early fourth her prophecies of judgment on the pagan world were juxtaposed with the Fourth Eclogue of Virgil in Latin apologies. Though Porphyry will not have lived to see it, this usurpation marks the climax of a war in which he had openly taken arms against the Church.

It may have been Diocletian who first canvassed the shrines for evidence that the Christians were offensive to the gods. Constantine, who in the elation of victory disseminated a Sibylline acrostic on the name of Christ, was present by his own account at an embassy sent by Diocletian to ascertain the cause of present evils from an oracle of Apollo. That the episode has precedents in Greek drama and Roman history is no proof that it is fictitious, since the theatrical evocation of myth was one of the chief devices by which Diocletian cemented his long tenure of the throne. The invectives which are hurled against Apollo by Christian writers of this period suggest that they blamed his acolytes for the crimes of their oppressors. Porphyry was another man whose name became synonymous in the Church with pagan malice, and if his three books *On the Philosophy to be Derived from Oracles* cannot be shown to have been the main cause of enmity, they were quoted at greater length, and with more obloquy, by our earliest Christian witnesses than the rest of his works combined.

Porphyry's *Philosophy from Oracles*[4]

The first extract in Eusebius, which appears to come from the proem to the opening book, declares that none of the oracles collected in the treatise has suffered change or augmentation, except for occasional corrections to the syntax, metrical supplements and pruning of otiose matter (Fr. 303.15-22 Smith). Wherever, then, the reader of this collection meets a philosophic doctrine, it is not because the editor has insinuated his own thoughts into the text but because the gods have a natural propensity to speak the truth. (Eusebius has evidently performed his own rites of exculpation here, for in the passages that he transcribes there is not an atom of philosophy.) The veracity of the oracles will be gauged best by those who, after years of fruitless labour in search of truth, have seen that there is no escape from perplexity except through revelation (303.30-4). This, however, the gods will not vouchsafe to those of dissolute life or sluggardly understanding: they reserve the gift for those whose one concern in life has been the liberation of the soul.[5] Such is the disparity between mortals and immortals that even Pan, a mere acolyte of Dionysus, has been known to leave nine men dead by a sudden epiphany.[6] Such formidable powers as Hecate, Hermes and Asclepius we must be content to know only from the verses in which they state their own name and lineage.[7] The sarcasm of Eusebius stifles Porphyry's defence of the ritual acts which enable worshippers to approach their gods without fear of annihilation, but his oracles prescribe the dedication of water to Hera (Fr. 309.11), the beating of timbrels in honour of Rhea (309.6), the mourning of Osiris (309.14) and the orgiastic cult of Dionysus (307.20ff).[8] Athena, we hear, delights in war, while Hecate, in whom the discordant sympathies of the universe are blended as in a single soul, can be bound as she binds others, by the adamant of a magical incantation.[9]

The principal expositor of divine mysteries is Apollo, and from him we learn that gods are of four orders – chthonic or earthly, marine, subterranean and celestial – each demanding the sacrifice of a different kind of victim.[10] To the gods of earth one offers four-footed animals – swine to Demeter, for example – which, in keeping with their habitat, must be black (Fr. 315.29-34). A trench must be dug for offerings to subterranean powers; to those who live above the soil we raise altars (315.35-7). Winged fowl suffice the other gods, and these again must be black for those who dwell in the dusky ocean (315.20). White birds are the portion of the supernal gods, the whole carcase being presented to those of the air, while those of the aether and upper heaven require no more than the extremities (315.21-5). Precepts for the fashioning of images follow. Those of Pan should be goat-legged, cloven-footed and two-horned;[11] Hecate's should be white-robed, shod in gold and in the likeness of Demeter, while her waxen effigies should bear a lamp, a whip and a sword and be encircled by the figure of a snake.[12] Her colours should be white and red and gold, which, like the three trophies, reinforce her triple character; this in turn corresponds (as we learn elsewhere[13]) to the three divisions of the soul and to the demiurgic and unitive power which Hecate exerts in all three provinces of matter.

It will be observed that the gods who figure most largely in this account are not those whose oracles were most frequently consulted in antiquity; there were indeed few local shrines of Hecate, who was most often invoked in witchcraft, though she was both a more public and a more potent deity in Hesiod.[14] In Porphyry's time, however, the famous oracles – as he himself admits, confirming the testimony of Plutarch – were extinct, and one was forced to look outside the Greek world for tidings of the gods. Porphyry names the Assyrians, the Phoenicians and the Chaldaeans[15] – though in fact the one work of Phoenician theology that he is known to have perused is that of his countryman Sanchuniathon, who had unmasked the gods as glorified impostors. Eusebius displays some of Porphyry's gleanings from this archive in his *Gospel Preparation*,[16] just before turning to the *Philosophy from Oracles*, from which he can cite a contrasting panegyric on the Hebrews. Numenius had praised the god of the Jews who has no fellowship with lesser beings; in Porphyry Apollo couples the Hebrews with the Chaldaeans as wise races who paid due reverence to the 'king who is born of himself'.[17] Does Apollo therefore agree with Paul in regarding the Hebrew scriptures as 'oracles of God' (Romans 3.2)? Not on the evidence of the next quotation – the last of our fragments from the first book of the *Philosophy from Oracles* – in which the Hebrews are said to have embraced the Chaldaean notion of seven heavens, each identical with one of the planetary spheres (Fr. 324.15-18).

Porphyry's second book defines the instruments and the bounds of divine activity. A long oracle divides angels into three classes: those who are always in the presence of the Almighty, those who depart to carry out his errands or convey his decrees and those who intone perpetual hymns of praise.[18] In addition to these ministers, there are evil daemons, subjects of the Egyptian god Sarapis, who must be exorcised in preparation for the approach of gods.[19] It is to them that the ignorant offer bloody and unwholesome sacrifices, and their reward is to be puffed up with crass vapours which give rise to wordless gibbering and bombast (Fr. 326.26-34). Whether these squatters are driven out by force or suborned by rituals of appeasement, the recipient of the prayers will be Pluto, tyrant of the nether world – whom the oracles know, however, to be identical with God (326.8-12). The daemons have their symbol, the three-headed Cerberus, who once again represents the three realms ensouled and ruled by Hecate.[20] This is perhaps another way of saying that these daemons, like the angels, have their own place in the polity of fate, from which they cannot be extruded by the gods themselves or by their most learned adepts. Apollo concedes as much when he tells one suppliant that he cannot reveal himself until the daemons have received their tribute of wine, milk, fruits and entrails;[21] on another occasion, when asked to foretell the sex of an unborn child, he replies that she will be a girl by the edict of the stars.[22] Hence it is that we turn to such consultants as the magi and the horoscope-casters; were it possible to be more than we are by nature – or, as Porphyry says to Marcella near the end of his life, to escape our natal daemon[23] – why would such a god as Ares still be a slave to the bellicose character that was allotted to him in his hour of generation? As it is, his temper must be restrained by Zeus, whose will is assumed in the oracles to be sovereign, not (it seems) because it countermands the decrees of fate but because the two never fail to coincide.[24] Yet Zeus is not the donor of any oracle in Porphyry's collection; his regular informants, if constrained to speak in an unpropitious season, will be caught between two millstones and can avoid deception only by giving notice that the response will be untrue.

Porphyry here betrays himself as the most superstitious of the Neoplatonists. Iamblichus, as we shall see, maintained that if the magician thinks that a god has lied to him, it is because he has mistaken either the sense of the words or the character of the visitant. When Porphyry writes that Plotinus studied the works of *genethlialogoi* or horoscope-makers and found them full of 'vanity' (*phluaria*), the report implies that he shares his master's estimate. Yet in the same biography he opines that it was by virtue of having 'more by birth than most men' that Plotinus escaped without injury to his soul when a rival turned the power of the stars against his body.[25] Plotinus himself might not have used the expression, which appears to have been borrowed from a eulogy of Pythagoras;[26] yet he admitted the practical efficacy of magic, and attributed it – like Porphyry, but in contrast to Iamblichus – to the natural sympathy between the elements. Vanity may not have been all that he hoped to find in the works of the *genethlialogoi*; and if (as Porphyry tells us) he refused to divulge his birthday and place of origin, it may not have been because he scorned such matters but because he was afraid that by disclosing them he would lay himself open to the sorcerer's arts.[27]

The excerpts that Eusebius appears to have culled from the third book of the *Philosophy from Oracles* mark little advance on the other two, except that Apollo warns us still more candidly of the impending deceit,[28] while Hecate finds a number of ways – all futile – of protesting against the coercive importunity of their suitors.[29] Verses ascribed to Pythagoras make Hecate submit to the conjurations of a 'mortal man', while other lines prescribe expressly that incantations should be accompanied by a 'mortal flute'.[30] Eusebius adds acid to his own scorn by citing Porphyry's exclamation that no teaching could be plainer, or more consonant with the character of the gods and the physical world (Fr. 349.11-16). He has, however, overlooked a passage, eagerly cited by Augustine, which declares that only ignorant and brutish folk would worship any god below the heavens, and that even the higher deities are subject to one whose Law has been enshrined in the Hebrew scriptures.[31] But for this passage, Porphyry's regulations for animal sacrifice in this treatise would have stood in bald contradiction to his repeated advocacy of bloodless sacrifice in other work. That is some evidence of its authenticity, and, if a Christian had interpolated the reference to the Hebrews, he would surely have deleted two other texts which are hostile to followers of Christ, though they spare the man. Man he was and all that man can be, declares an oracle (attested in Eusebius, and expressly assigned to the third book[32]) which is attributed to Hecate, though Augustine hints that Porphyry himself had more than a hand in it;[33] the oracle goes on to lament that worshippers of Christ parade their folly by paying to his exalted soul the honours due to a god alone. Another passage, cited only by Augustine, relates that when a pagan asked Apollo how to reclaim his Christian wife, the god replied that one might as well attempt to write on water as to cure those who have succumbed to this disease.[34]

Porphyry and the Chaldaeans

While Porpyhry lays down precepts in this treatise for the worship of lesser beings, the cardinal aim of the *Philosophy from Oracles* is to commend the bloodless worship of the one god. We have seen that an oracle quoted in his first book denied the knowledge of this 'self-begotten king' to every race except the Hebrews and Chaldaeans, and among the lost works of Porphyry were two books (or perhaps the same book under two titles) on the interpretation of the cryptic verses known to antiquity as the *Chaldaean Oracles*. In the *Suda* we find the title *On the Writings of Julian the Chaldaean*, and in Augustine a hectoring paraphrase of a treatise *On the Regression of the Soul*.[35]

Augustine's source concurs with the *Philosophy from Oracles* in distinguishing daemons from angels, and in separating those of the latter group who speak on God's behalf from those whose appointed business is to praise him. Of the highest order of angels in the *Philosophy from Oracles*

117

– those who live always in the presence of the Father – nothing is said, unless we are to equate them with the gods. Gods and angels alike are subject to incantations – even, it seems, to the petulant and self-serving kind that Porphyry stigmatised by the name *goêteia* (witchcraft). Again it is consistent with the *Philosophy from Oracles* that this treatise requires that the daemons be appeased before any rites can be applied to the higher entities; in these arts even a good man skilled in magic cannot prevail if a stronger rival elects to counteract his efforts.[36] Even a prosperous outcome can at best effect the deliverance of the inferior, or spiritual, soul; the higher, or intellectual, portion, is of one nature with the Father, and achieves reunion with him not through enchantment but through moral purification. It is sent to the world in order that the experience of transgression and its consequences may teach it to prize the unsullied life in the presence of the Father; there is a soul, perhaps of the inferior kind, that roves from body to body, though Augustine reports that Porphyry departed from his teachers by maintaining that a human soul can pass only to another human, never to a brute.[37]

Small wonder then that an able scholar has argued that the *Philosophy from Oracles* and the *Regression of the Soul* were a single work.[38] But, if this is so, it is curious that Augustine, in Book 10 of the *City of God*, should have used this unconventional title, while in Book 19 he is happy to join Eusebius and Philoponus in referring to the *Philosophy from Oracles*. Furthermore, it is hard to see why Eusebius, if his text of the *Philosophy from Oracles* had contained all the passages cited by Augustine, should have overlooked the pagan adumbration of the Trinity which Augustine professed to find there. From him we learn that Porphyry had named as transcendent principles of being not only the Father but a 'paternal intellect' which he also styled the Son of God.[39] The human soul is subordinate and posterior to both, but the immediate successor to the Father is not the Son but a coadjutant to which Porphyry does not seem to have given a name. Although Augustine detects an allusion to the Holy Spirit,[40] this intermediary appears to precede the Son in Porphyry's triad, rather than issuing jointly from both like the Spirit in the Augustinian Trinity. Adding that Porphyry fell into the error of describing the three participants in his triad as three gods, Augustine neglects to explain what office the second and third perform in the government of the cosmos or the liberation of souls; on his account, it is with the Father alone that the soul attains beatitude once it has purged all traces of embodiment. Once cleansed of its scars and brought into communion with the Father, the soul does not return to the carousel of transmigration. It appears that both the spiritual and the intellectual element will be saved, the one by theurgy and the other by virtue; as there is no migration to animal bodies, the appetitive soul, of which nothing is said, must be assumed to perish. When Porphyry despairs, then, of a 'universal way' to purge the soul, he means no doubt that there is none that redeems the soul in its entirety, not (as Augustine thinks) that no one way is suitable for all. When he declares that no such way is opened by the 'truest philosophy', nor by the customs of India or the rituals of the Chaldaeans, he cannot mean to deny that the first would suffice to perfect the virtues of the intellectual soul. He would deny, however, that it can release the lower or spiritual soul; that is the business of the Indians and Chaldaeans, whose arts would be of no avail, however, to the intellect seeking union with God. That Porphyry has a high esteem for both races is apparent from his citation of verses praising the Chaldaeans in the first book of his *Philosophy from Oracles*, and from his statement in the *Life of Plotinus* that India was the true goal of the philosopher when he attached himself to Gordian's campaign.

Pagans of the Roman era, even those who scoffed at Christian martyrdoms, seldom failed to admire the world-renouncing fortitude of the Indians, and reserved their loudest applause for those who built their own pyres in order to free the soul by the holocaust of the living body. The otherwise fastidious Lucian praised this custom in the second century (*Runaways* 1), but it is Porphyry's treatise *On Abstinence* that offers the fullest account of the Samanaioi, fasting celibates who, in contrast to the Brahmins (a hereditary and priestly caste), had abandoned family ties for a life in which the fruits of the harvest were a luxury, and were ready to crown this at any time, as soon as they received the word, by cremating themselves amid the hymns of their fellow-mendicants.[41] Yet the Indians were only occasional visitors to the Roman world – the most famous being one who had staged his own funeral in the forum[42] – whereas in Porphyry's time the utterances of the gods to the Chaldaeans had become current in the more durable form of verse. The *Chaldaean Oracles* – soon to acquire an authority among Platonists almost surpassing that of the founder – owe their name to Julian the Chaldaean, who appears to have been treated as the sole author in Porphyry's commentary, though later witnesses hold that they were jointly composed by Julian and his son.[43] This attribution implies that the *Oracles* date from the latter half of the second century, as Julian was one of a number of sages who were said to have conjured up the miraculous rain which brought relief to a stranded legion during the reign of Marcus Aurelius. It cannot be shown beyond doubt, however, that anyone made use of them before 250: Plotinus never quotes from them, except perhaps in the opening sentence of a vestigial treatise.[44] A florid aphorism in Numenius – 'O humanity, that which you call mind is not the first' – has a parallel in the *Oracles*: 'The Father has perfected all things and committed them to the second mind, which all of you, race of humans, call the first'.[45] Since the apostrophe seems more at home in verse than in prose, it might seem evident that priority lies with the *Oracles*,[46] but this conclusion cannot be sustained if the modern estimate of 150 for the *floruit* of Numenius is correct.[47] Porphyry, to judge by the list of his writings in the *Suda*, was the first to devote an entire book to the collection. While little of this is extant,[48] it is clear from the reports of other witnesses that the *Oracles* taught a doctrine all but identical with the one that he expounded in his treatise *On the Regression of the Soul*.

The commentaries on the *Oracles* by Porphyry, Iamblichus and Proclus[49] are lost; when they invoke the *Oracles* in their extant works, it is generally to reinforce some proposition already ascribed to, or derived from, Plato. There is seldom a gloss on the quoted verse or an indication of context; we have no systematic epitome of the whole collection from the Roman era, and when we encounter a series of quotations we have no reason to suppose that they reproduce consecutive passages in the original. For continuous exegesis – and then only of select verses – we must turn to the eleventh-century polymath Michael Psellus, who disclaims (as a Christian must) any inclination to the teaching of the *Oracles*, but contrives to intimate from time to time that they come nearer to orthodoxy than the philosophers.[50] Whereas the Greeks, he says, confine the lower soul to a region below the moon after its departure from the body, the Chaldaeans hold that, once the proper rites have been administered, the entire soul will ascend to a higher plane (*Patrologia Graeca* 122, 1124c1-1125a4). Both, no doubt, are wrong to affirm the natural immortality of the soul, but they at least escape the error of divorcing the salvation of the soul from that of the body. Their doctrine that the soul's vehicles can be purged by ineffable fire and rendered capable of ascent is expressly said to have been verified by the translation of the Biblical patriarchs Enoch and Elijah (1125c1-5); Psellus is gratified to see that the *Oracles*, like scripture, style the blessed abode a paradise (1129c1-14)[51] and proclaim that no redemption can be effected without the assistance of the gods. He reports, this time without favour, that the soul is said in the *Oracles* to possess two 'tunics', the spiritual and the intellectual: the first we must keep unblemished, and the second unencumbered (1137c10-13). Each of the soul's three faculties of knowledge – the opinionative, the discursive and the contemplative (1137c2) – must be purified by the fire of heaven and made to participate in the divine illumination, for we should not forget that she too is a pliable entity, and that we cannot always be exercising the contemplative faculty to the exclusion of the others (1133c10-d7). In her purification she must make use of natural forces – the 'supportive' powers, for example, which enable her to resist the lure of the senses – and to master such tools of Hecate as the bullroarer and the magic knot, or *iunx* (1133a5-9; 1149a12). She must learn to compel the gods without fear: the constellation Leo, for example, is the house of the sun, and must therefore be invoked until it appears to claim the whole of the firmament, blotting out the moon (1133b9-c5).

It must be remembered, however, that this apparition is only an accommodation to human senses: daemons assume a variety of shapes (1137a5), but the only true perception is that whose object is without shape or form (1136c6) . Powerful as the physical rites may be, their purpose is only to rid the practitioner of his vices, and to ensure that the flight of the soul

120

will not be retarded by the daemons. In order to rise she must cultivate rectitude and inward piety; those who draw down Hecate will see that the source of souls wells from her left flank, the fount of virtue from her right (1136a11-b10). That is to say that virtue is indigenous to us: if the practices of religion were foreign to nature, they could never lead the soul to the height of her natural capacity. Thus there can be no profit in such popular but irrational observances as ornithomancy, the taking of omens from the flight of birds, or haruspication, the scrutiny of entrails in a sacrificial carcase (1129a7-b4). All bloody immolations are prohibited, and a genuine manifestation of divinity is received not through the eye but through the fiery intellect (1140b3-4). The philosopher, we might say, is a rationalist, the Chaldaean holds a rational superstition. He will not presume to substitute Greek for the formulae handed down to him by barbarians,[52] but neither will he imagine that the gods prescribe any action that philosophy abhors.

As we have seen above, Porphyry concludes in his *Philosophy from Oracles* that it is only the daemons who crave the sacrifices of conventional religion. The gods, who demand to be worshipped with pure hands, convey their will to us through oracles; the daemons use the same medium, but our own reason tells us which commands betoken true divinity. If Augustine's annotations follow the plan of his treatise *On the Regression of the Soul*, it was not until after describing the rituals of purity that he unveiled the God who awaits the soul at the end of the purification. The commentary of Psellus observes the same order, and what he says of the divine is intended chiefly to show what knowledge the soul must have, and what limitations to her knowledge she must confess, in order to consummate her labours. The Father, we are told, is the source of every goal, and his light the terminus of the soul's ascent; and yet he remains ineffable, incomprehensible, noetic yet grasped only by the supranoetic faculty which is called the 'flower of *nous*'.[53] Hidden from all below as if by rapture, he does not even communicate his peculiar fire to his *dunamis* or power, whom Psellus takes to be the counterpart of the Son or Logos in Christian theology.[54] By this power the character of the Father is made known and his bounties communicated. The triad is completed by the *patrikos nous* or 'paternal intellect', with whom the soul deposits the motions of the will when she has overcome her forgetfulness and recovered her perception of the divine *logoi* and *sumbola,* principles and ectypes, in which her own essence resides.[55] Every soul is a compound of these principles and ectypes, every soul therefore an image of the noeric realm. No soul therefore lacks the power to free herself from fate and the tutelage of evil daemons;[56] those who rise above the carnal senses and embrace the life of the intellect will be succoured by good daemons, and be ruled – in perfect freedom, since they will it – by the providence (*pronoia*) of the gods.

I have spoken of a triadic Godhead, though up to the end of the commentary little is made of the number three.[57] In some texts, as we have seen, the powers of the soul are reduced to the opinionative, the discursive and the contemplative; another assumes the existence of three orders – that of existence, that of life and that of mind – and of three corresponding orders of comprehension, the ontic, the vital and the noetic (1145a9-10). The last fragment in the commentary is, however, a digest of the entire theology: it posits before all else the paternal *buthos* or abyss,[58] and then three triads of triads, each a *iunx* or ligature between superior and inferior extremes (1149a10-b11). The elliptical gloss in Psellus must be eked out from his three *Ektheses*, or short outlines of the Chaldaean system, in which the doctrine of God precedes and all but eclipses the ritual precepts.[59] From these we learn that all three triads – each comprising a Father, the Father's *dunamis* and his intellect – were brought forth by meditation from the abyss of the primal Godhead. It is in consequence of the Father's deliberations through this intellect that the Father, his *dunamis* and that very intellect form the first, or noetic, triad. All three members remain inscrutable, though reason apprehends them through their objectified *energeia* or activity. The complement to the noetic or intelligible is the noeric or intellectual, the first connoting the object thought, the second the act of thinking. Since perfect knowledge implies the union of knower and known, the thought and the thinking too coalesce in the incorporeal realm, yet remain distinct enough in sense to ensure that even the highest intellect is not a simple unity, but a plurality in oneness. Whether this distinction of terms – acknowledged only in passing by Plotinus[60] – was already made in the *Oracles* we lack evidence to say, but the second triad is said by Psellus to be 'noetic-and-noeric', the third noeric. The second is comprehended by the mind, the third by soul. But absolute primacy cannot be accorded even to this, for above all triads the *Oracles* placed the unfathomable and unparticipated ground of unity, which Psellus, like Plotinus, styles the One.

Below the transcendent principles sit their progeny, the architectonic triads of the physical realm. First of these *iunges* or ligatures is the noetic; the second is a 'constitutive' triad of empyrean, ethereal and material agents; the members of the third triad are 'teletarchic' or consummatory. Then follow the cosmic rulers – first the 'once transcendent', after him Hecate, lastly the 'twice transcendent'. And so the catalogue proceeds, embracing seven material universes and a medley of gods, barbarian cheek by jowl with Greek.

The noetic triad

It is in the noetic triad of the later school that the influence of the *Oracles* is most frequently discerned by modern critics. In this, the first of the triads below the One, Being is constituted by mind, and mind by being, through the medium of life. That is to say, the process of thinking begets its object, while the object circumscribes the act of thinking. Complementary and inseparable as the two sides of a line, they aspire to unity while remaining two; life makes a third because the eternal dialectic must be sustained by a dynamic bond which acts simultaneously as a divisor. Though being takes priority in the triad, its terms are equipollent, at least insofar as each necessitates and presupposes the other two. As Proclus observes, however, in the physical realm there are objects that possess being and life but not mind, and some that possess no other property than being, while there are none that possess either life or mind alone.[61] Only being therefore is ubiquitous in its action outside the noetic triad – though if we infer that being is the highest of the three we must add, as a logical corollary of its pre-eminence, that the objects over which it presides alone are of less dignity than those that it governs in conjunction with life or with life and mind.

Is the noetic triad derived from the *Oracles*? Proclus is known to have written a ponderous commentary on these verses, which he deemed equal to the *Timaeus* and superior to any other essay in philosophy. The triad of triads – noetic, noetic-and-noeric and noeric – is the foundation of his metaphysical system in his commentary on the *Timaeus*; Iamblichus too, whose commentary on the *Oracles* ran to 28 books, maintains a strong distinction between the noetic and the noeric triads in exegesis of Plato. The sequence 'being-life-mind' assumes an almost scholastic rigidity when he explains that intelligence, life and being exist monadically in the noetic realm, the first giving rise to noeric or discursive intellection, the second to noeric life, the third to the differentiated forms.[62] Again the source is a commentary on the *Timaeus*, and here the question arises: would these terms have come to hand so readily had they not already occurred as a constellation in Plato's *Sophist*? The *Sophist*, a standard text in the school of Iamblichus, is clearly the source from which Plotinus drew the terms 'being, life and mind' when he used them in combination.[63] There is, on the other hand, no clear precedent for the combination in the *Oracles*: Psellus once avails himself of the triad, but whenever he undertakes the anatomy of the Chaldaean system, the intermediate term in the triad whose other members are being and mind is *dunamis*, not life.

Nowhere in his treatise *On the Regression of the Soul* does Porphyry designate the members of the noetic triad, being, life and mind. The polar terms are Father and Son, while the meaning of the third is opaque, at least to his Christian periphrast. Damascius employs much the same nomenclature when he reports that the 'father of the noetic triad' is the first cause in Porphyry's exposition of the *Chaldaean Oracles*.[64] Another passage in his *Commentary on the Timaeus* has been adduced to show that Porphyry recognised three modes of approach to the transcendent – ontically through the ontic, vitally through the vital and noetically through the noetic – but the doctrine is in fact attributed jointly to Porphyry and to Theodorus of Asine, a later and lesser thinker, whose name would have added nothing to the testimony had his views been merely coterminous with those of his predecessor.[65] We may guess then that it is to him that we owe the artificial symmetry of a speculation which Porphyry had expressed more tentatively, and perhaps (as his custom was) in the language of the *Oracles*. There is one other work, however – now anonymous, but attributed to Porphyry by a number of scholars – in which being, life and mind provide the scaffolding for a study in metaphysics which is expressly said to be consonant with the teaching of the gods. It is once again a commentary on a Platonic dialogue, this time the *Parmenides*, though, as we owe our knowledge of it to a chance discovery, its authorship and date remain unknown.

The commentary is assigned to the second century by Bechtle, to the fourth by Kroll,[66] but to Porphyry by Hadot with the approbation of a number of eminent scholars.[67] Yet verbal correspondences, and occasional coincidence of thought, between this text and works securely ascribed to Porphyry do not suffice, in my view, to prove his authorship. It might be the work of a follower with a stronger architectonic bent – Theodorus of Asine cannot be excluded – or even another disciple of Numenius, since (as we have seen) he may have known the *Oracles*, and he appears to have elicited a primitive version of the noetic triad from the *Timaeus*.[68] While few endorse Bechtle's dating of the text to the second century it would at least explain the presence of the triad – still retaining the vocabulary of Plato – in Gnostic treatises whose archetypes were already known to Porphyry.[69] The affinities between the anonymous *Commentary on the Parmenides* and the Gnostic *Zostrianus* suggest that, if Porphyry was the author of the former, he made clandestine use of a work to which in public he was sedulously hostile.[70] We should also be forced to conclude that he interpreted the Oracles according to their own idiom and Plato according to his, without allowing the two to coalesce, as they do in the commentary of Psellus.

The most remarkable lines that are said to have issued from an oracle in the third century – perhaps the most remarkable in antiquity – are those that appear in chapter 22 of the *Life of Plotinus*. Having recorded the verdict of other philosophers on his hero, Porphyry turns away as though to retrieve a forgotten affidavit. 'But what is all this talk of mine about a tree and a rock, as Hesiod says? For if one ought to use the testimonies that come from the wisest, who could be wiser than a god?'[71] Lest we should miss the allusion to Plato's *Apology*, he himself invokes the famous pronouncement of the Delphic oracle that Socrates was the wisest of mankind. The suffrage of Herodotus reinforces that of Hesiod and Plato, yet the oracle which Porphyry goes on to transcribe is not said to have been received at Delphi.[72] Amelius, the inquirer, was at that time living in Syrian Apamea, and would therefore have been as likely to consult the Asiatic shrines of Apollo at Claros or Didyma.[73] The lengthy piece of verse that he brought home, with its teeming echoes of Empedocles, Homer and Plato, would have been an uncharacteristic deliverance from any oracle, but it was only in Greece that the meagreness and infrequency of responses were proverbial. Whatever its provenance, just as Augustine wonders whether Hecate or Porphyry was the author of the oracle on the Christians, so we have every right to suspect that the oracle on Plotinus has been embellished, if not created, by some colleague of his who was more inclined to prolixity than the Sibyl. It seems, however, improbable that Porphyry himself could have performed more than the editorial function that he admits to having performed on other oracles, for the content of the verse does not agree in all respects with his own exegesis: as I have remarked elsewhere,[74] he takes it upon himself to correct the gods.

Plotinus is saluted in the oracle as a man who now enjoys, along with Minos, Rhadamanthus and the rest of the 'golden race', the 'more divine estate of daemons'; five times this term 'daemon' is applied to his new condition, but his soul in life already possessed this quality, and what he now receives from Zeus he has earned by his dauntless ardour in pursuing the goal illumined by the radiance from above. This notion of return to a primordial felicity is plainly derived from Empedocles,[75] who, eight centuries before, had proclaimed to the citizens of Acragas in Sicily that he had expiated the sin which had caused his fall from the daemonic state, and was now 'no longer a mortal but a god'. Plotinus used this expression of the emancipated soul, and hence of himself, and we know that Porphyry in his *Aphorisms* went so far as to say that one who has attained the summit of virtue is not only a god, but the father of gods; he will not then have Apollo's weaker accolade in the oracle, 'man erstwhile but now a daemon' – all the less so because Apollo seems to reckon himself a god, and one of those who have given light to Plotinus in his earthly struggles. The oracle describes his escape from the turbid sea of life in words and images reminiscent of the Odyssey, and hints that he made landfall under the tutelage of the gods, much as Odysseus drifted blindly home to Ithaca with the unsuspected guidance of Athena. The comments of Porphyry intimate, however, that the sage's were fixed on a higher mark than is dreamed of in poetry, even the poetry of gods:

> And as he kept on drawing himself [not, as the oracle says, being drawn] by this daemonic light towards the first and transcendent God, through meditation and according to the methods described by Plato in the Symposium, there appeared to him that God who has neither form nor any concept but is seated above the mind and all intelligible. I Porphyry testify that I also once approached him and was united in my sixty-eighth year.[76] So it was then that the nearby goal appeared to Plotinus (*Life of Plotinus* 23.7-14).

We shall notice in the last chapter the equally fleeting and incidental appeals to mystical experience in Plotinus and Christian authors. Here we need remark only that it is by virtue of this experience that Porphyry can presume to outdo the oracle in his definition of the true goal of philosophy. For all that it is sanctioned by the gods, the oracle is after all, as Plutarch says, a means of impressing truth upon minds that are not schooled in philosophy, and are capable of acquiring knowledge only through the senses. For minds that hold immediate communion with truth the noise and spectacle of mantic divination are superfluous, just as the rites of India and Chaldaea would be applied in vain to the intellect, and are otiose even to the lower soul once it is cleansed.

Magic and Occult Sciences

'A failure of nerve'[1] was J.B. Bury's judgment on the delusive science and Stygian chicanery that disfigured religious practice in the later Roman world. Injuries, it seems, were now avenged by covert malediction as often as by suits or honest satire; in prayer and private cult the humane Olympians gave way to a foreign bestiary; the fates of individuals and whole peoples were no longer thought to depend upon themselves but upon the inexorable motions of the stars. Imperial writers who traced these arts to Egypt, Persia and Babylon are readily believed, for there is little evidence of them in Periclean or Roman times and those who practised them in the Antonine or Severan age were often of eastern provenance.[2] What irks the modern classicist most of all is that the religious hypochondriac was so often a man of wealth and culture, steeped in the Greek tradition – often indeed an astute philosopher who had worked his way through Plato and Aristotle to a rational monotheism, if not beyond theism altogether. It is hard for us to believe that such chaste intellects could tolerate so much that appears to us simply chimerical, nebulous or arcane.

How would the four protagonists of the present study have answered Bury's charge? Longinus can be acquitted out of hand; Plotinus, Porphyry tells us, had the capacity without the inclination;[3] Porphyry is often thought to have put his superstitious youth behind him after encountering Plotinus. Iamblichus seems, on the other hand, to be convicted by his own plea. Yet Iamblichus was the author of the first extended commentaries on Plato and the architect of a syllabus that would shape the minds of Platonists up to the closure of the schools three centuries later. We cannot read him fairly if we assume, against the clear testimony of Plato, that the supranatural and the suprarational never touched the Greek mind till it entered an 'age of anxiety' under Roman domination. In the second half of this chapter I shall argue that, in his treatise *On the Mysteries*, he holds few beliefs that would not have been endorsed by one at least of his fellow-Platonists, and that here and there he tilts against superstitions to which some Platonists had subscribed on the authority of the age. As will be apparent from the first half of the chapter, only some of his tenets seem to be aboriginal to the Greek tradition, while others accrued to it after Greek had become the common language of the east. Even the latter, however – though it may not have been dishonest of him to put them into the mouth of an Egyptian priest – are supported by clear arguments which bespeak a coherent, rational and (as we might style it) Greek view of the world.

What arts are magical?

The word 'magic' is often used by anthropologists of any ritual, formula or traditional expedient which, without recourse to scientific principles as these are now understood, is designed to accelerate, reinforce or intercept the natural chain of causes. The field-work of anthropologists is generally conducted in societies where activities of this kind take a public, official and collective form, and it has sometimes been assumed that we have only to interrogate the participants in these modern rites to discover what a practitioner in the Roman world would have thought of his vocation. Yet this is to impose our own vocabulary on a different world, for it was not the ancient usage to apply such terms as *goêteia, mageia* and *pharmakeutria* – the equivalents of 'witchcraft', 'magic' and 'sorcery' – to any rite performed in public or for the common weal. Divination was a regular duty of the magistrates, but their business was to observe the phenomenon, not to arrest or change it. Astrology was a science for trained consultants, one in which political officers had no role but to determine what was lawful; alchemy too was an esoteric discipline, hardly noticed in the literary sources, and producing neither benefits nor injuries which might demand the attention of the law. The forbidden arts – the ones that we call magical – were carried on in secrecy and under suspicion of turpitude. The *goês*, when he is not a mere purveyor of counterfeit miracles, is one who can bend the hearts and minds of others by enchantment; the *pharmakeus* exploits the latent properties of herbs and drugs to induce death or insanity – most frequently, if the *pharmakeus* is female, the insanity of love. Her associates may include men who can charm the corn from another's field or cause a snake to burst asunder by incantation; those who desired to look into a hidden future crept, in peril of soul, to the cell where the necromancer wrung forbidden knowledge from the jaws of the newly dead.

Though pharmacology and necromancy are both attested in the *Odyssey,* there is little trace of either in Greek until the Hellenistic age, when a new fashion for the erotic made the enamoured witch a familiar type in poetry. In Plato, however, the noun *goêteia* (witchcraft) is habitually applied to rhetorical or sophistic trickery;[4] his premiss is that whatever binds the intellect is manmade and irrational, but what elevates it is godly and suprarational. Since nothing is more conducive to this rapture than the study of the heavens, both the *Laws* and the *Epinomis* urge that the stars, and the sun and moon above all, should receive the honours in Greece that they enjoy among barbarians. This, if we will, is the point at which Greek piety was invaded by the 'astral mysticism' of the Orient; we are still some way from astrology, though astronomy (if we mean by this the assiduous mapping of the planetary cycles and the correlation of these with harmonic ratios) was a discipline in which Plato and his followers set new goals.[5]

A sea-change in Greek culture begins a generation later, when the cities of the mainland lost their independence to Macedon. Within two centuries, Rome had annexed the whole of Greece, and another hundred years made her the heir to Alexander's conquests in Egypt, Alexandria and the Levant. Some mainland cities openly despaired of their ancient saviours, while Tyche or Fortune, a figure barely known in myth, was perhaps the one divinity to command the sincere devotion of the new Greeks.[6] It was, however, before the age of political subjection that Alexandrian Greeks took up the native practice of casting horoscopes;[7] when we try to account for this indiscretion we should perhaps not blame the climate, but remember that an unparalleled exactitude of observation and measurement gave the Egyptian charts a specious objectivity which was lacking not only in Greek cult, but in many of the sciences that had exercised the best minds of the classical era. No mathematical error of any consequence had occurred when the Babylonians marked out twelve signs of the zodiac on the ecliptic,[8] or when the Egyptians divided the heavens into quarters, each corresponding to a phase of human life.[9] The subdivision of these four regions first into eight and then into twelve, and the conflation of these twelve 'houses' with their Babylonian counterparts in the zodiac, seems to have antedated the Greek occupation of Egypt. It may, however, according to one authority,[10] have been the Greeks who matched a star to each part of the body, and it was certainly Hipparchus who discovered the precession of the equinoxes, a 'Copernican revolution' exceeding any other achievement of Greek science outside mathematics.[11]

The distinction between astrology and magic is strictly observed in Greek and Latin treatises, even when they pay homage to such figures as the Chaldaean Zoroaster or the Egyptian Petosiris and Nechepso.[12] It was, however, inevitable that, in those who were not content to know their own fate if they could not alter it, astrology would beget a desire for magic. An old myth, for example, taught that after death the soul ascends to the empyrean, yielding one of its vices in turn to each of the seven planets. In the Greek *Hermetica* – which contain some true Egyptian lore, but strain it through a parsimonious filter – this itinerary can be completed only by the departing soul, and only when it is free of error and innocent of purpose.[13] There are, however, a number of texts which promise to teach the means by which it can be anticipated in the present life, at little expense of study or moral labour. Platonists were familiar with these stratagems in reverse, for Numenius speaks of enchanters who lure souls from the Milky Way with milk and honey.[14] All Platonists were familiar with Hermes, the conductor of souls and messengers, and some had made the acquaintance of his counterpart Thoth, the Egyptian god of wisdom. Plato ascribes to 'Theuth' the invention of writing (*Phaedrus* 274c-275c), while Porphyry cites 'Taautos' as the source of the ancient matter in the *Phoenician History* of Sanchuniathon;[15] in Hermetic literature Thoth plays the pupil under the name of Tat. Only one extant work in the name of Hermes could be called occult – an alchemical treatise, entitled *Cyranides*[16]

– but in antiquity a cornucopian literature was ascribed to him, and one of the longest magical papyri was conceived as a refutation of a Hermetic tract, now lost. The Nag Hammadi codices, Coptic texts which preserve the vestiges of an erudite if opaque theology, also abound in senseless strings of syllables and cachinnatory formulae which suggest that they were designed for use in magic. This inference is confirmed by Plotinus' strictures on the 'hissings and incantations' which were employed by Gnostic readers of the Greek originals in the mid-third century (*Enneads* 2.9.14.2-8). This was a time (like the early twentieth century) when it would rather enhance than compromise one's standing in polite company to be versed in such pursuits.

Plotinus and the magicians

Since it was a commonplace that the wise man's soul remains untouched by the fate that rules his body – and a commonplace not only among philosophers but in authors who, like Zosimus the alchemist,[17] appear to us superstitious – we might expect a Platonist to declare that such a soul is also impervious to magic. Yet this is not quite the doctrine of Plotinus in *Enneads* 4.4, where he argues that the sympathy which entwines all sentient things, the stars included, allows the magician to coerce the irrational soul (4.4.40.22-5). The emancipated power of contemplation in the sage cannot be bound, as it cannot be induced to 'pursue what is not good as though it were a good' (4.4.44.30-37). The higher soul, although it will not consent to passions kindled in the lower soul by enchantments, will be sufficiently affected to respond with 'counter-charms' (4.4.43.8). It may be that Plotinus is alluding here to an episode recorded in Porphyry's life of him, where the malice and subterfuge of the assailant certainly warrant the stigma implied in the allusion to his 'magic':

> One of those with pretensions to philosophy was Olympius, an Alexandrian, who at one time had been a pupil of Ammonius and had a grudge against Plotinus through a desire to achieve pre-eminence. Such was his malignity that he endeavoured to make him star-struck through magic. But when he found that the attempt had turned against himself, he said to his cronies 'great is the power of Plotinus' soul, for it can reciprocate the attacks of those who try to do him harm'. Plotinus, for his part, resisted the machinations of Olympius, saying that his body at that time was drawn together 'like the contracted purses'[18] as his members were compressed. But Olympius, once he was in danger of suffering more himself than he inflicted on Plotinus, desisted. For Plotinus had something more by birth than the majority of men (*Plotinus* 10.1-15).

Porphyry's verb *helkesthai* ('draw together') is the one that Plotinus himself employs to describe the affliction of the soul at *Enneads* 4.4.43.22. The coincidence between the philosopher's tract and his pupil's anecdote gave

Philip Merlan grounds to describe Plotinus as a magician[19] – a misleading label none the less, as Plotinus is said to have overcome Olympius not by calculated wiles but by his 'uncommon power of soul'. Porphyry's aim is not to reveal Plotinus as the superior magician, but to extort his praise from the lips of an adversary, and to show that, like Pythagoras, he enhanced great birth by the greatness of his deeds.

Another of the philosopher's compatriots in Rome was an Egyptian priest, who undertook to evoke his guardian spirit in the temple of Isis – this being, as he pretended, the only undefiled locality in the capital.[20] When the spirit proved to be a god, the mortified priest pronounced a benediction on the philosopher, and he in turn (so Porphyry says) commemorated the episode in a treatise, *On the Guardian Daemon to which we are Allotted,* of which more will be said below (10.23-5). Here it will suffice to say that Porphyry had not yet entered the school when it was written, and his account of its origins may be mere surmise. The function of the episode in his memoir of Plotinus is clear enough: it wins for its hero once again the tribute of an adversary, who is not expressly portrayed as a fool or charlatan. Porphyry elsewhere commends the Egyptians as the wisest of the nations, even quoting one to verify Plato's teaching that the soul of one who takes his own life is doomed to linger unredeemed in the neighbourhood of the corpse. In this case, however, the priest has (perhaps unwittingly) essayed the dangerous practice of theurgy, the coercion of gods; what follows might be taken to imply (if we knew no better) that the philosopher has succeeded where the priest failed.

At the end of the chapter, Porphyry relates that when Amelius asked Plotinus to accompany him to a festival, he was answered with the enigmatic dictum, 'it is the gods who should come to me, not I to them' (10.35). It may be because these words would have come so aptly from the mouth of a theurgist that the biographer pre-empts interpretation in the last sentence, saying that 'none of us dared to ask what he meant by this'. He himself had already penned a gloss on them in his *Aphorisms*, where he states that one who attains the fourth and highest level of virtue is no god, but a father of gods.[21] In one of his earlier treatises (though the last in our present arrangement of the *Enneads*) Plotinus himself declared that as we approach the One we beget the gods within (6.9.9.18). This anecdote is apologetic rather than didactic: it exposes the simplicity of Amelius, without leaving Plotinus open to any charge of using arts that would have clipped the wings of an elevated soul.

Porphyry and theurgy

Yet there is one work by Porphyry in which he commends theurgy as a purgative to the lower soul, and hence as a means of freeing the higher soul from the contagion of the body. The conventional title *On the Return of the Soul* is attested only in Augustine's *City of God*, and even there was intended only as a description of its contents.[22] The excerpts in Augustine are compatible with the teaching of the *Philosophy from Oracles*, but coincidences of thought and style are not common enough to justify the thesis that the two works were identical. It is only in the Augustinian excerpts that the Chaldaeans are represented as the true adepts in theurgy, and only here that we find express quotations from the *Chaldaean Oracles*. By their precepts angels – not, as Augustine calls them, daemons[23] – are brought down from the fiery space beneath the firmament to assist in the exorcism of the passions; other rites must be observed to persuade our evil genius not to hinder the approach of a better guardian; offerings to the sun and moon, however, are proscribed because the destiny of the rational soul is to rise above the spheres and join the Father in incorporeal beatitude.[24] Theurgy differs from magic in aiming only at the good, and in being collaborative rather than coercive: one cannot be saved in ignorance, and it is not by charms but by the virtue of continence, nurtured inwardly, that ignorance is expelled from the rational soul.[25]

For all this, it cannot be denied that angels are prone to vice,[26] and that the venal or malicious acolyte always finds a daemon to assist him. 'A good man in Chaldaea', Porphyry writes, 'complains that his laboured efforts to purge the soul were baffled when a man skilled in the same arts, touched by envy, checked the powers from granting his petitions though he adjured them in sacred prayers'.[27] Such a man was clearly not the equal of Plotinus, and when Porphyry declares that he has not discovered a universal means of purification we may presume that he is speaking here, as throughout the treatise, only of the soul's irrational faculties.[28] What Christians falsely promise can be effected, though imperfectly, by the arts of many other barbarous peoples; the purgatives that Greek philosophy offers to the higher soul, on the other hand, are sufficient, and (for all that we know) unique.

The *Letter to Anebo*[29]

We have said above that Porphyry has no quarrel with the Egyptians in the majority of his writings. Nevertheless the shortest of his extant works – if the *Letter to Anebo* is an entire work, not an excerpt – he accosts the Egyptian priesthood with a series of paradoxes which, to judge by the growing acerbity and sarcasm of his tone, he considers fatal to their pretensions. Eusebius transcribes the piece with obvious gratification, and almost every sentence in his version finds a parallel in the great treatise *On the Mysteries* by Iamblichus, which answers Porphyry's questions one by one. Iamblichus does not quote the unctuous preface, which Eusebius himself reserves for a different book of his *Gospel Preparation*; for the rest, it would seem that if we paraphrase the most substantial extract in Eusebius, we may be confident that we know what both men read.

Since the letter shows Porphyry at his most incredulous, scholars have often read it as a palinode of his mature years; yet, while he might have renounced his old beliefs, it is hardly probable that he would have affected ignorance of matters that he had himself discussed in previous works. The hectoring and cursory style might just as well betoken a juvenile tendency to suppose that whatever one thinks of first is equally new to others; if it is indeed a late work, it may have been an exercise, designed to precipitate such a work as the treatise *On the Mysteries* – though if that is so, we must grant that Iamblichus missed the benign intent beneath the polemical veneer. The interrogation commences bluntly: how is it, Porphyry wonders, that the priests invoke the gods as their superiors, yet command them as inferiors? Why is spotless purity demanded of the postulant when the gods themselves not only assist us in lechery, but command it? Why does 'theagogy' make use of carcases when its adepts are required to abstain from meat and shun the smoke of sacrifice? How can gods as powerful as the sun and moon be awed into speaking the truth by threats which they know to be fictitious? Are they children, to believe that a man can open the pit of Hades or disperse the limbs of Osiris once again? The Egyptians may profess to have seen their deities ensconced in mud or seated on a lotus, or even changing form to match the constellations of the zodiac; but in that case they have failed to unmask the products of their own fantasy, having no conception (according to their apologist Chaeremon) of any deity who is not a physical element. If all this is said in riddles, can they not divulge the meaning of the riddle? Why are all their mysteries wrapped up in barbarous terms which (we are told) will not bear translation into Greek? We cannot suppose that Egyptian is the language of the gods, or indeed that they use any language heard among mortals. Clearly these are the sophistries of jugglers and impostors – all the more futile because, if the higher gods are impassible, then none of our menaces, prayers and immolations can subdue them, while the lower gods will be too weak to do us service. Useless as it is in securing happiness, this mummery is not even equal to its stated purpose: no god and no good daemon will be cajoled or intimidated by such arts.

This then is the assault to which the great treatise *On the Mysteries* replied under the pseudonym of an Egyptian priest, Abammon, who is generally assumed to be fictitious. That Iamblichus was the true author would appear to be proved, not only by the testimony of Proclus, but by the dense and convoluted prose of the treatise, by coincidences in detail with his undisputed writings, and above all by the theology of the eighth book, which concurs with his at the points where he diverged from his predecessors. In the following summary I shall argue that he makes his defence on grounds that would have seemed rational and cogent to fellow-Platonists, and indeed to the majority of Greeks. It will also appear that where he contradicts a view held by Porphyry, in the *Letter to Anebo* or elsewhere, it is not because he is reasoning less Platonically, less systematically or with less concern to vindicate the dignity of reason and the absolute transcendence of the gods.

Iamblichus, *On the Mysteries*

Gods and daemons (Book 1)

The aim of the work, according to its preface, is to give an account of the theoretical truths on which the mysteries are founded, and to justify the associated practices, so far as this can be done in words alone. Porphyry's manner of questioning has been so indiscriminate that, although Abammon is an Egyptian priest, he will be forced to speak from time to time on behalf of the Chaldaeans – an invidious promise if Porphyry had already written his treatise *On the Regression of the Soul*, since it would imply that he had not understood the rites that he himself professed to favour. Certainly any system of theology would be impoverished by the cardinal error that Abammon goes on to impute to Porphyry – that of assuming that all superhuman beings form a single class, differentiated only by locality and bodily condition. It is wrong, we are told, to imagine all such agents as a single genus, divided (as in Plato) by dichotomous characteristics or (as in Aristotle) by constellations of accidental properties which are notionally, if not physically, separable from the universal substance in which they inhere (*On the Mysteries* 1.4). The truth is, on the contrary, that the higher gods, the daemons and the heroes – the only species named at this point, though Abammon will later add angels and archangels – differ in essence as in rank, and that it is only when the properties which define each class are ascertained that we know what to hope from any member of it. In the class of gods, we cannot speak, in fact, of individuated members, for deity is pure intellect, identical with its thoughts and grasping all thought in the undivided unity of truth (1.6-7).

The contemplative faculty of a daemon or a hero, on the other hand, is limited and discrete – though this is not, as Porphyry seems to presuppose, the consequence of their being confined to the regions that furnish the elements of their bodies (1.5). Porphyry shows his ignorance by assigning an aerial body to the gods themselves, thus rendering it impossible for them to know, let alone to regulate, whatever is done outside their own sight and hearing (1.8). And he commits another fallacy when he supposes that the daemon or hero owes his identity to his corporeal envelope, for the principle of individuation at any level of being resides not in the substrate but in the form – that is to say, in the higher entities from which all form proceeds. The more remote a class of beings is from the unity of the ruling principle, the greater will be the difference among its members, but it is not the remoteness itself that differentiates. It is qualities, not the amorphous matter in which it is housed, that characterise the soul and the things above it (1.10); and matter itself, as we shall see, is a product of divine action, not (as in Platonism before this) the reified nothingness in which divine power expires. It is not, however, an attribute of any transcendent being: heroes, daemons and gods alike are properly incorporeal, and hence imperceptible to our physical senses. Bodies, when they employ them, remain extrinsic, so that if, for example, the gods employ such visible instruments as the sun and stars, they remain superior to the daemons, however tenuously the latter may be clothed (1.17). It is almost a logical consequence that heroes, daemons and gods alike are immune to the passions that afflict their votaries (1.10). It is in fact our own rebellious spirits that we propitiate when we offer prayers to wrathful gods, and the evils that we hope to avert by sacrifice are born of our own false reasoning and desire (1.11). If obscenity and licence are admitted in public rituals, it is not to amuse the gods, but to remind us that these ceremonies are tempered to human understanding – often to the grossest understanding – and can offer us at best a turbid image of the reality beyond sense and imagination (1.12). Yet even the volatile soul is immaterial, invisible and capable of grasping the intelligible through a disciplined use of reason: it cannot be doubted, then, that impassibility and incorporeality are universal properties in the transcendent realm, which, for all disparities of rank and nature, is as continuous as a field of radiant light.

Iamblichus will have been aware that Porphyry, in his *Philosophy from Oracles*, had espoused not so much a graded as a bifurcated notion of divinity, prescribing that black victims should be sacrificed to the chthonic powers and white ones to the true gods who dwell above. In the *Letter to Anebo* he continues to divide the gods into antithetical species, each with its natural abode, though he no longer holds that piety can ordain an animal sacrifice, or indeed permit any cult of beings who live beneath the firmament. Iamblichus has set out to prove in this first book that it is only because his premises are absurd that Porphyry's reasoning has a specious air of sanity. Arbitrary, vulgar and even sordid as the instruments and devices of the priests may appear, their very irrationality shields both worshipper and priest from the delusions of the overweening intellect. It is only the true idolaters – those like Porphyry – who cannot see that the rituals point to the very truths that they conceal (1.21).

Refinements of theology (Book 2)

In the second book,[30] Iamblichus undertakes to explain the difference between a daemon and an archon. His general premiss is that, whereas daemons represent the creative and generative powers of deity, heroes represent those which communicate life and shape the conduct of the soul (2.1). Porphyry's questions now oblige him to introduce three new orders – the archangelic, the angelic and the archontic, whose activities and virtues he delineates with scrupulous exactitude, contrasting them at every stage with gods, daemons and souls – though only occasionally with heroes, who (as he tartly notes) are omitted in Porphyry's inventory of superhuman powers (1.3). Archangels and angels rank between the gods and daemons; archons of are two kinds, the cosmic or sublunary and the material or hylic. The first resembles the gods in its stability while the second is diverse in aspect, turbulent in action. In most of the subsequent catalogues, the heroes (if present at all) precede both categories of archon, and the soul holds the lowest place, although it often seems to be the hylic archons who sit furthest from perfection. The properties of each order are now described, with a scholastic predilection for taxonomy far more redolent of Iamblichean commentary on Plato than of any ancient work from a priestly hand:

1. Gods are simple and uniform in aspect; archangels and angels may fall short of their simplicity, but do not adopt such heterogeneous guises as the daemons. With archons, it would seem, a new chain begins. When they preside in the cosmos, they exhibit variety, but not without order; variety is more pronounced in those who inhabit matter, while souls present themselves 'in every form' (2.3, p. 71).

2. Again gods are benign, archangels gentle in their solemnity, angels solemn and not so gentle, daemons formidable. Heroes are gentler, the cosmic archons striking, while the hylic may cause pain to the beholder; souls display the qualities of heroes, though not in the same degree (2.3, p. 71).

3. Gods are immutable, even in semblance; archangels fall short of them in 'sameness', but even angels, though inferior, cannot yet be said to change. Daemons, however, 'appear at different times in different forms' – as Plato in the *Symposium* says of merely phenomenal beauty in contradistinction to the Beautiful. The sublunary archons are not so vulnerable, the hylic are at least equally so; heroes resemble daemons, while the soul is once again a weak simulacrum of the hero (2.3, p. 72).

4. Gods are tranquil, angels subject to motion, while disorder enters at the daemonic level. Sublunary archons are more steadfast, but the hylic succumb to the turbulence of matter. Heroes too are not exempt from motion; souls are inferior once again (2.3, pp. 72-3).

5. Gods shine forth in undivided splendour; archangelic beauty is less sublime, angelic beauty more divisible, while daemons possess the beauty of proportion and heroes all that is beautiful in courage. The beauty of cosmic archons is spontaneous, but that of the hylic archons comes by artifice, while that of the soul falls short of the heroic because it is dominated by a single form (2.3, pp. 73-4).

6. Gods, as we observe them, are swifter than thought, though in themselves they do not experience any motion. Archangels and angels are engaged in errands which retard their movements; daemons are not so swift as they appear. Heroes are still less swift, for all their occasional magnificence; the acts of cosmic archons are potent, those

of the inferior kind abortive, and the labile soul is weaker in operation than the hero (2.4, pp. 74-5).

7. Gods bestride earth and heaven in their epiphanies, while an archangel has only so much light as he has authority. The radiance of an angel is still more circumscribed, while that of a daemon is prone to fluctuation. Heroic apparitions are smaller in bulk but nobler in bearing. Cosmic archons are capable of great epiphanies, hylic archons only of pretending to greatness; once again the soul is more mercurial than the hero (2.4, pp. 75-6).

8. Gods are enveloped in a tenuous fire that threatens to suffocate their votaries; the radiance of the archangels is not so oppressive, while that of angels is easily tolerated. Daemons emit neither heat nor light, while heroes trouble us only by the noise that accompanies their apparitions. There is much discomfort, but nothing preternatural in the appearances of archons, whether cosmic or hylic, and souls can manifest themselves without difficulty, their nature being akin to that of air (2.4, p. 76 and 2.8).

9. Through the approach of a god we receive perfection and deliverance from passion; archangels bring serenity of contemplation, angels rational wisdom, daemons a longing to complete the works required of us in the sphere of generation. From heroes we derive zeal, and from the archons an inclination of the soul to heaven or earth; care for our bodies and desire to propagate are inspired by the encounter with a soul (2.8, p. 87).

It may be that the mention of the archons is a concession to Porphyry: the author hardly seems to know where to place them, and even when they intervene between hero and soul, the soul is always characterised by reference to the hero. He will not concede that the arts of the magician are deceitful, or that vicissitude in the mode of appearance proves that the higher powers themselves are mutable. Whereas Porphyry, in his treatise *On Statues*, commends such artefacts as ciphers of the ineffable,[31] Iamblichus holds that we see the gods only because they reveal themselves and only insofar as our worthiness permits us to behold them.[32]

Prophecy (Book 3)

In his third book Iamblichus answers Porphyry's objections to the use of irrational stimuli in prophecy. The faculty of divination, in Porphyry's view, is wakened in the soul when it has risen above the turbulence of common life and attuned itself to the harmonies that sustain the universal web of causes. Prescient dreams occur in sleep because it is then that the soul is least encumbered by the appetites and gross senses of the body (3.2); but it can hardly be supposed that this or any other mantic art is peculiar to women, or that even in men it can be induced by the inhalation of vapours, by the cultivated ecstasy of Corybantic dances or by the soul-deafening clangour of devotions to Sabazius and the Great Mother (3.9). Least of all can knowledge of the future be elicited from the flight of birds, from carcases after sacrifice or from lifeless wood and stone (1.15-17). Consequently it is ludicrous to suppose that even a daemon would descend at a magician's behest, accompanied by such talismans, to assist in our predictions (1.18); the coercion of higher powers would be at once impossible, impious and redundant, since we have 'small sparks' within each of us (1.20) which enable us to shape more in imagination[33] than we perceive with the outward senses.

The allusion is perhaps to the rational daemon which is said in the *Timaeus* to be implanted by the gods in every soul that they send to earth. It appears that certain Platonists before Porphyry had identified this tenet with the Stoic teaching that the individual mind contains the seeds or 'seminal principles' of divine reason; under philosophical discipline, they argued, these may germinate to yield direct intuitions of the truths that elude experience and reflection. While Porphyry too is likely enough to have held this, it is strange that he should deny the rationality of animals, since Plato's maxim that all souls are akin was one that his followers had never ceased to press against Stoics and Christians.[34] Porphyry himself maintains at length in his treatise on abstinence that dumb brutes are as rational as humans (188.11ff); human *phantasia* or imagination, on the other hand, is not so highly esteemed in any other surviving work of his.[35] More often he treats it as a perfidious faculty which burdens the soul with memories of the contingent and ephemeral, thus retarding its deliverance from the body after death.[36] Such observations suggest that, if the *Letter to Anebo* was an expression of Porphyry's views and not a whetstone for his pupils, it belongs to his philosophical apprenticeship, and is not, as Bidez thought, the apologia of a Greek Renan, abjuring in middle age the superstitions of his youth.[37]

Iamblichus' rejoinder would appear to be addressed not only to critics but to injudicious champions of the mysteries. There are some, he remarks, who hold that mantic dreams are the product, not of a second power in souls (as Porphyry might have argued), but of a second soul, released in the hours of sleep (1.3). Such theorists are unaware that veridical prophecy often comes not as a dream but as a voice to the receptive soul that tarries on the frontier between sleep and waking. Such receptivity is at times perfected by an exquisite attenuation of the senses, as at Colophon, where the prophet's soul is purified by certain waters until it becomes amenable to the same fiery inspiration to which these waters owe their virtue (1.11). More frequently, however, the less rational souls of women, or of males unmanned by ecstasy, are favoured because they offer less resistance to divine communication. The prophetess at Delphi, for example, yields herself wholly to the 'fiery spirit that comes up through the aperture', while her counterpart at Branchidae is willingly overwhelmed, if not by vapours, then by the radiance that proceeds from her sacred wand (1.11). The orgies of Sabazius and Bacchus are all the more efficacious because they expel all 'human and natural qualities'; Corybantic rituals do indeed equip men to govern, but – whatever Porphyry chooses to insinuate – the majority of the great mother's adepts are women (1.10). It is not, as Porphyry thinks, because the soul contains scintillae of divinity (1.20), but because it submits to powers that it does not possess by nature, that it serves the gods as a vessel of inspiration. To propose, as Porphyry does, that it is only through cosmic sympathy that the irrational and inanimate can become portents is to suggest that we acquire knowledge from something lower than the intellect, and thus to overthrow the very premiss on which Porphyry attributes vaticination to the soul (3.15-17). It is true that the harmonious and immutable revolutions of the stars furnish the data of astrology, because this motion has been impressed upon them by the eternal gods (3.30); it is also true, on the other hand, that augurs base their predictions in anomalies which, if they contradict the instincts of the bird, must be deemed preternatural (3.16).

In the closing chapters of this book Iamblichus takes up and expands his previous strictures on the representation of the gods in statuary. There is some temerity in this, for in the classical tradition – of which he was, like Porphyry, a connoisseur – the human body had been regarded as the most fitting natural image of the divine. Even among philosophers, who were apt to protest when the culture of the body preponderated over that of the rational soul, it was a commonplace that humans, as the only creatures who stood erect, were also the ones who were most disposed to elevated thoughts. After the rise of Christianity philosophers took up the defence of images, though only the anthropomorphic specimens – chiefly Phidias' statue of Zeus at Olympia[38] – were thought worthy of comparison with the essays of philosophers and poets. Porphyry's treatise *On Statues* was perhaps the earliest Greek attempt to vindicate the ascription of bestial properties to the gods in iconography:[39] sacrifice to these effigies, and the use of them in divination or coercive magic, he does not defend either here or in his *Letter to Anebo*. Iamblichus denies that anything natural can point beyond the natural, or that supernatural knowledge is accessible because of some affinity between the daemon and its purported image (3.28). He concludes with a harangue against false practitioners who, by courting evil spirits for their own ends, bring disrepute on the true theurgist, whose performances, in the mantic art as in others, are at all times 'sacerdotal and undefiled' (3.31).

Working upon the gods (Books 4-6)

The fourth book (as the work is now divided) reveals the fallacy in Porphyry's question how the gods, if just themselves, can be coaxed into unjust actions by their servitors (4.1). It is often the case, Iamblichus explains, that the gods appear to condone injustice because they see that it conduces to a more distant goal, which we too – could we perceive it – would acknowledge to be just (1.5). Again, there is no truth in the innuendo that the gods themselves enjoin unrighteous conduct on their worshippers, whose characters they none the less require to be without blemish (4.3). Iamblichus replies that, when an act performed in the name of the gods miscarries, it is not because there is ignorance or error in the divine realm, but because the practitioner lacked the means to make better use of the strength that he acquired by exploiting the sympathy of the elements (1.6). It is true that there are daemons who effect their illicit purposes through just but unlearned ministers (1.7), but that is only a further proof that the wisdom by which gods judge good and evil is not immanent to the world or to our own unassisted faculties. The object of theurgy is in fact to make a science of our religion, purging the mind (with divine assistance) of its natural hence superstitious propensity to imagine that a crime against one's neighbour may be a duty to the gods.

Should we deduce that matter, which the gods shun, can never be of service to their devotees? Priests are required, as Porphyry notes, to keep themselves unpolluted by the smoke of animal sacrifices (5.1); but how are we to harmonise this requirement with their collusion in the ritual, or the ritual with philosophy, since we can hardly entertain the popular notion that the gods are allured by the 'odours of living things'? Iamblichus disposes quickly enough of the innuendo – since gods possess no matter, nothing material can nourish or pollute them (5.4) – but his chief aim in this fifth book is to show that the altar has at least a pedagogic role in the economy of worship. Sacrifice is, as many say, a channel of cosmic sympathy, though Iamblichus means by this not a mechanical chain of causes but the friendship that obtains between creator and creature, the ruler and the ruled (5.8-9). As there are many such relations, so there are many forms of sacrifice, each (when duly performed) releasing the influence of the god to whom it is offered (5.10). This is not the highest or the least fallible mode of intercourse with the gods, as we learned above, but it serves for those – the great majority – who have not progressed so far as to live entirely in the intellect. The prayers of the true theurgist – of the mind set free from the carousel of worldly desire and sensuous delusion – are extolled and illustrated in the last chapters of Book 5.

Iamblichus had depicted such a figure in the first volume of his Pythagorean encyclopaedia. The hero of *On the Pythagorean Life* eschews both meat and the killing of beasts throughout his sojourn in the body, and even bloodless sacrifices are left out of the question when he introduces the cocksure priest Abaris to the numerological method of theurgy. When Porphyry drew his namesake in the *History of Philosophy*, he allowed him to regulate rather than abolish animal sacrifice, and even flirts with the strange report in Heraclides Ponticus that he acted as a dietician to athletes. We have noted another example of his inconsistency or promiscuity in the *Philosophy from Oracles*, where he seems to endorse prescriptions for the sacrifice of animals, though of different colours, both to gods above and to gods below. Egyptian science, according to Iamblichus, is less concerned to identify the recipient of an offering than to ensure that the affinity between the law of sacrifice and the order of the divine world is respected. No sacrifice, whether to heavenly or to chthonic powers, will advance the business of the true theurgist; Abammon therefore deprecates the labours of certain priests – his own compatriots, as he tells us – to account for the utility of such practices by establishing numerological or lexical correlations between the colours or names of victims and such visible deities as the sun and moon (1.8).

The sixth book addresses Porphyry's question, 'why are priests enjoined to refrain from contact with the dead, when they habitually avail themselves of the carcases of beasts in their invocations?' (6.1) Iamblichus replies that priests are not required to hold aloof from every corpse, but only from those of human beings, since the animal form has never housed a divine soul and is thus not rendered unclean by its departure. It is in any case not through the animal's flesh but through its emancipated soul that we approach the divine, for, while this soul retains some likeness to ours, it acquires some kinship with the daemons by the mere fact of having shed its carnal envelope (5.3). A corpse creates no defilement in a daemon, because these superhuman beings are not susceptible of corruption (5.2). But now it seems that Iamblichus has bared his flank to the next thrust: how can beings so impassible be intimidated by the threats of mortals? The great ones, he replies, suffer no coercion (6.5): it is not such potentates as the sun and moon but lower agents – senseless, limited, irrational – who permit themselves to be overawed, or perhaps the terrestrial daemons, not because they are compelled but because they are not so indifferent as the higher powers to the threat of sacrilege (6.6). Furthermore, it is possible that the magician gains an ascendancy over lesser gods by becoming one with their overlords, whose symbols he employs (6.6).

Divine symbolism, human understanding (Books 7 and 8)

Iamblichus proceeds to explain these symbols in his seventh book, with the caveat that a symbol fails of its purpose unless we grasp the intellectual truth behind the pictured emblem (7.1). Mud, for example, signifies the corporeal, and (by virtue of this) whatever gives life and nourishment, hence the generative principle, and finally (for those who can ascend so far) the First Cause (7.2). The lotus enthroned on mud betokens mastery of the corporeal, while the image of a piloted ship bears witness to the divine administration of the cosmos (7.2, p. 252). Just as the gods forbid their acolytes to renounce these symbols, so they will not permit them to replace the Egyptian names and imprecations in their prayers by Greek equivalents (7.4). That would be to ratify the false disdain of the Greek for his 'barbarian' teachers, and once again to substitute human wisdom for divine self-revelation. The same position is taken in the *Hermetica*,[40] and could hardly be denied by any Platonist who believed, on the authority of Socrates in the *Cratylus*, that certain names belong naturally to their referents, and that Homer had these in mind when he distinguished the speech of men from that of gods.[41]

We have spoken of mud as a symbol of the First cause; but what, asks Porphyry, do the Egyptians mean by this? In his eighth book Iamblichus confesses that he has no time to review all the matters canvassed in the 36,525 books that the Egyptian priests ascribe to Thrice-Great Hermes (8.1). Leaving aside subsidiary and supervenient causes, we must be content to know that the cause of all is One, 'remaining immovable in the singularity of his own onehood' (8.2). From him proceeds the 'first god and king', the self-fathering Good, who, as the monad prior to essence, is the transcendent source of intellect and its objects. Hermes, we are told, could not give a full account of these transcendent principles in less than a hundred volumes: after them he places another monad, the unitive principle of the intellectual realm, in whom resides the 'primordial object of intellection', to be worshipped only in silence (8.2, p. 262). The intellectual realm takes shape through Kneph,[42] the 'self-thinking mind', who is the leader of the celestial gods; the visible world, however, is shaped and governed by a demiurgic intellect, who is called Amoun when he brings forth, Ptah or Hephaestus when he perfects his work, and Osiris when he makes this work productive of further goods (8.3).[43] In another text the elements are assigned to an Ogdoad or group of eight, in which four masculine deities are paired with their feminine counterparts under the regency of the sun, while the generated world itself is subject to the authority of the moon (8.3, p. 265). Of matter the Egyptians say – in contrast to the Greeks – that it is not a mere passivity but a source of life, abstracted from the principle of essence by the self-fathering god who entrusts it to the demiurge (8.3, *finis.*). Consequently their sacred guides are not ashamed to parcel out the heavens into spatial quarters, the twelve signs of the zodiac, or even thirty-six decans (8.4). The more exquisite the measurement, the more accurate will be the horoscopes that we cast for those whose bodies are in the moon's keeping. It would not be true, however, to say with Porphyry that the Egyptians imagine human life to be subject to the stars, for soul and intellect have their origins outside the natural realm. We have in fact two souls, the higher and more elusive of which is naturally receptive to divine influence. It can indeed afford to despise the lower manifestations of divinity, for it is only the supracosmic gods who are able to assist it in its ascent from the toils of matter (8.6).

In his reference to the Ogdoad, Iamblichus may be thinking of the sodality of eight gods, male and female, who are depicted in a famous relief at the city of Hermopolis.[44] Iamblichus would appear to have been aware that these powers were thought to be projections of the sun; perhaps he was also aware that in Egyptian verse the return of the sun is heralded each morning by the opening of the lotus, while his eight projections were also said to personify qualities of the primaeval ocean, and were therefore often represented as 'creatures of mud and slime'. The decipherment of Egyptian myth had been an occasional recreation of Platonists since Plutarch's treatise *On Isis and Osiris*; even the austere Plotinus held (without claiming the privilege of a native) that the Egyptians had encoded their wisdom in images rather than sounds or written characters (*Enneads* 5.8.6.1-9). In the Greek Hermetica 'Ogdoad' is a name for the heaven of the fixed stars, to which the soul ascends after giving up its vices, one by one, to the seven planets (*Poimandres* 24-7). In Porphyry's treatise *On Statues* there is no mention of an Ogdoad, but Kneph's winged helmet is said to betoken the mystery from which the creative word proceeds, while the egg coming forth from his mouth prefigures the birth of Ptah, the demiurge, who is also called Hephaestus.[45] We see, not for the first time, that a question posed in the *Letter to Anebo* is one to which Porphyry himself could have given a competent reply.

The doctrine of two souls is not attested in any extant writing of the Hermetic corpus. Plotinus, however, states in an early treatise that the gods have given us both a fabricant soul to inform the body and its actions in the present world, and a higher one – impassible, immobile and divine – which is the source of reason and, even when we are unaware of it, constitutes the real self (*Enneads* 2.1.5). This is clearly the daemon of the *Timaeus*, a divine spark which endows the embodied soul with the power of ratiocination. Commenting elsewhere on the *Meno, Phaedrus* and *Republic,* he accounts for the *anamnêsis* or latent memory of the supercelestial heaven in the earthbound soul by saying that the higher soul remains unfallen even when its companion must descend. Porphyry, with the majority of modern commentators, sees in this no more than a colourful and hortatory mode of speaking; to him the soul is an integer, which cannot subsist without reason even in beasts, and which, though manifold in capacity, is only metaphorically divisible into parts. This was his position in an essay on the tripartite soul in Plato, now surviving only in fragments,[46] and it prompted him to disown the literal reading of Platonic texts which sentence the erring souls of men to penal servitude in the irrational frames of animals and women. When he encounters a doctrine of two souls in his treatise *On Abstinence*, he rebuts it as a grave but uncommon error;[47] yet among those who had maintained it was Numenius, as Porphyry remarked in his book *On the Faculties of the Soul*.[48] Abammon's fissiparous conception of the soul is hardly less Greek than that of Aristotle, who thought the human intellect too sublime to be of merely natural origin.[49]

Platonists, while not scoffing at all astrology like their cousins in the sceptical Academy, contested the authority of horoscopes, and applauded a soul that lived in opposition to its stars. Plotinus wrote a treatise to show that even if the future is prefigured in the stars, it is determined by a higher cause, which the soul can approach without their mediation (2.3.15). Porphyry tells us also that he examined the pretensions of the *genethlialogoi,* or horoscope-casters, and found them baseless (*Plotinus* 13.21-6). Yet astrology cannot have been all imposture, for we see that Plotinus suffered when a rival turned the power of the stars against him (*Plotinus* 10). Abammon is making a concession to freedom, not to Platonism – though he echoes a statement made elsewhere by Iamblichus in his own name – when he says that the gods may intervene to save their worshippers from an inclement fate.

From birth to death (Books 9 and 10)

Book 9 acquits the Egyptians of maintaining that our destiny is fixed for us at birth by a personal daemon, or that a soul can procure its happiness by appeasing it with material sacrifices (9.1). The daemon – not a product of one element but of all the elements in due combination – represents the lot that the soul elects for itself before descent into the body. It is therefore not the agent of the soul's release but only its coadjutor in fulfilling the sublunar decrees of fate. The object of theurgy is that the soul should be not only at peace with the hylic powers but free of them; at this point the daemon yields to a higher god, whom the astrologers style the *oiko-despotês,* 'master of the house' (9.2).

Platonists before Plotinus recognised three species of daemon: the souls of the great departed, the intermediaries who deliver oracles and convey our prayers to heaven, and the tutelary spirits (Latin *genii*) who accompany the soul from birth to death.[50] It is of the third class, if any, that Iamblichus is speaking, though our early witnesses do not associate this natal guardian with the stars. A precedent can be found, however, in *Enneads* 3.4, where Plotinus undertakes to determine 'who is the daemon to whom we are allotted' on the threshold of each new life. The title alludes to *Republic* 620b, where we are told that when the soul has chosen its lot it comes to Lachesis, who assigns it to the daemon that it has chosen as the 'fulfiller of its choice'. Plotinus understands this to be the same daemon who, at *Timaeus* 90b, is 'the most authoritative portion of the soul' (*Enneads* 3.4.4.22-3), and concludes that for every pilgrim in the cosmos the allotted daemon is that condition of soul which lies immediately above his present state. The character of the daemon being determined by one's present level of being, it could not be said that its guidance robs the soul of freedom or her works of merit. In the philosopher's case at least, the word daemon is a misnomer, for he lives already at the level of intellect, and his self-in-prospect therefore must be as high as any god – perhaps higher still, though Plotinus leaves this to conjecture. Once the philosopher's soul is liberated from the maelstrom of becoming, it will come to the star that has always ruled it 'in harmony with its character'; it is 'this star, or the power set above it, that he will possess as his daemon and his god' (3.4.6.27-30). It is hard to believe, whatever Porphyry tells us, that the attempt of an Egyptian priest to evoke the guardian spirit of Plotinus could have had any palpable outcome; he may, however, be stating a fact (though burying the motive) when he tells us that Plotinus was reluctant to divulge his date of birth.

The tenth book is a peroration on happiness, which in Greek thought is defined as the realisation or enjoyment of the Good. The Good, as has been shown, is the inscrutable source of intellect and the intelligible (10.7); the soul that aspires to union with it, therefore, must not only attain the 'plenitude of intellect' but submit to divine assistance, and for most this will entail some use of theurgical machinery (10.5). Theurgy, while it is not the art of virtue, is the art of making a virtue of necessity – a necessity which, as Bacon has it, can be commanded only when obeyed.

Platonists and Christians

Enough has been said to show that our four philosophers are also four custodians of Greek tradition, all unconscious of any failure of nerve, any shift to the east or any supersession of reason by authority. Plotinus, in the name of the Greeks, excludes or subordinates everything that he, like Plato, finds profane or frivolous in the canon; the maxim of Longinus, on the other hand, is that everything Greek is equally Greek, though he handles none of the classics with the same reverence that Plotinus accords to Plato. Porphyry holds that the wisdom of many nations flowed into one stream in the teaching of Pythagoras, and that the first springs may be revisited with profit by his Greek contemporaries; yet everything is subjected to the *interpretatio graeca* in his researches, and as mentors of Plotinus he acknowledges only the masters of Greek philosophic schools. Iamblichus has the most eclectic canon in such works as his compendium of opinions on the soul; he is the author of a treatise on the Egyptian mysteries under a native pseudonym, and the first commentator on the *Chaldaean Oracles*; yet he is also the mathematician among the Platonists, and the most fastidious theist. While he maintains, in contrast to Plotinus, that the soul descends entire from the noetic realm, he does make this a reason either for shunning the visible cosmos or for worshipping the inferior powers within it; in arguing that matter is of divine origin and that the soul, in its earthly toils, is accountable only to the gods, he proves himself the most optimistic of the Greeks.

Rejection of the world, and of the philosophies that embrace it, is a tenet of Christianity, which taught that, since the fall of Adam, humans are immersed in a night of sins from which only God could pluck them, and only by permitting the world to crucify his son. None of our four philosophers is likely to have lived until 324, when a Christian seized the eastern throne and issued the first in a series of edicts which, by the last years of the fourth century, were to rob the gods of sanctuary and sacrifice, their priests of legal privilege and their votaries of the right to pursue a livelihood as lawyers or civil servants. Porphyry and Iamblichus, however, will have witnessed the persecution of Christians under Diocletian and Galerius, revoked in 311 but continued under Maximinus Daia in the east up to 313. Porphyry, whether or not he endorsed these measures, certainly held that Greeks and Christians were irreconcilable enemies, and that the laws could not countenance both.[1] So many have thought the contrary, from his day to ours, that more than a brief excursus is required to test the strength of his position.

Unshared postulates

Augustine – the young Augustine – was perhaps the first to see in Neoplatonism a Christless Christianity, which demonstrated the unity and incorporeality of the Godhead, offered hints for a philosophical doctrine of the Trinity, and underwrote the promise of resurrection with a proof of the immortality of the soul.[2] To humanists of the Renaissance it served chiefly as an antidote to scholasticism, giving rise in some hands to a critique of all religion;[3] yet the Anglican divines of the seventeenth century turned the same arsenal against the materialism and Unitarianism of Protestant freethinkers.[4] The most popular apologist of the twentieth century told young neophytes, 'It's all in Plato', while a Dean of St Paul's was the pioneer of modern English scholarship on Plotinus.[5] In the Roman world, however, no affinity was admitted by the pagans; so intense was their opposition that 'Porphyrian' became an invidious synonym for 'heretic' among Christians, while the death of the Church's bugbear, the Emperor Julian, marked the beginning of the epoch by which Platonists reckoned dates in the subsequent history of the school.[6]

When did these hostilities commence? There is little in Plotinus to suggest that he was aware of the new religion. In his treatise against the Gnostics (*Enneads* 2.9), of which more will be said below, the interlocutors are depicted as lost friends and renegade Platonists, not as an aberrant Christian sect. Porphyry, on the other hand, knew well enough who his adversaries were when, as he tells us, he exposed the Gnostic Book of Zoroaster in a series of refutations (*Life of Plotinus* 16.14-18). The *Suda* in its catalogue of Porphyry's works says nothing of these, but mentions fifteen *logoi* or discourses against the Christians. Of these only fragments remain – how many we cannot say, though the title *Against the Christians* is attested in Augustine, and Eusebius seems to quote the work by name on five occasions in his *Gospel Preparation*. His evidence makes it clear that *Against the Christians* and the *Philosophy from Oracles* were not the same work, as one critic has surmised. But neither in Eusebius nor in Augustine do we hear of fifteen books, and it has been doubted whether a work of such dimensions would have left so poor a trail.[7] It may be that the writings against the Gnostics were included among the *Suda*'s fifteen *logoi*; Porphyry has also been identified with the anonymous philosopher whose strictures on Christianity were rebutted in the fourth century by one Macarius Magnes. Timothy Barnes's argument that Porphyry would have written with most effect against the Christians during the reign of Diocletian is confirmed for some (though not for Barnes himself) by a Christian diatribe against an unnamed philosopher who had stridently condoned the persecution of 303.[8] Yet even the most hospitable collation of

147

possible testimonies and fragments yields a jejune and largely anecdotal case against Christianity – grist to the mill, perhaps, of those who hold that the two philosophies had more in common than either would avow.

In fact, as I shall argue here, the differences between the two were profound, and always remained so in antiquity, though it is possible that Porphyry elided them in setting up his own brand of Platonism as a rival to Christianity. One aim of this chapter is to demonstrate that in the ancient world there could have been no such thing as Christian Platonism; for illustration it cites the works of Origen, who is often supposed to have been just such a hybrid. The last word will be given, however, to Porphyry, whose *Letter to Marcella* shows that enemies in religion need not always be strangers in piety, and that virtue can be fashioned by the same norms under many gods as under one.

Theism in Porphyry and Plotinus

First, we should not overlook the simple platitude that to be a monotheist one must be a theist. That is to say, one must habitually use God as a name for the sovereign of the universe, and must be disposed to acknowledge that sovereignty in acts of worship. On this definition it may be said that the more one is a Platonist the less one is a theist. God is a proper name in Christianity; to a strict disciple of Plato like Plotinus it is a title of esteem, which the philosopher employs at his own discretion.[9] John Rist observes an incipient distinction between *ho theos* (the proper name of the One) and *theos* (the titular appellation of Nous), and we find a parallel in John 1.1, where God the Father is *ho theos* while the Word who will become Christ is simply *theos*.[10] It is also true that Christ is both the image and the Son of the Father, while Nous is both the image and the offspring of the One. Analogies in nomenclature, however, cannot outweigh the fact that deity is more often predicated of Nous than of the One in Plotinus' writings, and that in neither case is it used to inculcate any duty of worship. By contrast the Father is typically the sole referent of the term *theos* in the New Testament, which concurs with the Hebrew scriptures in assuming that any being so called is worthy of veneration. 'Thou shalt have no gods before me' (Exodus 20.3) would be a nonsensical injunction to the Platonist who believed that he himself could become a 'father of gods' through wisdom. Plotinus, who surmised that the soul gives birth to the Olympians as she approaches the fount of unity, went so far as to say 'the gods should come to me, not I to them'.[11] For such a philosopher theism is simply the demography of the invisible world, and while it may be true that the One is God, it does not follow that God is one.

Porphyry's title for *Enneads* 5.1 is *On the Three Hypostases*. If he was as familiar as he purports to be with the works of the Christian Origen (his older contemporary and acquaintance), he will have known that this was the formula under which the Church subsumed the Father, the Son and the Holy Spirit.[12] While it would have been blasphemy to deny that they constituted a single Godhead, there was no creed which forbade one to hold that the Father and the Son were of different *ousiai* or essences. This was a position held by Origen, at least with respect to the Son incarnate,[13] and one that his admirer Eusebius seems to have entertained of the Son as Logos (Word) before his incarnation.[14] It was Eusebius who suggested, in his reply to Porphyry's work against the Christians, that the Platonists had an inkling of the Christian Trinity. If, however, Porphyry was referring to the One, Intellect and Soul, he was departing from the usage of his teacher. A hypostasis in the *Enneads* is the realisation of a transcendent principle in a lower plane, so that *nous* is the hypostasis of the One, and soul of *nous*.[15] Only once, at *Enneads* 6.8.15.28, do we read that the One itself possesses a hypostasis, and this remark is at odds with an earlier statement in the same treatise that the One is 'before hypostasis' (*Enneads* 6.8.10.35). Unless then the three hypostases of *Enneads* 5.1 are Intellect, Soul and nature – not an established triad in Plotinus, though he does sometimes speak of nature as a hypostasis – it would seem that Porphyry's title is polemical, a hint that any occasional felicities in Christian thought are surreptitious gleanings from the harvest of the Greeks.

At the Council of Nicaea in 325 the Church determined that the Son is 'of one essence' (*homoousios*) with the Father.[16] Neither this tenet nor the opposing view that the Son and the Father are of different *ousiai*[17] could have been expressed in the vocabulary of the *Enneads*. Nous is the realm of essence, and the One is thus, as Plotinus states repeatedly, superior to essence (*hupekeina tês ousias*). The meaning of this claim is examined in *Enneads* 6.8, one of the richest and most original, though not the most characteristic, of Plotinus' meditations. Its premiss is that in every permanent entity we can distinguish between the essence, the *ousia,* which is wholly or partially actualised, and the energy (*energeia*) which transforms it from potential to actuality. As every act is grounded in the nature of the agent, so the essence is logically prior to the energy, yet it is only through the energy that essence is realised in the discrete particular. Only in Nous is the energy wholly converted into essence, and even here the two remain logically distinct. Even such a notional or conceptual duality is, however, incompatible with the simplicity of the One. If the One had an essence, the antithesis between essence and energy, thought and thinking, act and activity, would be inescapable, and we should be required to posit a higher principle of unity. If the One is itself to be this principle, it must be energy without essence, cause itself but with no selfhood to circumscribe its own causality, infinite power that never terminates in finitude. In this treatise, and only here, Plotinus ascribes to the one both free volition (*to autexousion*) and love, two attributes of the Christian deity.[18] Yet there is no will to create, no love of anything below, and in the *Enneads* such locutions serve to accentuate, though not to define, the otherness of the One.

Almost seventy years ago, a Lutheran theologian, Anders Nygren, drew a celebrated contrast between erotic or acquisitive love, the only kind of which unredeemed humanity is capable, and the agapetic or charitable love which Christ embodies in the Gospels.[19] The cultivation of virtue and intelligence under the discipline of *erôs*, he maintained, is the philosopher's attempt to storm the heavens: what he hopes to achieve by loving God he will receive only when he levels himself with the poor, the weak and the ignorant, confessing that all depends on God's inscrutable love for him. Humility – the admission of one's unworthiness – and charity – the love of the strong for the weak – are the two concomitants of faith, unknown by name to the Greek philosophers and imparted to Christians only by divine mercy. Undoubtedly the contrast is overdrawn, for the disciple of Christ is not forbidden, even in the New Testament, to love God or to please him by good works, while on the other hand, the superabundance of the Platonic Demiurge – his propensity to communicate his own goodness – is surely a manifestation of *agapê*, though it entails no sacrifice. It is true none the less that the words denoting charity and humility in the Greek Bible are neologisms; true again that neither revelation nor salvation, as the Christians understood these terms, is represented in the Platonic lexicon. All that the Platonist has to say of the One is the product of his own logic, and no increment to it is logically conceivable. Christians professed to know a great deal more – that God is loving, merciful, wise and just, that he works miracles, that he intervenes to enforce his own laws – but only by supernatural disclosure. Origen declared that Plato had fallen short of the truth in his aphorism that 'it is difficult to find out the Father of all';[20] but for the Father's condescension, he argued, it is not difficult but impossible, and where does he condescend if not in Christ and in the scriptures which preserve Christ's voice today?

Having convicted the Platonist (fairly enough) of wishing to pay his own fare to heaven, some theologians urge – not quite so fairly – that he would not have needed to pay at all had he not put an infinite gulf between his god and the creation. Lacking the condescension and humility of the true god – for the worshipper cannot bestow on his idol what he lacks himself – this deity is unconscious of the world and hence incapable of governing it. The prayers of those below cannot reach him, nor is it even possible to speak of him except in negatives. Plato was now compelled to fill this vacuum of his own making by the invention of an intermediate power in whom the hyperbolic attributes of the sovereign god are commuted to spare the weakness of his subjects. He or some successor of his (the fact is too well-known to require a footnote) styled this second god the Logos, and there were heretics in the early Church who superimposed this qualified polytheism on the Biblical doctrine of the Word incarnate. Yet the incompatibility of the two creeds (it is said) is plain enough: the Christ of the Church is God in man, the Logos of philosophy is the man-made silhouette of an absent God.

This story is false from the outset, because its premises are not Plato's.

Instead it takes for granted the Biblical axioms that there can be only one God and that nothing exists apart from him and his creation. The God of Christianity, who transcends his creatures as cause transcends effect, distinct in nature and operation from every being that depends on him and imparting even to man, his image, only a reflection of his attributes – such a God would indeed be sought in vain unless he himself compressed the void, while those who declined to seek him would indeed be 'without God in the world' (Ephesians 2.12). For the Greeks, however, there was no void – not because the philosophers had filled it with intermediaries, but because even the philosophical notion of God was itself derived from, and continued to accommodate, a polytheistic culture in which the gods were made present through statuary, poetic recitals, civic holidays and domestic prayers. These were Plato's gods as they were Homer's: it would not have occurred to either that the petty and quotidian needs of mortals should be an object of concern for the highest deity, whether we call him Zeus, the Demiurge or the One. And if these needs were customarily satisfied by agents near at hand, then why (they might have asked) should anyone demand access on all occasions to the highest God, any more than one would insist that all petitions should be carried to the first magistrate in a city where local officers were appointed for local purposes? It was only those who had risen above the appetites, and had learned to look with indifference on the changes and disappointments of the world, who had the motive or the right to turn away from the civic pantheon and ascend, through the deification of their own intellects, to the place of the Good, from which even Zeus and his retinue are excluded. Such a soul, having fled the body, would not wish that its god should become incarnate if this were possible; all intermediaries would disappear because no scope would remain for providential government; nor, since there would be no one to cajole and nothing to pray for, will the soul engage in worship when it has come to rest 'alone with the alone' (6.9.11.51).

Plotinus, in his treatise on providence, scoffs at superstitious folk who call on God to amend their affairs when they themselves have shown no prudence in them (*Enneads* 3.2.8). It has been surmised that Christians are his targets here, and certainly it is Christians of a sort whom he upbraids in *Enneads* 2.9.11.57 for imagining that the formula 'you are the son of god' will suffice to make true by fiat what has not been proved by works. Porphyry records that when Plotinus taught in the capital there were 'Christians of divers kinds, especially certain heretics',[21] and one of his two titles for this tract is *Against the Gnostics*. Christian polemicists agreed that the salient tenet of the Gnostics was the one that furnished the second title, *Against those who maintain that the author of the cosmos is malign.* Porphyry claims that he himself, with Amelius' help, exposed the counterfeit scriptures of the sect, and we possess Coptic texts of writings with the same titles, which confirm that Plotinus gives a fair epitome of the Gnostic myth in *Enneads* 2.9.[22] According to this, a superfetation of aeons or hypostases in the godhead engendered Wisdom or Sophia as the last and most unable of the divine powers. Wantonly looking away and catching sight of her own reflection in the underlying darkness, she descended and, avoiding a fall herself, deposited souls and 'members of wisdom' in captivity. From her benighted fancy sprang the Demiurge, a mere shadow of a shadow,[23] who proceeded to fashion, not a beautiful image of the Ideal like his namesake in the *Timaeus*, but a lifeless adumbration of the divine realm which he glimpses at secondhand. The regular course of nature, superintended by the stars, is fatal rather than providential, and, of the two orders of soul, those consubstantial with Sophia will be redeemed by nature, while those compounded of matter are doomed to perish. All works are predestined, discipline and abstinence effect nothing, and the elect are saved by knowing that they are saved.

Spokesmen of the episcopal church made common cause with Platonism against this saturnine 'tragedy of fears' (*Enneads* 2.9.13.7), affirming both the goodness of the created order and the soul's power to co-operate with Christ in her own redemption. Yet there are passages in Paul, not to speak of sayings ascribed to Jesus, which imply that the salvation of the elect is foreordained, while in the Gospel of John it is strongly intimated that this world is lost, and its denizens already separated into children of darkness and children of light.[24] Was it therefore disingenuous of these critics to seek the roots of Gnostic thought in Greek philosophies, including Platonism? Not entirely, because, although they upheld the freedom of the will against the Stoics, the Platonists also taught that our freedom in the present is restricted by our remembered choices in past lives. They also held that our lower world of *genesis* or becoming is but a copy of one in which there is no present, past or future; this, they opined, is the soul's true home to which she can return only by escaping from the body. No more than in Christianity is there any Gnostic cheapening of the world here. By arguing that the essences of natural kinds exist above, the Platonist justifies our use of common names for diverse individuals in the lower sphere; by peopling an invisible realm with archetypes of justice, beauty and goodness, he affirms the objectivity of justice, beauty and goodness as we know them. It is better that there should be a material universe than that matter should remain untouched by form; its flaws arise inevitably from the truculence of the substrate, not from any primordial trespass, as in the Gnostic myth or the Biblical tale of Eden. There is thus no charge to be laid against an omniscient God, no reverie of a 'new earth' in which the evils of the present will be miraculously annulled (cf. *Enneads* 2.9.5.25). The Gnostics were, of course, not the only Christians to anticipate the end of the world, and the following passage, often quoted to illustrate the optimism which Platonists shared with orthodox Churchmen, also reminds us where they parted company:

This All that has emerged into life is no amorphous structure – like those lesser forms within it which are born night and day out of the lavishness of its vitality – the Universe is a live organism, effective, all-comprehensive, displaying an unfathomable wisdom. How, then can anyone deny that it is a clear image, beautifully formed, of the intellectual Divinities? No doubt it is a copy, not original; but that is its very nature, it cannot be at once symbol and reality (*Enneads* 2.9.8, trans. McKenna).

In Christian thought the world bears witness to God not because it resembles him, but (as Augustine says) because he made it (*Confessions* 10.6). The image of the Father – his *monogenês*, unique or only-begotten, is not the world (*Timaeus* 92c) but Christ, who framed it before the fall and condescended to inhabit it, the Word becoming flesh to make all things new (John 1.14 and 1.18; Revelation 21.5). Christian theology was not required to prove – indeed it denied – that humans presently live in the best of all possible worlds. Nor, on the other hand, did it join the Platonists in asserting that it was the worst of actual worlds. It refused to countenance any theory of Forms outside the mind of God or any notion of matter as an independent substrate.[25] Some inferred from the opening chapter of Genesis that God produced matter first and then the cosmos; some maintained that matter was only logically, not temporally, prior to the creation;[26] some doubted whether a thing that was defined only by the absence of such qualities could be said to exist at all.[27] The Greek view of matter accounted for the discreteness of the world at the cost of denying its original perfection; Christians affirmed both and traced them to one cause, the omnipotent will of God. The world, as we have seen, was his creature rather than his image, and, because the two were so disparate in nature, it was capable of perfection in its own kind.

This is not to deny that in Christian thought a distinction can be drawn between the temporal and the eternal. The Pentateuch states that the tabernacle, the prototype of the Temple, was fashioned by Moses in accordance with a pattern revealed by God, and Christian writers constantly recur to this text to corroborate their claim that the entire Law was designed to foreshadow the mysteries that were openly proclaimed in the Incarnation.[28] Paul himself averred that, while the things that are seen will pass away, the unseen will endure for ever (2 Corinthians 4.18). Yet he and his readers differed from the Platonists in that they understood the temporal to be temporary, the end of the world having been ordained by the same God who had brought it into being. During this interval creatures lived or died in time without hope of liberation or return; the eternal was hidden from them, though not from God, until the final day, and, if there was a sense in which the elect were already saved, already regenerate, it was only by virtue of the Incarnation, which was itself an event in time. In Platonism, by contrast, the distinction between the temporal and the eternal was not chronological but qualitative. One was subject to change and one exempt from it, but, since there could be no reason for the eternal to be more productive at one time than at another, there could be no beginning or end to the vicissitude of the lower realm, any more than there could be beginning or end in the timeless universe of Forms.

Christians replied that, since there is no time when there is nothing for it to measure, it is futile to ask why the temporal world was not created sooner, or for ever.[29] Before the rise of Neoplatonism they read the *Timaeus* (with Atticus, Numenius, Philo and Plutarch) as a philosopher's testimonial to the unity of the world and its creation in time by God (Justin, *First Apology* 59). The case against a temporal creation, generally regarded as Aristotelian, could be rebutted with the argument that if the world had no beginning the number of humans who have inhabited it will be infinite, whereas Aristotle himself had shown that infinities cannot be realised in nature.[30] Neoplatonists could meet this quibble, and at the same time overthrow the literal reading of the *Timaeus*, by citing Plato's dictum 'all soul is immortal' (*Phaedrus* 245c), with the associated doctrine of the transmigration of souls. Each tenet confirmed the other, since, if the soul could even once survive the extinction of the body, it had no reason to perish at all, but it would survive without a function if it did not continue to animate a body. It followed that souls, though finite in number, were destined to pass through an infinite number of cycles; only the soul of the world could retain uninterrupted possession of one abode. All such wanderings, whether from one human to another or from humans to beasts, the Christians denied, adducing scripture to prove that everyone will rise again in the body to receive judgment for the deeds of a single life.

Origen and his followers, indeed, were accused of teaching that the soul exists from eternity with God, that it has fallen into the body through its own lassitude, that even souls in heaven may fall again, and that new worlds will be created to chastise them. The most that he can be proved to have said, however, is that souls descend from the hand of God at the moment of conception, for the sins before birth of which he speaks may all have been committed in the womb, and the one surviving text in which he envisages penalties for the soul in future worlds is a *reductio ad absurdum*.[31] He undoubtedly denied the transmigration of the soul from human to human, let alone from humans to beasts; on the evidence of works that remain intact, and in the original Greek, it is generally agreed that he did not expect the soul to quit this world without a real though tenuous body.[32] Origen held, as firmly as any Christian in antiquity, that the present life defines the self and its destiny for ever.[33]

When did this life commence? Christians held abortion to be a sin: as one apologist says, they marry, but they do not kill their children (*Epistle to Diognetus* 5). Origen cites an episode from the Gospel of Luke (1.41), in which John the Baptist leaps in the womb to salute the birth of his cousin Jesus, as evidence that the foetus is ensouled (*First Principles* 1.7.4). Elsewhere he explains the subordination of Esau to his younger sibling Jacob as a requital for the sins of his 'former life'; while this is often taken to mean the life of the pre-existent soul, the Jews of this epoch had already been exercised by the question whether sin can be committed in the uterus.[34] Greeks asked only whether the rational soul begins to animate the embryo at the moment of conception. Porphyry, in the longest extant treatise on the subject,[35] holds that no powers are communicated in pregnancy but those of the lower, or vegetative soul, which will suffice to explain the motions of the foetus and the inheritance of those traits (including traits of sensibility) which bear witness to the bond between child and parent. Only at birth does the rational soul, the heir to its own free choices in previous lives, accept the stewardship of a body that has been fashioned by the ineluctable processes of nature. Thus Porphyry maintains the Platonic doctrine that the soul is the artisan of her own misfortunes at a time when it was coming to be widely held among Christians that we are all born sinners because of Adam's sin. The theory that we inherit it biologically, the entire soul being transmitted to the child in the father's semen, had already been propounded by Tertullian, and Augustine in the fifth century regarded this as one of two doctrines licensed by the scriptures.[36] Freedom, as we conceive it, was of less concern to such authors than the unity of the human organism; how, they asked, could those who denied this unity account for the independent fall of a multitude of beings from perfection, or explain why soul and body should fare differently in the afterlife when both had been a party to the same sins?

As we have seen, the Christian ideal was not a life of conscious and self-authenticating virtue; in a monotheist it would be idolatrous folly to aspire to be a god or the father of gods. It was nevertheless an axiom of the New Testament, as of the Old, that human beings are made in the image of God.[37] Since it appears, in the opening chapter of Genesis, that God proposed to make Adam in his image and likeness but gave him only the image at his creation, it was widely held that Christ had taken flesh to reveal the likeness, and was presently at work in the Christian, moulding him into the form of a 'perfect man'.[38] Likeness to god is also the goal of philosophy in Plato's *Theaetetus*, and there is no doubt that the outward marks of sanctity in a Christian bear a strong resemblance to the Platonic virtues. Both Platonists and Christians live as citizens of an unseen world, eschewing the pleasures and comforts that are commonly mistaken for goods in this. Both, despising the perishable body, can meet torture and death without fear; both hold that it is better to suffer an injury than to do one; both admit that a man who is wise on his own account will be a fool to his neighbours. For all, their lives are directed to different ends, for whereas a Christian acts from obedience to God and in the hope of divine reward, the Platonist believes that he can fashion his own perfection, and that even if the gods help him for a season, his salvation is in his own gift rather than theirs. This likeness in unlikeness is most apparent in those fleeting anticipations of beatitude that would now be described as mystical experiences. For a Christian it is always the presence of God that is experienced, but Plotinus remembers only the elevation of the soul:[39]

> Often, having stirred into inner waking from the body, and coming to be outside other things but within myself, beholding beauty of wondrous intensity, having felt a conviction that then I possess the highest possible lot, and having exercised the best life through becoming one with the divine and making my seat in it – having arrived at that activity and made my seat above all else that is intelligible – after abiding in the divine, I descend from intellection to discursive thought and wonder how it is that I now descend (*Enneads* 4.8.1-8).

Porphyry reports that during the period of his own studies with Plotinus, the latter was united with the 'first and transcendent deity' on three or four occasions (*Life* 23.8-12). Yet this is not a mode of speech that Plotinus would have favoured; it is the Christian mystic Origen who assumes that if there is knowledge there is someone to be known:

> Often, as God is my witness, I have seen the Bridegroom suddenly approaching me, and I have enjoyed the fullness of his presence; then suddenly he has withdrawn, and I have not been able to find what I sought (*Homily on Song of Songs* 1.7, p. 39 Baehrens).

This is the true erotic, a cathartic intensification of love in which mutual desire is sublimated but not outgrown as in the Platonic itinerary from the Beautiful to the Good. Origen uses the appellation Bridegroom because it is in his text, the Song of Songs. For him there is no illumination except in the perusal of scripture, and no word in the scriptures that is not an embodiment of Christ the Word. As Platonists set out to discover a hidden text in Homer, so Origen held that the scriptures may be interpreted in three senses. It is not, however, the wisdom of the author or the discernment of the reader that reveals the three strands, but the incarnation of Christ himself in body, soul and spirit (*First Principles* 4.2.4). By virtue of this miracle the scriptures which bear record of him are susceptible of a bodily, a psychic and a spiritual reading, of which only the first corresponds to what we should call the literal sense. All three are true, though for simple readers the literal sense may occlude the others, just as the flesh of Jesus temporarily veiled his Godhead. If the Incarnation were a fable, Origen's threefold exegesis would be fanciful; the commentator's task, as he conceives it, is to refine but not extrude the literal meaning, whereas a Platonist seeks insight even in myths that he knows to be literally untrue.

Porphyry's *Letter to Marcella*

If a wife in late antiquity ever received a gallant letter from her husband, it has not survived. If she was not married to a Tertullian who sentenced her to a cold bed and a chaste widowhood, her spouse might be a Plutarch who eased her publicly into benign submission with his 'conjugal precepts'. Porphyry's *Letter to Marcella* is, by contrast, a meek and affectionate piece – the more so if one reads it as a teacher's valediction to his pupil. The opening paragraphs assure Marcella that she is too wise to suppose that Porphyry married her for money or companionship. Of the first, he tells her, we both have little (p. 273.11 Nauck); and one may well believe that few incomes in this age of high inflation would have sufficed to support her two sons and five daughters (273.1-2). As to the second, Marcella is too infirm to nurse a husband (273.13-16). It is not to love, not even to carnal appetite, but to the duties of his station that he alludes when he explains that his purpose in marrying a friend's widow was to appease his natal daemon (274.5-25); passion has not blinded him to Marcella's age or the ill-repute that accrues to him from this union (274.2-3), but rumour, as we have seen, is put to flight by the absence of the customary attractions in his bride. This is no perfumed letter but a defence of the author's character; having vindicated his marriage, he has next to explain the desertion of his wife as a sacrifice forced on him by a summons to public business in the interest of the Greeks.[40] What this means we cannot now say, but the words of consolation which he addresses to her would serve as an epitome of practical philosophy for any disciple who had been suddenly left to his own devices. Pain, he reminds Marcella, is unavoidable in the virtuous life, so long as our standard of pleasure is supplied by the reckless and dissipating appetites of the body into which we have descended (274.24ff). Salvation for her, as for everyone, lies in escape from the sensible world, and therefore not in the physical presence of her consort, but in the mental recollection of him, which absence cannot mar, and in his precepts, which are engraved in indelible characters on her soul (279.14-280.9). Porphyry intimates, with an echo of Plotinus, that the body is but a shadow or *eidôlon* of the true self; he is not, however, so like Plotinus when he admonishes Marcella to make god her overseer in all affairs (282.5-6), to consider that wisdom lies in paying honour to the god whom the wise know best (281.16-17), and to cultivate prayer under the tutelage of this god, remembering only that she is not to ask for anything without need, and not even for needful things without merit (282.12-22). The wise man is to be unknown to all others, but known to god; his mind, as it follows god, should see his likeness in its own reflection (283.10); let his soul and mind be dedicated to god, his body free from taint, every act and word concordant, and he will never be guilty of falsehood or insincerity, though he will be aware that he honours his guardian more by reverent silence than by multiplying words (284.17-22; 285.12-14). The servant of the gods should frequent their altars; he will not, however, credit them with a propensity to anger when neglected, as the vulgar do (286.10-13), and will take more care to please them by his life than by formal homage (285.2-7). It is certainly not for him to offer sacrifice or to join the untutored suppliant in showy lamentations (284.3-11); a true deity will make his temple in the upright mind (281.14).

Our choice, in fact, is to be the seat of god or of evil daemons (281.24-282.1; 287.23-4). If we choose god, we must also pay due reverence to the angels and good daemons whom he employs as his subordinates in the administration of rewards and punishments; it is they who ensure that, while the gods flee the wicked, the wicked cannot flee the vengeance of the gods (288.8-289.4). As Plato testifies, we are the authors of our own woes, the gods being guiltless;[41] they will not yield to the petitions of the vicious soul (289.14-18), but will answer prayers that are tempered by the four elements of virtue – faith, truth, love and hope (289.18). We are governed in the present world by three laws – that of god, that of mortal nature, and the positive law of the nation or commonwealth to which we belong in the present life (289.25-290.1). The positive law exists by contract only; it is not the same in all societies, checks the deed but cannot touch the conscience, and protects us from injustice without teaching us to be just (290.4-6 and 13-17). The law of nature is common to all who inhabit the present cosmos; it is recklessly transgressed by the *philosômatos*, the lover of the body, but solemnly transcended by the philosopher in pursuit of goods superior to the body and its concerns (290.9-13). The divine law is inexorable, though few heed its demand that we should sacrifice without blood and live without luxury; the business of philosophy is to make us rich within, and not, as many are, rich in fond conceit and paupers to the gods (290.18-20; 292.7-9 and 16-22). What do we learn through philosophy? Nothing less than to jail our jailers – that is, the stomach and other members by which souls are weighed down and robbed of understanding. Only when the soul rids itself of 'all that is feminine' can it achieve such mastery (296.2-3); as Plato slighted the progeny of heterosexual unions in the *Symposium*, so Porphyry declares that the most blessed offspring are born of a virgin soul and a godly intellect (296.4-6; cf. 273.4-6). If we would live the philosophic life, we must be ready to die for it (296.10-11), and in the meantime to eliminate the passions of the soul and eschew the pleasures of the body. But for an injunction to be forbearing in the punishment of slaves (296.16-20), the rest is lost.

Porphyry alludes in the course of the letter to a number of myths: the fall of the soul resembles the abandonment of Philoctetes on Lemnos (276.10-11), while her labours to return will be inspired by those of the demigods Asclepius, Heracles and Dionysus, all of whom sojourned in hell (278.19-20). When Porphyry contrasts the rugged ascent to the gods with the easy but discursive path of virtue, any reader of moderate learning would remember the choice of Heracles in Xenophon;[42] a reader who knew the cave of the Nymphs would perceive that when he placates his natal daemon Porphyry follows the path that Odysseus failed to take in his early wanderings (*Cave of the Nymphs* 80.8-81.1). The warning to shun *polutropous logous* ('tricksome words') is surely another reference to the early peregrinations of the hero for whom *polutropos* ('of many wiles') is the stock Homeric epithet.[43] Yet his argument is bound to no one scripture, and his purpose in writing the letter is perhaps above all to sketch that ideal portrait of himself which he expects his correspondent to have inscribed upon her soul.

Porphyry and Paul

Analogies are easily drawn between this letter and those of the early Christians, who employed epistolography as a medium of both doctrine and exhortation. Yet the result would be a catalogue of like motifs contrastingly applied, and thereby illustrating not so much the difference as the incommensurability between the two forms of piety:

1. When Paul tells the Corinthians that he is with them in spirit though absent in body (1 Corinthians 5.3), he means that he is present through his letters and through his prayers. He varies the conceit on one occasion by declaring that the Corinthians themselves are his epistle (2 Corinthians 3.2). In neither case is the presence of the teacher divorced from the bearing of witness: in the New Testament, as in the Old, the service of God consists in hearing rather than in seeking, and the truth conveyed by the logos, whether in Christ or in scripture, cannot be discovered until it is disclosed.

2. Paul offers himself as a model to his flock, but when he urges them to be 'imitators of me', he is careful to add, 'as I am of Christ' (1 Corinthians 11.1). For Porphyry all human beings are capable of attaining the likeness of god, but no one human being is god, and therefore no one man is a paradigm for all.

3. Likeness to God is also the goal of the Christian life, but this, as Paul explains, cannot be perfected until the body has been 'conformed to the likeness' of Christ's immortal body (Philippians 3.21). The climax of salvation is therefore not the soul's deliverance from the body, but the deliverance of the body from corruption (Romans 8.23; 1 Corinthians 15.53). Paul affirms what Porphyry expressly denies – that the body is as much a part of the person as the soul – and thus denies in his turn that the soul has the power to consummate her own destiny without the assistance of an external god.

4. Paul advises Christians not to marry, on the grounds that their attachment to domestic affairs will sever them from God (1 Corinthians 7.33-4). The children that he hopes to produce in place of carnal offspring are not, however, timeless creatures of the intellect, but new Christians, begotten (as Paul says) by their evangelist (Philemon 10), but properly sons of God.

5. Paul maintains that the man is the head of the woman (1 Corinthians 11.3); he does not, however, state that the distinction between the sexes is abolished by her subjection.[44] He rather implies, indeed, that it is not, for he appeals to the Book of Genesis, in which this bifurcation

159

of humanity is willed by God before the Fall, and therefore surely destined to endure.[45]

6. Paul draws an antithesis between flesh and spirit (Galatians 5.17; Romans 8.13), Porphyry between body and soul. Body gives way to flesh on one occasion in his *Letter to Marcella* (292.22), but even here the infirmities of the flesh are those of the body, whereas in Paul they include such ailments of the soul as jealousy, anger, pride and malice (Galatians 5.19-21). Porphyry admits that the soul communicates certain vices to the body, which the body returns with interest: he does not appear to share the view of Christ and Paul that all uncleanness comes from within, the body being not so much the instrument as the victim of the Fall.

7. Porphyry's tetrad – faith, hope, love and truth – contains one more term than the Pauline triad 'faith, hope, charity' at 1 Corinthians 13.13. In the Old Testament truth is almost a synonym for righteousness, and in the New it is a title of Christ himself (John 14.6). It therefore does not suggest itself as an independent virtue to Paul; still less would he have regarded it as a gem that the mind can cut for itself with the adamant of reason. Aspiring reason in Platonism takes the form of *erôs*, the thirst for beauty which renews the plumage of the fallen soul; but the Pauline word for love is *agapê*, a Biblical neologism more often denoting love of neighbour than love of God, and seldom without allusion to the sacrificial love of God in Christ.

8. Paul cites a number of illustrative stories form his own tradition, not all of them canonical, but all, in his estimation, true: had these things not been 'done among them', they would not have 'been written for us' (1 Corinthians 10.11). Truth is not what we find but what God reveals, and since the medium of revelation is history, a belief in the actual death and resurrection of a man named Jesus Christ is indispensable to faith. While there is no evidence that Paul had heard of the virgin birth of Jesus, this appears to have been a universal article of belief among the Christians of Porphyry's time. Their ideal and founder was a man born of the virgin Mary and the Holy Spirit; Porphyry hints that this is true as metaphor, not as fact, when he commends to Marcella the offspring of a 'godly intellect' and a 'virgin soul'.

In Christian thought, it is not the innate divinity of the mind, or the indefeasible simplicity of the soul, that secures immortality, but the covenant made with Adam by a benign creator, who did what he need not have done by framing this one creature in his image and endowing it with the foretaste or the promise of his likeness. Even had humanity never fallen, it would have owed its preservation to God and not to its own capacities; in the fallen state, where moral infallibility is unattainable, it is only in Christ, the one man who has kept and surpassed the Law, that Adam's posterity can find the righteousness that brings salvation. Paul proclaims both the necessity of good works and the insufficiency of all works (Romans 2.6 and 3.23 etc.); for him there is no virtue in the self-reliant imitation of God enjoined by Porphyry, and still less is it conceivable that the soul might become its own god, as in Plotinus. Christians and Platonists might employ the same vocabulary, deny themselves the same pleasures, sometimes preach the same morality; but they could never be united, unless a Platonist abjured his belief in his sovereignty of reason or a Christian came to think that a man-made god would be as powerful to save him as God made man.

Notes

Introduction

1. After Inge, Festugière and Dodds had disabused professional classicists of this fallacy, it survived in other academic disciplines: see e.g. L'Orange (1951).

2. De Blois (1989).

3. Dodds (1965).

4. *On the Soul* 430a15-25.

1. The Platonic Tradition

1. The editor has asked me to remind readers that a female scholarch (head of a school) was rarer in antiquity than a black swan.

2. Dillon (2005), 1-2.

3. Plato, *Protagoras* 314e-315b.

4. Diogenes Laertius, *Lives of Philosophers* 6.2, 8.2.

5. Dio Cassius 72.31. Dillon (2005), 926 observes that the Academy which was born of this endowment was assumed by later witnesses to be a continuation of Plato's school.

6. Dillon (2003), 2-11.

7. See Jaeger (1948), 111, citing Strabo, 13.57.

8. The technical term for one who succeeds to the headship of a school.

9. Numenius, Frs 24-8 Des Places. Neoplatonists were hardly aware of Antiochus of Ascalon, who is said to have restored the dogmatic spirit, styling his own school the Old Academy so that his sceptical predecessors came to be known, paradoxically, as the New Academy. See further Barnes (1989). Philo of Larissa, the tutor of Antiochus, had already abjured the sceptical tradition which forbade the wise man even to entertain a belief which could not be demonstrated irrefutably: Brittain (2001), 129-68.

10. *Meno* 81a-86b; *Phaedrus* 245c-257a. Note also the definition of the person as a soul using a body at *First Alcibiades* 129e-130a. Most scholars now consider this text apocryphal, but Iamblichus believed it to be Plato's introduction to his own corpus.

11. *Timaeus* 28a-38e; but cf. Cherniss (1944), 423-31.

12. See Chapter 4.

13. Cf. Annas (1981), 124.

14. On the conjecture that he was a Stoic see Dillon (1993), xii. On the restoration of his name to the Didascalicus see Whittaker (1987).

15. See Dawson (1992).

16. The 'companion' of Numenius, according to Porphyry, *Cave of the Nymphs*, 70.26 Nauck; little else is known of him.

17. See e.g. Cicero, *On Ends* Book 5 on the ethics of Antiochus of Ascalon.

18. Eusebius, *Church History* 6.19,8, naming Numenius, Cronius, Apollophanes, Longinus, Moderatus, Nicomachus and other Pythagoreans. Most authors in this catalogue fall under the last description; Apollophanes is little more than a name to us; the intrusion of Longinus, Origen's junior by about twenty years, is a riddle not solved in Origen's extant works.

19. Seneca, *Letters* 33.4; Epictetus, *Discourses* 1.4.9; Snyder (2000), 14-44. The other founders of Stoicism were Zeno and Cleanthes.

20. Sedley (1989). The most famous Roman expositors are Lucretius and Diogenes of Oenoanda.

21. See Julian's admonitions to uneducated Cynics, *Orations* 6 and 7.

22. Cf. Porphyry, *Life of Plotinus* 24. Against those who would relegate the exoteric writing to a phase of callow Platonism in Aristotle's career, see Gerson (2005), 47-75.

23. Diogenes Laertius 3.56-61; Tarrant (1993), 17-30.

24. Tarrant (1993), 58-71.

25. Albinus, *Isagoge*, p. 150 Hermann.

26. Simplicius, *Commentary on Physics* 453.25-455.14.

27. *Metaphysics* 1036a9, 1037a4, 1045a34-6. On the notion of matter and its relation to space see the discussion of the *Timaeus* in Chapter 3.

28. Aristotle, *Metaphysics* 1028b, 1072b; cf. Iamblichus, *Theology of Arithmetic*, p. 61 Ast and Lang (1965), 53-6 and 68.

29. Dillon (2003), 107-23; Theophrastus (*Metaphysics* 6b) attributes to Xenocrates the view that mathematicals hold the intermediate place between intelligibles and sensibles.

30. Aristotle, *On the Soul* 404b27-8. Dillon (2003), 121-2 explains that number is a composite of the one and the Dyad, to which Sameness and Otherness must be added to produce the mobile principle called soul.

31. See Kingsley (1995), 187-204.

32. Dillon (1977), 352-60; Porphyry, *Life of Pythagoras*, p. 50.12 Nauck.

33. Dodds (1928).

34. Gerson (2005), 278 suggests that he would have separated the Form but not the nature of the Form; Crombie (1963), 319-25 is one of a number who argue that Plato's theory need not entail the separability of the Forms.

35. See *On the Soul* 429-30; for the simile of the sun, assimilating *On the Soul* 430a15 to *Republic* 508b-c, see Themistius, *Paraphrase* p. 103 at Schroeder and Todd (1990), 104.

36. *Metaphysics* 1074b-1075a. See Kahn (1992), 374 for the argument that the Forms constitute the mind which is the object of its own thought.

37. See Armstrong (1960), 406-14. On Platonic theories that the Forms are thoughts in the mind of god see Rich (1954); the fountainhead is *Republic* 597c.

38. Cf. Alexander of Aphrodisias, *On Fate*.

39. See Eusebius, *Gospel Preparation* 815d.

40. Ibid. 798c-801a.

41. Ibid. 801b-804a.

42. Ibid. 794c-798b.

43. Ibid. 808d-811a.

44. Ibid. 804b-806b.

45. *On the Generation of the Soul in Plato's Timaeus* 1114d-e.

46. See further Hijmans (1987).

47. In deference to Whittaker (1987).

48. Origen, *Against Celsus* 6.23-6.

49. *Enneads* 2.9.6; Porphyry, *Life of Plotinus* 16.

50. *On the Soul*, p. 357 Wachsmuth.

51. Origen, *Against Celsus* 6.23ff.

52. Eunapius, *Lives of the Sophists*, p. 455 34-5 Boissonade.

53. Eusebius, *Gospel Preparation* 1.9-10; Baumgarten (1981).

54. Murray (1935), xiii.

55. *Timaeus* 22c; *First Alcibiades* 121-2.

56. Porphyry, *Life of Plotinus* 17.1 and 20-1. The four canonical Platonists whom Longinus pronounces inferior to Plotinus are Thrasyllus, Cronius, Numenius and Moderatus.

57. At *Life of Plotinus* Porphyry records that, after collating the works of Numenius, Amelius took up residence in Apamea. On Porphyry and Numenius see Proclus, *Commentary on Timaeus* I, 77.21-3 Diehl (Numenius Fr. 37.24-6 Des Places).

58. Eusebius, *Gospel Preparation* 411c (Numenius, Fr. 1.7-8 Des Places).

59. Clement of Alexandria, *Stromateis* I.150.4 (p. 93.11 Staehlin); Eusebius, *Gospel Preparation* 527a, but with a hint of doubt; Numenius, Fr. 8.13 Des Places.

60. Porphyry, *Cave of the Nymphs* p. 63 Nauck; Numenius, Fr. 30.3-6 Des Places.

61. See Whittaker (1967) on Numenius Fr. 13.4 Des Places (Eusebius, *Gospel Preparation* 538b); Edwards (1989). See Lydus, *On the Months* 4.53 (Fr. 56 Des Places) on the inscrutability of the Jewish God.

62. Eusebius, *Gospel Preparation* 412a; Origen, *Against Celsus* 4.51; Frs 9 and 100 Des Places; Fr. 1a9 Des Places.

63. Frs 24-8, cited above.

64. Eusebius, *Gospel Preparation* 544a-b (Fr. 16 Des Places).

65. Ibid. 536d0537e (Fr. 11 Des Places).

66. Proclus, *Commentary on Timaeus* I, 303.27-304.7 Diehl (Fr. 21 Des Places).

67. Frs 30-37 Des Places; see Pépin (1967), 243-8.

68. Dillon (1977), 362.

2. Four Philosophers

1. *Enneads* 1.6.8; *Life of Plotinus* 1.1.

2. O'Meara (2003), 40-4.

3. Iamblichus, *On the Pythagorean Life* 108, 129-30, 258; O'Meara (1993).

4. *Augustan History, Alexander Severus* 29.2.

5. Olmstead (1942); on Philip as the murderer see *Augustan History, Gordian* 29 and *Sibylline Oracles* 13.20.

6. On the content and purpose of this see Rives (1999).

7. Porphyry, *Life of Plotinus* 2.7.

8. Once a scholarly truism, but contested now by Swain in his introduction to Swain and Edwards (2004), 2ff.

9. Rostovtzeff (1926), ch. 11.

10. Philostratus, *Life of Apollonius* 8.28; cf. Marinus, *Life of Proclus* 17.

11. *Lives of the Sophists* 456.3 Boissonade.

12. Said to have been the teacher of Porphyry by Athanasius Syrus (Testimonium 29 Smith), who may have taken him for the Christian of that name. Weiske (1809), lxxxiv-lxxvii makes him the tutor of Longinus.

13. *Life of Plotinus* 3.32. For the title of this second work cf. Plato, *Philebus* 79d and Weiske (1809), lxxvii. My argument for a date after 263 is ignored by Böhm (2002).

14. Eusebius, *Church History* 6.19.8; Porphyry, *Plotinus* 20.49-52; Philostratus, *Lives of the Sophists*. See further Edwards (1993a).

15. Kalligas (2001) surmises that the remnants of his library furnished Eusebius with the excerpts from Plotinus in his *Gospel Preparation*.

16. *Augustan History, Aurelian* 30.2-3; Zosimus, *New History* 1.56.

17. *Life of Plotinus* 17.11, 20.103, 20.15, 14.18-19.

18. Porphyry, *Life of Plotinus* 20.1-2.

19. See Chapter 6 below.

20. Porphyry, *Life of Plotinus* 3.46-8; Brisson (1987).

21. Eunapius, *Lives of the Sophists* 455.34-5 Boissonade. On Lyco and Lycopolis see Zucker (1950); on the credibility of Eunapius see Edwards (1988).

22. Theodoret, *Remedies for all Ills* 6.61.

23. See Dörrie (1955); Edwards (1993), and on the other side Langerbeck (1957).

24. *Life of Plotinus* 3.15-24; Edwards (1994).

25. *Contra* Harder (1960).

26. Praechter (1916). If he was indeed the teacher of Apuleius and Alcinous, the Neoplatonists knew nothing of him and little of his pupils.

27. Lydus, *On the Months* 4.80 (Fr. 57 Des Places). I suspect that Lydus is in fact quoting an apocryphal work ascribed to a Jewish Numenius, whose visit to Rome *c.* 133 BC (Maccabees 1.14.16ff; Josephus, *Antiquities* 13.5.8) is said to have won both privilege and honour for his people.

28. *Life of Plotinus* 1; cf. Edwards (1993b).

29. My interpretation of *Life of Plotinus* 26.33.

30. See Edwards (1990) for discussion and bibliography.

31 *On Abstinence* 1.1; see Chapter 5.

32. Henry (1934), 26-9.

33. Keaveney and Madden (1982). See further Grmek (1992).

34. Firmicus Maternus, *Mathesis* 1.20-1.

35. *Life of Plotinus* 2.25; cf. Most (2003).

36. On variants in the manuscripts see Henry (1953).

37. Eunapius, *Lives of the Sophists* 456.24-36. On the numerous discrepancies between Eunapius and Porphyry, see Goulet (1982).

38. Cumont (1919), interweaves Macrobius, *Commentary on the Dream of Scipio* 1.13.9-10 with *Enneads* 1.9.

39. Eunapius, *Sophists*, 456.44-8 Boissonade.

40. Bidez (1913), 103-10. Cf. Barnes (2003), x: 'Porphyry was never the head of a philosophical school'.

41. *On Abstinence* 1.1; see Chapter 5.

42. *Life of Plotinus* 7.31 and 20.16, though we cannot say whether both passages refer to the same Marcellus.

43. Socrates, *Church History* 3.23.37 (Testimonium 9 Smith). On Marcella as Jewess see Test. 10.6.

44. Chadwick (1959), 142.

45. Barnes (1973). The *Suda* speaks of fifteen logoi against the Christians, and while these may not have constituted a single work, they must have amounted to something more than the three books *On the Philosophy from Oracles* which Beatrice (1991) inaccurately declares to have been the only polemic answered in Christian sources. See Edwards (2007).

46. Lactantius, *Divine Institutes* 5.1. For bibliography, see Edwards (2007). Lactantius seals his polemic with a string of jibes in which I can detect only a frigid parody of his enemy's claims to enlightenment, and not, as Barnes surmises, an allusion to physical blindness.

47. Bidez (1913), 5-36. On p. 33 Bidez notes that Longinus had written a treatise entitled 'Whether Homer was a Philosopher', but this does not suffice to prove that Porphyry's animadversions on the poet were composed under his supervision.

48. See Chapter 5.

49. O'Meara (1959).

50. On the ascription to Iamblichus, which is assumed throughout this book, see Saffrey (1971), and Dillon (1973), 312, comparing *On the Mysteries* 8.3 with Fr. 38 on the *Timaeus*.

51. *Lives of the Sophists*, p. 457 Boissonade. On Anatolius see also Eusebius, *Church History* 7.32.21 with Dillon (1973), 8-9.

52. Dillon (1973), 10. On Iamblichus as a pupil of Porphyry see also Testimonia 6 and 33c Smith (from David on the *Isagoge* and a Greek theosophy).

53. Lactantius, *Divine Institutes* 5.1; Simmons (1995), Digeser (2000).

54. *Sophists* 459; Dillon (1973), 11 conjectures that he broke with Porphyry before the latter's death *c*. 305.

55. Dillon (1973), 12, citing Bidez (1919), 32ff and Libanius, *Letters* 1389.

56. *Chronographia* 12.312.11-12, quoted by Dillon (1973), 12-13, with the observation that Malalas confounds Galerius with the western usurper Maxentius.

57. Bidez (1919), 32 on the grounds that he is said to have been dead when his pupil Sopater decamped to Constantinople shortly after the execution of Crispus and Fausta in 326/7. But can we put such faith in the exactitude of Sozomen, *Church History* 1.5.1?

58. Dillon (1973), 7. Cameron (1968), tenuously identifying Iamblichus with the (future) father-in-law of Amphicleia, a woman old enough to have been a pupil of Plotinus, proposes a date of 245 for his birth. If he is not a chance namesake, why should not this Iamblichus (Porphyry, *Life of Plotinus* 9) have been the grandfather of the philosopher?

59. *Sophists* 460-1 Boissonade.

60. Testimonium 1.76 Smith.

61. Eunapius, *Sophists* 458.30-40.

62. Dillon (1973), 15, 21.

63. Dillon (1973), 15, 22.

64. O'Meara (1989).

65. Dillon (1973), 23.

66. Since one cannot write about Greek philosophy without using the word protreptic as a synonym for 'hortatory', most scholars leave this title untranslated.

67. Proem 8, 13 and 17 at 37.8, 37.27 and 38.16 Des Places.

68. Proem 6 at 37.1 Des Places.

69. Proem 21 at 39.4 Des Places. Cf. 131.16-151.11 Des Places.

70. 81.9-12 Des Places; cf. Aristotle, *On the Heavens* 271a33.

71. 115.22-7 Des Places, with the Aristotelian premiss that *eudaimonia* or happiness is the end of life.

72. 75.16-19 Des Places; cf. *Nicomachean Ethics* 1174a1.

73. 73.9-19 Des Places.

74. 81.15-20, though Des Places observes a parallel at Aristotle, *Eudemian Ethics* 1216a11-15.

75. 43.17-48.19 Des Places.

76. 48.10 Des Places; cf. Plato, *Theaetetus* 176c.

3. Platonists on Plato

1. See e.g. Reale (1997).

2. See e.g. Krämer (1990), 53-64 on the unwritten doctrines; Krämer (1968), 115-24 and Reale (1997) 62-9 on the *Seventh Letter*.

3. The thesis of Cherniss (1944) and (1945). On the other side see De Vogel (1969), 256-92.

4. Cf. Syrianus, *Commentary on Metaphysics* 105.25-30 Kroll on the coexistence of ideas and intellect in the exegesis of Longinus.

5. See *On the Soul* 429b-431a etc., with Schroeder and Todd (1990).

6. Rich (1954).

7. See Rist (1962) etc.

8. See *Metaphysics* 1075 against the notion of an external creator; *Physics* 251b and *On the Heavens* 280b-282b against the temporal origin of the universe; Cherniss (1944), 417-31 against the literal interpretation of the *Timaeus*.

9. See especially Frs 11 and 22 Des Places.

10. On Calvisius (or Calvenus) Taurus, a polymath of the early second century, see Philoponus, *On the Eternity of the World*, p. 145 Rabe and Dillon (1977), 242-3. Compositeness, contingency, mutability and affinity with the things that emerge in time are all characteristics of the *genêton* in this discussion.

11. See especially Plutarch, *On Isis and Osiris* 372e; *On the Generation of Soul* 1026e-f.

12. De Vogel (1969), 226-35.

13. Proclus, *Commentary on Timaeus* I, 307.1; 322.1-12.

14. Proclus, *Commentary on Timaeus* III, 103.18ff Diehl; Corrigan (1987), 978-84. See also Chapter 7 on the intelligible triad.

15. Charrue (1978), 127-33 observes that Plotinus draws his metaphors from nature rather than from the workshop.

16. *Enneads* 3.8.2-7; Deck (1967), 69 and 72, concludes that nature possesses its object in 'immobile contemplation', whereas the higher soul aspires to what it cannot possess as soul.

17. *Enneads* 2.3.17; 4.3.10; 4.4.12 etc.

18. See n. 12 above.

19. *Enneads* 1.1.4; Atkinson (1983), 4-6. For soul as *nous* in a state of *tolma* see *Enneads* 1.8.9.18.

20. *Enneads* 4.3.17.21ff; 4.8.2.42-4; 1.8.4.7; Rist (1967), 124-9.

21. Alt (1993), 236 remarks that the soul is never daemonic for him, as for Plutarch.

22. *Enneads* 1.8.14. 51-2; O'Brien (1981). For refinement of this position, which O'Brien does not endorse, see Corrigan (1985).

23. *Timaeus* 52b2 at *Enneads* 2.4.11.

24. *Enneads* 2.8.14, opposing Aristotle, *Physics* 192a3-4. See Rist (1961), 167.

25. Proclus, *Commentary on Timaeus* I, 109.25-6 Diehl; also I, 119.16-23.

26. Ibid. 63.25-64.11. Origen, here as elsewhere, appears to have sided with Longinus against the strict philosophers of the Plotinian school; perhaps it was as a pupil of Longinus that Porphyry overheard his strident defence of Homer (ibid. 63.29-64.3) Cf. ibid. 66.29-32.

27. Ibid. I, 277.10-14, in company with Plotinus and Iamblichus.

28. Simplicius, *Commentary on Physics* 454 (Fr. 174 Smith).

29. Damascius, *Commentary on Philebus* 10.1-9 (Fr. 173 Smith).

30. Simplicius, *Commentary on Physics* 135.1-14 (Fr. 134.24-35 Smith).

31. Fr. 236.33-4 Smith (Simplicius, *Commentary on Physics* 231).

32. See Dillon (1973), 15, with the anonymous *Prolegomena* 26.

33. Proclus, *Commentary on Timaeus* I, 152.28 Diehl (Fr. 16 Dillon). At Fr. 10 (ibid. I, 93.15) he explains that Solon employed a poetic figure because 'all the works of nature come into being through imitation'.

34. Dillon (1973), 33; *Timaeus Commentary* Fr. 47.

35. Olympiodorus, *Commentary on First Alcibiades* 110.13 (Fr. 8 Dillon).

36. Proclus, *Commentary on Timaeus* II, 36.24ff Diehl (Fr. 48 Dillon).

37. Ibid. II, 240.4ff (Fr. 54 Dillon).

38. As the distinction, explained on p. 57, between the noetic and the noeric will make clear, the word 'intelligible' is merely a conventional equivalent for 'noetic', and is not to be understood in any of its usual senses.

39. See Dillon (1973), 35.

40. Fr. 16 above, but also Fr. 34.2 (Proclus, *Commentary on Timaeus* I, 307.14 Diehl).

41. Simplicius, *Commentary on Physics* I, 702.20ff (Fr. 62 Dillon).

42. Ibid. 793.23 (Fr. 63 Dillon).

43. Sorabji (1983), 37-41; Simplicius, *Commentary on Physics* 793.3-7; *Commentary on Categories* 354.9-26.

44. Ibid. 794.26ff (Fr. 68 Dillon).

45. Proclus, *Commentary on Timaeus* II, 45.5ff Diehl (Fr. 65 Dillon).

46. Ibid. I, 307.14ff (Fr. 34 Dillon).

47. Ibid. I, 431.23 (Fr. 44 Dillon).

48. Ibid. I, 426.3-4 (Fr. 43 Dillon).

49. Fr. 43.23-9.

50. Proclus, *Commentary on Timaeus* I, 72.6 (Fr. 49 Dillon).

51. Ibid. I, 399.28f (Fr. 40 Dillon).

52. Fr. 43.16-17.

53. Proclus, *Commentary on Timaeus* I, 87.6 Diehl (Fr. 9 Dillon).

54. Stobaeus, 372-3 Wachsmuth.

55. Proclus, *Commentary on Timaeus* I, 386.8 (Fr. 38 Dillon), with Dillon (1973), .313.

56. Damascius, *Commentary on Philebus* 115 West (Fr. 7 Dillon), with Proclus, *Platonic Theology* 143.45ff and Dillon (1973), 262-3.

57. Damascius, *Commentary on Philebus* 5 West (Fr. 1 Dillon).

58. See Dillon (1973), 262.

4. Logic, Number and the One

1. *Sophist* 218d-236b; *Statesman* 274b-292a; cf. *Phaedrus* 264e-266b.

2. *Metaphysics* 1028b-1029. The meaning of the terms is much contested, and an investigation of them lies outside the scope of the present work.

3. Graham (1987); Gerson (2005), 99-100 suggests that the illusion of two systems arises only because *On Interpretation* 23a, which seems to espouse a 'Platonic' notion of substance, is extruded from modern readings of Aristotle's works on logic.

4. E.g. *On the Soul* 429a23-b4 – though it follows from this that there must be some mode or plane of mind, the active reason, which does not coalesce with any external form.

5. Gerson (2005), 14-16.

6. See 238T and 240T in Smith's edition of the fragments: the first title, from Elias, is *On the Discrepancies between Plato and Aristotle*, while the second, from the *Suda*, is *That the Philosophies of Plato and Aristotle are One*. See further Hadot (1990).

7. *Isagoge* 6.5; Simplicius, *Commentary on Physics* 92.26-8; Barnes (2003), 115-24.

8. See Barnes (2003), 138-40 on 6.22 and 7.25.

9. Dillon (1977), 12-18.

10. Charrue (1978), 59-115.

11. Simplicius, citing Porphyry, *On Matter* (Fr. 236 Smith), in *Commentary on Physics* 230.36-231.7. See Chapter 1 and Tarrant (1993), 150-61.

12. Dodds (1928).

13. Cf. *Enneads* 5.5.12 and 1.6.9.

14. *Enneads* 6.9.6.10.

15. Rist (1962).

16. Cf. 6.9.8.8: that which is conjoined with it is *theos*.

17. Cf. 6.9.5.40: we call it One in order to communicate.

18. Maier (1992), 27-57.

19. Longinus makes no mention of it at *Life of Plotinus* 20.41.

20. See Maier (n. 17) for a summary and critique of these positions.

21. As it does in Gerson (1994), 15.

22. See Chapter 9 on *Enneads* 6.8. Thinking, of a different kind than that of *nous*, is attributed to the One at *Enneads* 5.4.2.19-20. Lloyd (1987), 162 terms this an 'indefinite thinking', doomed to fail in its attempt to grasp the One. The first determinate product of this thinking is existence, which may be characterised, with Lloyd, both as the 'internal *energeia*' of the contemplative intellect, and as the 'external *energeia*' of the One. On the 'second entelechy' which was regarded by Aristotelians as the invariable concomitant of being-in-act, see Rutter (1956).

23. Beierwaltes (1999).

24. See the remarks of Gerson (1994), 27 and Schrodeder (1996), 242-9.

25. Armstrong (1936), 28.

26. Cf. Lloyd (1987), 167 on the Stoic understanding of solar emissions.

27. *Enneads* 6.9.2.8-10 with Maier (1992), 109-12.

28. 1053-5 with notes of Dillon (1987), 412.

29. I should add to my caveat in Chapter 3 that the term 'intellectual' is not used here, any more than the complementary term 'intelligible', in its normal English sense.

30. Hermeias, *Commentary on Phaedrus* 150.24 (Fr. 6 Dillon); Shaw (1995), 108-9, 118-21.

31. *On the Soul*, at Stobaeus I, 264; *Common Science* 40.12-41 and 41.24-42 Festa; Shaw (1995), 191-4.

32. Proclus, *Commentary on Timaeus* II, 277.26ff (Fr. 57 Dillon), though in his note, p. 388, Dillon opines that the true offender is Theodorus of Asine.

33. See Dillon's edition (1973), 29-34.

34. 15.6-14 and 18.1-13 Festa. See Dillon (1984) in support of Merlan's theory that chapter 4 of the *Common Science* was taken bodily from Speusippus.

35. *Common Science*, 16.10 Festa.

36. *Parmenides* Fr. 2A6 Dillon from Damascius, *Problems and Solutions* I.151.

5. The Pilgrim Soul

1. Cf. Plato, *Phaedo* 88d-95b.

2. See *Phaedrus* 245c-e; *Timaeus* 35a-37c.

3. *Meno* 81a-d, where the knowledge seems to be acquired empirically and contingently in a life before the present one.

4. At *Phaedrus* 247a-c every soul is said to have imbibed the knowledge of at least one virtue, with a concomitant yearning for the unseen Good, in the place above the heavens which it inhabits before embodiment.

5. Beauty is the spur to recollection of the supercelestial forms at *Phaedrus* 250b-252b.

6. *Enneads* 4.8.2.19-24; cf. 3.9.3.

7. *Enneads* 5.1.1; 5.2.2.1-7. Dodds (1965) opines that Plotinus renounced this notion after his conflict with the Gnostics, and began to maintain the necessity of the soul's descent in such passages as *Enneads* 4.3.13.7-12. But cf. Atkinson (1981), 5-6.

8. See 4.8.7.9-10 with Rist (1967), 123-9.

9. *Enneads* 4.8.3.21-2: it is the function of the rational soul to think, but not only to think. On the coincidence of the voluntary and the involuntary see 4.8.5.1-4.

10. *Enneads* 4.8.2.15; cf. 2.9.21-2 on the absence of audacity in the creations of the World-Soul.

11. *Enneads* 4.1.1.11; 3.4.3.24.

12. See Fr. 87.15-22 Dillon on *Timaeus* (Proclus, *Commentary on Timaeus* 3, 334.7-15 Diehl): if the will chooses badly, the entire soul sins, and if the ruling faculty is glad, the whole is glad.

13. *On the Soul*, pp. 375-80 Wachsmuth; Finamore (1985), 91-114.

14. *Against the Nations* 2.11-52, with Courcelle (1953).

15. Irenaeus, *Against Heresies* 4.39.1; Edwards (2002), 102-7.

16. See Alt (1993), 147-53 with Alcinous, *Didascalicus* 25, where the soul is said to have a natural yearning for the body.

17. For the person as *sunamphoteron*, a union of two, see Corrigan (1985).

18. See *Enneads* 6.4.14 on the loss of identity in descent. At *Enneads* 5.3.4 we are properly the intellect, though not (at least yet) identical with it; the 'we' is rather the highest function of the soul.

19. Gerson (1994), 141.

20. Rist (1963); Blumenthal (1996), Kalligas (1997), O'Meara (1999).

21. The allusion to particulars may be juxtaposed with *Enneads* 5.7 by those who wish, like Langerbeck (1957), to reconstruct the teaching of Ammonius Saccas from anomalous tenets held in common by Plotinus and the Christian Origen.

22. *Aphorisms* 32, esp. p. 29.8-31.8 Lamberz.

23. Ibid. 28.1 and 29.5; cf. Plotinus, *Enneads* 1.2.6.19.

24. Ibid., p. 27.8. Cf. Plotinus, *Enneads* 4.8.3.13 and 23.

25. *Aphorisms* 32, p. 31.9-35.3 Lamberz.

26. *Enneads* 1.1.12.35-9; Lamberton (1986), 102.

27. *Aphorisms* 29, p. 18.12 Lamberz.

28. *Phaedrus* 246a; cf. Deuse (1983), 213-30 on Porphyry, Finamore (1985), 17-27 on Iamblichus.

29. Porphyry, *Aphorisms* 29, p. 18.14-20.6 Lamberz.

30. Fr. 382 (Stobaeus 1.49.60). Frs 373-80, also drawn from Stobaeus, can be assigned with confidence to this treatise.

31. *City of God* 10.30 at Bidez (1913), appendix 2, *38.12-15; ibid. 13.19 at *41.28-32. See also Smith (1984).

32. *On Abstinence* 1.1 (p. 85.2ff Nauck).

33. Ibid. 1.26 (104.1-12).

34. Ibid. 1.28 (106.10-21).

35. Ibid. 2.47 (175.7-9).

36. Ibid. 1.40-1 (116.11-117.10).

37. Ibid. 1.14 (97.14-15), adding that the pig is spared by a number of other peoples.

38. Ibid. 3.13 (202.5-10), with the observation that in extremities we do not spare one another.

39. Ibid. 3.11 (201.8-14).

40. Ibid. 3.24-5 (219.5-221.20).

41. Ibid. 3.19 (209.5-15); 3.26 (222.7-14). Those who eat flesh are said to be especially prone to inhumanity. The argument that beasts do not form cities is rebutted with an allusion to the Scythians at 3.15 (204.17-20).

42. Ibid. 3.16 (205.17) and 3.17 (206.5-10).

43. If they eat them it is because passion overcomes reason, as in humans, and as in humans, such defeats are not irresistible: ibid. 3.14 (203.6-11).

44. Ibid. 3.20 (210.23-211.7)

45. *On the Intelligence of Animals* 2-5 (pp. 959-63) is avowedly the source for *On Abstinence* 3.11-24 (211-20 Nauck).

46. Ibid. 2.1-15 (132.18-154.22), citing Theopompus, Theophrastus, Empedocles and others.

47. E.g. at 2.12 (142.1-5).

48. Ibid. 2.36 (165.21-2); 2.58 (183.1). The first passage allows that the daemons may be 'good'.

49. Ibid. 2.51 (177.19).

50. Ibid. 2.58 (182.22-183.20).

51. E.g. at 2.16 (146.5-19); 2.17 (147.3-7); 2.61 (185.1-15) on the offerings of the upright soul.

52. Ibid. 2.11 (141.10-24).

53. Ibid. 2.26 (155.4-8); 2.53-7 (179.3-182.21).

54. Ibid. 4.17-18 (256.1-259.18) on Brahmans and Samanaioi; 4.14 (251.6-24) on the Essenes of Palestine.

55. Fr. 255.21-2 (Stobaeus 3.25.1 from the treatise *On the Powers of the Soul*), citing Aristotle, *Minor Works on Nature* 449b6-8 and 453a4-14.

56. See further Rohde (1871-2).

57. *Life of Pythagoras* 19.23-20.2; Diogenes Laertius 8.3.3.

58. See 23.8 on Zaratas; 38.16-18 on the magi.

59. Burkert (1972), 192-208.

60. O'Meara (1989), 32-40.

61. *Pythagorean Life* 80-2; Burkert (1972), 192-208.

62. Cf. chapter 1, the first of many sneers at Amelius; on Porphyry's self-aggrandisement see Edwards (1993b).

6. Literature and Dogma

1. Chroust (1973), 29-42.

2. Hippolytus, *Refutation* 6.42.2; Proclus, *Commentary on Timaeus* I, 304.4 Diehl (Numenius Fr. 21.6 Des Places).

3. *Art of Rhetoric*, 552.1 Walzer (as cited in Prickard); Aristotle, *Rhetoric* 1355b26-36.

4. *In Tim.* 1,83.15ff (*on Timaeus* 20e/21a); ibid. 94.4 (on 21d).

5. Heath (1999).

6. Walzer (1949), 11; Numenius, Fr. 30.3-6 Des Places.

7. Porphyry found in the Septuagint not only a more exalted notion of God than one could glean from any Greek oracle, but a confirmation, at Genesis 2.7, of his own belief that the embryo is not ensouled at the moment of conception. See *To Gaurus*, 48.18 Kalbfleisch.

8. Philostratus, *Life of Apollonius* 6.19; Porphyry, *Life of Plotinus* 1; Edwards (1993b). See generally Watson (1988), and Chapter 5 above, nn. 35 and 36.

9. Heraclitus, *Allegories* 19.5, 67.2, 73.10.

10. See Chapter 1.

11. For commentary see Brisson (1990) and Chapter 7 below.

12. Maximus, *Discourses* 11.10; Numenius, Fr. 33 Des Places (Porphyry, *Cave of the Nymphs* 79.19-80.2 Nauck).

13. Porphyry, *Plotinus* 22.

14. *Enneads* 1.6.9.31; *Enneads* 1.6.9.13 = *Phaedrus* 252c.

15. *Timaeus* 37d; *Enneads* 5.8.12.

16. Origen, *Against Celsus* 4.45.

17. Cf. *Meno* 80e-81a.

18. *Enneads* 5.8.10.1ff alludes to *Phaedrus* 246-7, and 5.8.13.6-9 to *Theogony* 459 and 478.

19. *Enneads* 5.8.13.6-10; cf. Porphyry, *Cave of the Nymphs* 68.5-7 Nauck, where Cronus suffers the castration.

20. For the locution *sômatopoiein ton logon* (give body to the discourse) in this period cf. Origen, *Against Celsus*, proem 6; Eusebius, *Against Marcellus* 1.1.

21. Fr. 416 Smith, from Syrianus, *Commentary on Hermogenes* II.14, 11-14 Rabe. This appears as Fr. 4 of Porphyry's treatise on rhetoric in Heath (2002). A commentary on the textbook of Minucianus, perhaps the first of its kind, this work included a definition, an anatomy, a history and a defence of the art. On its modest originality, and on the reasons for its obsolescence, see Heath (2003).

22. Proclus, *Commentary on Republic* 1, 59.13 Diehl.

23. This would be p. lx, 30-1 in Prickard's edition, if the pages were numbered.

24. Frs 399, 390.12-21, 397, 400, the first three drawn from the commentary on the *Iliad*, the last from that on the *Odyssey*. All are securely attributed to Porphyry, though Smith is not certain whether 399 and 400 ought to be assigned to the *Homeric Questions*.

25. Fr. 377.50-83, citing Empedocles, Fr. 31 DK.

26. 79.20; cf. 63.11, 71.1 for references to Numenius. Plato's application of the term *eikôn* to his own parable at *Republic* 514a is cited at 62.4-5.

27. *Odyssey* 13.102-12; *Cave of the Nymphs* 60.5-14 and 71.15-16 Nauck.

28. The verb *allêgorein* occurs at 56.8 and 57.20. At 81.1 Porphyry denies that his conjectures are violent (*bebiasmenas*), deprecating the term that Plutarch had used of Stoic exegeses. Porphyry slights the Stoics in his comments on Origen at Eusebius, *Church History* 6.19.8.

29. *Republic* 514a, cited at *Cave* 62.1-3.

30. See 81.9-10, where the poem is the matter or *hupokeimenon* and the treatise the *hermêneia*.

31. 55.18, 58.1, 58.11, 81.6. Cf. 62.22, where *poiein* is used of the fashioning of the cave, with the use of *poiêtês* to designate both the human bard (58.1) and the creator of the universe (60.7).

32. On the possible allusion to his own suicidal melancholy at 80.11f, see Lamberton (1986), 131.

7. Philosophy from Oracles

1. Plato, *Apology* 21a.

2. Plutarch, *On the Decline of the Oracles* and *On the Pythian Oracles*; in Parke and Wormell (1956), the responses from 30 BC to 'the end' – an epoch of some four centuries, almost half the life of the oracle – occupy only pp. 186-228.

3. Whittaker (1969).

4. For the title see Fr. 303.4-5 Smith (Eusebius, *Gospel Preparation* 4.6.2).

5. This would be an arrogant claim for one as young as Porphyry is often supposed to have been when he produced this compilation.

6. Fr. 307.15-18 (Eusebius, *Gospel Preparation* 5. 6.1).

7. Frs 310 (Eusebius, op. cit. 3.14.4); 312-13 (3.14.6-7); 317 (5.12.1); 319 (5.13.3-4); 320 (5.14.2); 311 (5.14.4).

8. Eusebius, op. cit. 5.6.1-2, 5.6.4-5.

9. Frs 308.21-2, 309.8 (Eusebius, op. cit. 5.6.2-5).

10. Frs 314 and 315 (Eusebius, op. cit. 4.8.4-9.7).

11. Fr. 318 (Eusebius, op. cit. 5.13.2)

12. Frs 319 and 320 (Eusebius, op. cit. 5.13.3-4 and 5.14.2).

13. Fr. 308.21-2 (Eusebius, op. cit. 5.7.2).

14. *Theogony* 411-522. On Hecate in the third century see Johnston (1990).

15. Fr. 323.14-15 (Eusebius, op. cit. 9.10.2); 324.7-12 (9.10.4).

16. Collected by Baumgarten (1981).

17. Fr. 324.11-12; cf. Numenius, Fr. 57 Des Places.

18. Fr. 325.15-23, from a theosophic collection.

19. Fr. 326 (Eusebius, *Gospel Preparation* 4.22.15-4.23.1). Cf. Frs 318.3 (Eusebius 5.13.1) and 306.19-21 (Firmicus Maternus, *Errors of Profane Religion* 13.5) for less hostile allusions to Serapis.

20. Fr. 327 (Eusebius, op. cit. 4.23.6).

21. Fr. 329 (Eusebius, op. cit. 4.20.1).

22. Fr. 333 (Eusebius, op. cit. 6.1.2).

23. On *Letter to Marcella* 274.6 Nauck see Chapter 9.

24. Fr. 336 (Eusebius, op. cit. 6.2.1).

25. See Chapter 8.

26. Aelian, *Miscellaneous Knowledge* 4.17.

27. Edwards (2000a), 4-5.

28. Fr. 341 (Eusebius, op. cit. 6.5.2-4).

29. Fr. 342 (Philoponus, *Creation of the World* 201.18-202.16).

30. Frs 347.23 and 349.9 (Eusebius, op. cit. 5.8).

31. *City of God* 7.23 (Fr. 346).

32. *Gospel Preparation* 3.7.1-2 (Fr. 345 Smith).

33. *City of God* 19.23.107 (Fr. 346.1-2); cf. 19.23.43-73 (Fr. 345a).

34. *City of God* 19.22.17 (Fr. 343.8-14).

35. Testimonium 2 Smith (pp. 6-7 of his edition); Frs 283-302 Smith and appendix 2 Bidez.

36. See following chapter for detailed exposition.

37. See *City of God* 10.30.6-7 (Fr. 30.6-7 Smith) and 13.19. 40-1 (Fr. 300 Smith), with Deuse (1983), 130-1.

38. O'Meara (1959).

39. *City of God* 10.23.10-19 (Fr. 284.10-19 Smith).

40. *City of God* 10.29.1-3 (Fr. 284a Smith).

41. *On Abstinence* 4.17-18, pp. 256.1-259.18 Nauck.

42. Lucian, *Runaways* 1.

43. Saffrey (1981).

44. *Enneads* 1.9.1.1: 'You shall not drive it out, that it may not go out' is reminiscent of Fr. 166 Saffrey (Michael Psellus, *Patrologia Graeca* 122, 1125d1-2): 'You shall not drive out [the soul], that it may not depart bearing some [evil]'. This seems to be a prohibition of suicide.

45. Numenius, Fr. 14 Des Places; *Oracles* Fr. 7 Des Places (Psellus, *PG* 122, 1140c10-11).

46. Dodds (1960), 6.

47. Dillon (1977), 362.

48. Lewy (1956), 1-60 maintains that his debts to the Oracles exceed what is declared or can be securely demonstrated. Cf. Hadot (1967).

49. For what remains of Proclus see pp. 202-12 in the edition of Des Places (1971); on Iamblichus see pp. 24-9 and Cremer (1969).

50. *Exposition of the Chaldaean Oracles, Patrologia Graeca* 122, 124a-1153b, at Des Places, pp. 162-95.

51. The flaming sword of Genesis 3.24 appears at 1137c9 – an indication, perhaps, that Porphyry's oracle which coupled the Chaldaeans with the Hebrews is from this collection. The term *autogenethlos* (self-begotten) also recurs at Fr. 39.1 Des Places (Proclus, *Commentary on Timaeus* 2, 54.10 Diehl).

52. 1132c1-11; cf. Hirschle (1979) and Iamblichus in next chapter. Psellus adds that Hebrew names possess an ineffable power in incantations; cf. Origen, *Against Celsus* 6.32 and 1.24.

53. 1144b6-11; 1148d1-1149a5; on the noeric actions which engage the highest capacities of the soul see 1145a10, 1145d2, 1148b8.

54. 1144a14-b5, commenting on the 'rapture' or concealment of the father's fire within his noeric power.

55. 1148a12-b13, where Psellus avers that we are icons of noeric essences, images of incognoscible ciphers.

56. 1145c9-d6; 1148b14-c14.

57. Except by Psellus at 1140c12.

58. Cf. the depth or *bathos* of soul at 1137c5, the appeal to the depth or *bathos* of the intellect by the Gnostics at Porphyry, *Plotinus* 16.3, and the Valentinian representation of the ineffable father as an abyss or *buthos* at Irenaeus, *Against Heresies* 1.1-2. The Valentinian teaching that the fullness or *plêrôma* of the Godhead is circumscribed and therefore rendered comprehensible by a *horos* or limit finds parallels at 1145b11 and 1144b5 (although the language in both cases is that of Psellus).

59. See the edition of Des Places (1971), pp. 189-91.

60. E.g. at *Enneads* 4.8.3.13 and 23.

61. Proclus, *Elements of Theology* 101.

62. *Philebus Commentary* Fr. 4 (Damascius, *Commentary on Philebus* 105.49-51 Westerink, with Dillon (1973), 260.

63. *Sophist* 248e-149a; Hadot (1960). See e.g. *Enneads* 6.6.8.

64. Damascius, *First Principles* 1.86.3-15 (Fr. 367.9 Smith). It is not clear to me that such a thesis belies the ineffability of the first cause, as Dmascius seems to hint by his comparison with Iamblichus.

65. Proclus, *Commentary on Timaeus* 3, 64.8ff. On the eccentricity of Theodorus, and his debt to 'Chaldaean' teachings, see Dillon (1973a).

66. Kroll (1892); cf. Edwards (1990b).

67. Bechtle (2000); Hadot (1967), supported by Majercik (2005), 278 and now, I believe, by Dillon.

68. Fr. 21 Des Places on *Timaeus* 39e. Cf. Amelius at Proclus, *Commentary on Timaeus* 3, 103.18ff.

69. Zambon, 35-41.

70. For fuller discussion see Majercik (1992).

71. *Life of Plotinus* 22.1-4, citing Hesiod, *Theogony* 35.

72. Plato, *Apology* 21a; Herodotus 1.47.

73. Parke and Wormell (1956), 193 urge that Porphyry was too learned to have been duped by a spurious oracle, but fail to draw the most natural conclusion.

74. Edwards (2000b).

75. Edwards (1990d).

76. It is not clear whether Porphyry means to indicate that he is now in his sixty-eighth year: see Igal (1972), 212.

8. Magic and Occult Sciences

1. Oral communication, quoted in Murray (1935), xiii.

2. Tester (1987), 49.

3. See below on *Plotinus* 10.

4. *Meno* 80a; *Phaedrus* 271c-d; *Protagoras* 329d; *Republic* 336c; *Symposium* 203d.

5. *Laws* 898c-899d; *Timaeus* 35b-37d and 43c-d.

6. Nilsson (1926), 264-5.

7. Tester (1987), 12.

8. Gleadow (1968), 206.

9. Tester (1987), 25-6.

10. Tester (1987), 23.

11. Cumont (1912), 5 and 34, though priority in the calculation of lunar cycles is here accorded to the Babylonians.

12. On these figures see Festugière (1944), 102-7.

13. *Poimandres* 24-7, as below.

14. Fr. 35.26-31 Des Places (Proclus, *Commentary on Republic*, II, 130 Kroll); Fr. 32.61-2 (Porphyry, *Cave of Nymphs* 75.16-76.1 Nauck).

15. Eusebius, *Gospel Preparation* 1.9.24.

16. Fowden (1986), 87-9.

17. Scott (1936), 103-53; on his relation to the Gnostics see Edwards (1990a).

18. Plato, *Symposium* 190c7-8.

19. Merlan (1944); cf. Armstrong (1955-6).

20. *Plotinus* 10.20. The rite included an abortive sacrifice of chickens, on which see Eitrem (1942).

21. *Aphorisms* 32, p. 31.8 Lamberz.

22. Augustine, *City of God* 10.29; see Bidez (1913), appendix 2, *38.3. A commentary on the [oracles] of Julian the Chaldaean is also attested in the *Suda*.

23. *City of God* 10.9 (*27.19-20 Bidez).

24. *City of God* 10.23 (*36.5-14).

25. Ibid. 10.29 (*37.11-21). Cf. *35.12-15 (ibid. 10.27).

26. See ibid. 10.26 (*33.9-13) on the different orders.

27. Ibid. 10.9 (*29.16-21).

28. Ibid. 10.32 (*42.6-*43.22), alluding to the Indians and Chaldaeans (*42.19-20) as at *Plotinus* 3.

29. For text and commentary see Scott (1936), 28-102.

30. As Clarke, Dillon and Hershbell (2003), xlvi observe, the division into books is a convenience of renaissance scholarship, as are the chapter divisions and the conventional pagination.

31. Eusebius, *Gospel Preparation* 3.7.1 (Fr. 351 Smith). The fragments also appear as an appendix to Bidez (1913).

32. See especially the allusion to *eidôlopoiia* (image-making) at p. 95.1.

33. A *dunamis phantastikê* at 3.22.

34. *Meno* 81c; Origen, *Against Celsus* 4.40.

35. Though Watson (1988), 105-6 concludes that a 'discriminatory power' is attributed to this faculty at *On Ptolemy's Harmonics* 13.15-14.3 Düring. At Fr. 78.69-75 Smith (from Boethius, *Commentary on Aristotle's* On Interpretation 2.28), *phantasia* is defined as an interweaving of truth and falsehood in cognition.

36. Watson (1988), 107-9; cf. *On the Styx*, Frs 372-3 Smith. Thought without *phantasia* is impossible for embodied beings (Fr. 78.75), but even at its most plausible it sometimes makes a puppet of the soul (Fr. 269.10, from Stobaeus 2, 167.16-17).

37. Bidez (1913), 77.

38. Maximus of Tyre, *Discourses* 2; Dio Chrysostom, *Oration* 12.

39. See Frs 359.55 on Cerberus, 360.57 on the Egyptian Typhon, 360.95 on Apis, though the majority of the figures that he interprets are anthropomorphic. He ignores, for example, the horns of Zeus at Fr. 354.23.

40. *Hermetica* 16.2; Copenhaver (1992), 201-3.

41. *Cratylus* 391e-392a; cf. Hirschle (1979).

42. Otherwise Khnum: Gwyn Griffiths (1996), 81-2 see ibid. 105 on the substitution of Khnum for Osiris.

43. See Gwyn Griffiths (1996), 80 for a triad including Ptah and Osiris; 103-4 and 108 for triads including Ptah and Amun. The Leiden Hymn to Amun declares that all gods can be subsumed under the one who is Re in aspect and Ptah in body but conceals his name as Amun: ibid., 89.

44. Copenhaver (1992), 117-19; Gwyn Griffiths (1996), 88 notes that Hermopolis is the original seat of Amun. Fowden (1986), 138 suggests that Iamblichus will have derived his information not directly from native sources but from Greek intermediaries, such as the 'books of Hermes' known to Plutarch (*Isis and Osiris* 61).

45. Eusebius, *Gospel Preparation* 3.11.45 (Fr. 360.3-12).

46. Frs 251-4 Smith (Stobaeus 1.24-6). See especially Fr. 253.110-22: the soul is partible only in its relation to the body, not in itself.

47. *Abstinence* 116.11-118.21, rebutting the inference that the higher soul is not defiled by the vices of the lower.

48. Fr. 52.64-75 (Chalcidius, *Commentary on Timaeus* 297); Fr. 44 (Stobaeus 1.49.25 = Porphyry, Fr. 253.18-21 Smith).

49. *On the Soul* 408a29; cf. 430a23.

50. See Apuleius, *On the God of Socrates*; Plutarch, *On the Sign of Socrates*.

9. Platonists and Christians

1. See his comment on the defection of Origen's tutor to a more lawful way of life at Eusebius, *Church History* 6.19.8.

2. See *Soliloquies, Confessions* 7 and Edwards (1999).

3. Pico della Mirandola, *De Gloria Hominis*; Hankins (1990).

4. Cudworth (1820), 77-146.

5. Inge (1911-12).

6. Gelasius of Cyzicus, *Church History* 2.36 and *Theodosian Code* 16.5.66; Marinus, *Proclus* 36.1.

7. Beatrice (1991); cf. Edwards (2007).

8. Barnes (1973); Simmons (1995), 216-303; Digeser (2000), 91-104; Edwards (2004).

9. Rist (1962), 180 maintains that in the *Enneads* the divinity of the One entails the divinity of the world; to Augustine (*Confessions* 10.6) it is equally apparent that the work a divine creator is not itself divine.

10. Origen, *Commentary on John* 2.2; Rist (1962), 178 concludes that the One is *ho theos* on fifteen occasions, *theos* on eleven.

11. *Enneads* 6.9.9.18; *Life of Plotinus* 10.35.

12. Eusebius, *Church History* 6.19.8; Origen, *Commentary on John* 2.10.

13. Origen, *On Prayer* 15.1.

14. Eusebius quotes a paraphrase of the Prologue to the Gospel of John by Amelius at *Gospel Preparation* 11.19. On his assimilation of the Trinity to the Platonic triad see Strutwolf (1999), 129-47.

15. Atkinson (1983), 55-8.

16. Kelly (1972), 215-16 and 242-54.

17. Eusebius, *Against Marcellus* 4.25 Klostermann; but cf. 133.13.

18. *Enneads* 6.8.3.6 and 6.8.15.1ff with Leroux (1990), 255 and 344. Against his view that Plotinus advances from apophatic to positive theology in this treatise, see O'Meara (1992).

19. See Nygren (1932), I, 119-96 against Platonism.

20. *Timaeus* 28c; Origen, *Against Celsus* 7.42.

21. On the translation of *Life of Plotinus* 16.1-2 see Igal (1982).

22. See Puech (1960), Elsas (1975), Edwards (1990).

23. *Enneads* 2.9.10; cf. *Life of Plotinus* 1.

24. 1 Corinthians 2.8, 2 Corinthians 4.4, Ephesians 6.12, John 3.31 and 8.44.

25. See e.g. Origen, *First Principles* 3.5.6, 4.4.6.

26. Justin, *First Apology* 10.2; Augustine, *Confessions* 12.29.

27. [Origen], *Philokalia* 24 etc.

28. Exodus 25.40; Origen, *First Principles* 4.2.6 etc.

29. Origen, *First Principles* 3.5.3; Augustine, *City of God* 11.4-6.

30. Philoponus, *Commentary on Physics* 428.25-429.12 Vitelli, commenting on *Physics* 204b7.

31. Edwards (2002), 89-101.

32. *Commentary on John* 2.10-14; Methodius, *On the Resurrection* in Epiphanius, *Panarion* 64. Cf. *Commentary on Romans* 7.8, *First Principles* 1.8.4 and Pamphilus, *Apology for Origen* 10.1.

33. Kruger (1996), 35-132.

34. Urbach (1973), 220, though the 'pagan' Antoninus persuades Rabbi Judah to give up this position.

35. *To Gaurus*, with the commentary of Festugière (1954), 265-305.

36. Tertullian, *On the Soul* 27; Augustine, *On Genesis according to the Letter* 14.23-17.31.

37. Genesis 1.26-8, 1 Corinthians 10.111; Irenaeus, *Against Heresies* 5.6.1; Origen, *First Principles* 3.6.1.

38. Colossians 1.15; Philippians 2.6; Irenaeus, *Against Heresies* 5.16; Ephesians 4.9.

39. O'Meara (1974) maintains that this describes a habitual state of intellectual rapture rather than a fugitive experience of communion with the ineffable. It is certainly not accompanied by self-consciousness, as Rist (1989) demonstrates, citing *Enneads* 1.4.10.22f and 4.4.234f.

40. 275.19. Chadwick (1959), 142 surmises that the allusion is to the writing of a work against the Christians.

41. 282.9; cf. *Republic* 617e.

42. 277.22.

43. Cf. *Odyssey* 1.1.

44. Or rather, not yet: cf. Galatians 3.28. That the feminine must become male is, however, affirmed in writings later declared to be heterodox: *Gospel of Thomas* 105, Clement, *Excerpts from Theodotus* 63.

45. Certainly to Genesis 2.22 at 1 Timothy 2.13 (though Pauline authorship is disputed); probably to Genesis 6.1, and to the associated tradition about the fall of angels, at 1 Corinthians 11.10.

Glossary of Historical and Philosophical Terms

akousmatikos: one whose conduct is governed by a literal construction of the precepts handed down in the name of Pythagoras.

consul: one of the two chief officers of the senate, appointed annually to lead the armies. In imperial times, the Emperor was often one of the consuls and the office itself was vestigial.

Cynic: a philosopher distinguished by frugality and habitual insolence.

demiurge: divine creator of the visible and/or the intelligible universe.

diadokhos: the head of a philosophical school, considered as a successor to the founder.

dunamis: power to cause an effect, or (in a substrate) the capacity to be affected.

dyad: the archetypal number two.

eidos: the idea, particularly when it informs matter.

energeia: the perfect actuality to which a thing aspires, or the activity which expresses this perfection.

Epicurean: follower of Epicurus, who taught that the goal of life is to cultivate pleasure and extinguish pain.

form: see *idea*.

Hellenistic: belonging to the period between the death of Alexander the Great in 323 BC and the Roman conquest of Egypt in 30 BC.

hermêneia: semantic content, lexical meaning or the critical investigation of these.

hulê: matter, i.e. the substrate of properties, source of divisibility and possibility in the products of soul.

hypercosmic: superior to the visible universe.

idea: the eternal archetype of a virtue, quality or natural kind.

intellect: see *nous*.

intellectual: see noeric.

intelligible: see noetic.

impassible: not liable to suffering.

mathêmatikos: one who professes to follow the esoteric teachings of Pythagoras; also, a mathematician or an astrologer.

matter: see *hulê*.

monad: the archetypal number one.

noeric: intellectual, pertaining to the discursive intellect.

noetic: intelligible, pertaining to the non-discursive intellect.

nous: intellect, especially the non-discursive intellect.

Peripatetic: a follower of Aristotle.

Principate: that period of Roman imperial history (ending, at the latest, in 284) during which the sovereign professed to be merely the leader of the senate.

protreptic: a rhetorical summons to virtue or philosophy.

psukhê: soul, i.e. the universal principle of life and motion; that which gives form and life to body.

reductio ad absurdum: the disproof of an argument by the exposure of its untenable consequences.

Republic: the Roman commonwealth before the troubles which followed the death of Julius Caesar in 44 BC.

senate: the ruling body of the Roman Republic, the prestige of which in Roman survived the extinction of its political authority under the Empire.

sophist: a man who earned his livelihood by public oratory.

soul: see *psukhê*.

Stoicism: Hellenistic philosophy which taught that the goal of life is to live in accordance with nature, and that virtue consist in the efforts of the will to achieve this goal.

supramundane: see hypercosmic.

tetrarch: one of four rulers of the Roman Empire under the polity introduced by Diocletian in 285. The two most powerful were Augusti (one for the east and one for the west), while the other two were their nominal subordinates and bore the title Caesar.

world-soul: the principle which communicates vitality, regularity and form to the visible universe.

Chronology

Date	Political events	Events in lives of Platonists
204/5		Birth of Plotinus Longinus roughly contemporary
211	Caracalla begins to reign with Geta	
213	Caracalla sole ruler	
215	*Constitutio Antoniniana*	
217	Accession of Heliogabalus	
222	Accession of Alexander Severus	
231/2		Plotinus studies with Ammonius Birth of Porphyry
235	Accession of Maximinus Thrax	
238	Accession of Gordian III	
242/3	Persian campaign	Plotinus leaves Alexandria
244	Accession of Philip the Arab	Plotinus in Rome
245		?Birth of Iamblichus
249	Accession of Decius	
250	Edict for universal sacrifice	
251	Accession of Gallus	
253	Accession of Valerian with Gallienus	
260	Gallienus sole ruler	Longinus teaching Porphyry in Athens
263/4	Decennalia of Gallienus	Porphyry comes to Rome
268	Accession of Claudius Gothicus	Porphyry and Amelius leave Rome
269	Plague in Rome	Plotinus mortally ill
270	Accession of Aurelian Fall of Palmyra	Death of Plotinus Death of Longinus
275	Accession of Probus	
282	Accession of Carus	
283	Accession of Carinus and Numerian	
284/5	Accession of Diocletian	
299	First measures against Christians	*?Life of Plotinus, Enneads*
303	Great persecution of Christians begins	?Porphyry, *Against the Christians* *?Letter to Marcella*
305	Abdication of Diocletian and Maximian Constantius and Galerius made Augusti	?Death of Porphyry
306	Usurpation of Constantine and Maxentius	

Date	Political events	Events in lives of Platonists
308	Licinius made Augustus	
311	Death of Galerius	
	Licinius and Maximinus contest power in the east	
312	Constantine defeats Maxentius	
313	Licinius defeats Maximinus	
324	Constantine defeats Licinius and rules as sole Emperor	
326/7		?Death of Iamblichus

Bibliography

Primary sources

Texts and translations of most classical authors (including Plato, Aristotle, Philo, Plutarch, Augustine) are available in the Loeb Classical Library. Plato, Aristotle and Plutarch are cited by standard pagination, others by the recognised chapter divisions. Most of the following works are cited by editor's pagination or numbering of fragments.

Albinus, *Isagoge*, and Alcinous, *Isagoge* or *Didascalicus*, ed. C.F. Hermann in *Platonis Opera*, vol. 6, 1880, 147-89 (Leipzig). Text (as *Epitome*) with French translation: J. Whittaker, 1990 (Paris). Translation: Dillon (1993).

Alexander of Aphrodisias, *De Fato* (*On Fate*), ed. and trans. R.W. Sharples with excerpts from *Mantissa,* 1983 (London). Many other works now translated in Ancient Commentators on Aristotle series, ed. R. Sorabji (London).

Apuleius, *Oeuvres Philosophiques*, ed. J. Beaujeu, 1973 (Paris).

Atticus, *Fragments*, ed. with French translation: J. Baudry, 1931 and E. Des Places, 1977 (Paris).

Boethius, *Commentarium in Librum Aristotelis* Περί Ἑρμηνείας (*Commentary on Aristotle's On Interpetation*), vol. 2, ed. C. Meiser, 1880 (Leipzig).

Chaldaean Oracles, ed. as *Oracles Chaldaïques*, E. Des Places, 1971 (Paris).

———— ed. with English translation, R. Majercik, 1989 (Leiden).

Clement of Alexandria, *Excerpta ex Theodoto* (*Excerpts from Theodotus*), ed. & trans. R.P. Casey, 1934 (Cambridge).

———— *Stromata*, I-VI (*Werke*, vol. 2), ed. O. Stählin, 3rd edn, 1960 (Berlin).

Damascius, *In Platonis Philebum Commentaria I et II* (*Commentary on Philebus*) ed. L.G. Westerink, 1959 (Amsterdam).

———— *Dubitationes et solutiones de primis principiis* (*Problems and Solutions*), ed. C.A. Ruelle, 1889 (Paris).

Epiphanius, *Panarion* II, ed. K. Holl and J. Dummer (Berlin).

Eunapius, *Vitae Sophistarum* (*Lives of the Sophists*), ed. J.F. Boissonade, with Philostratus, *Vitae Sophistarum,* 1849 (Paris). Text with translation also in Loeb Classical Library.

Eusebius of Caesarea, *Contra Marcellum* (*Against Marcellus*) and *De Ecclesiastica Theologia* (*Ecclesiastical Theology*), ed. E. Klostermann, 1972 (Berlin).

———— *Praeparatio Evangelica* (*Gospel Preparation*), ed. with translation E.H. Gifford, 5 vols, 1903 (Oxford).

Firmicus Maternus, *Mathesis*, ed. W. Kroll and F. Skutsch, 1913 (Leipzig).

———— *De Errore Profanarum Religionum* (*On the Error of Profane Religions*), ed. R. Turcan, 1982 (Paris).

Heraclitus the Allegorist, *Allégories d'Homère*, ed. F. Buffière, 1962 (Paris).

Hermetica, ed. A.D. Nock and A.-J. Festugière, 4 vols, 1946-54 (Paris). Translation: Copenhaver (1992). See also Scott (1936).

Hippolytus, *Refutatio Omnium Haeresium* (*Refutation*), ed. M. Marcovich, 1986 (Berlin).

185

Iamblichus, *Commentaries*, see Dillon (1973).

———— *De Anima* (*On the Soul*), cited from Stobaeus 1, 353.23-458.23 Wachsmuth.

———— *De Communi Mathematica Scientia* (*On the Common Science of Mathematics*), ed. N. Festa, 1975 (Leipzig).

———— *De Vita Pythagorica* (*On the Pythagorean Life*), ed. F. Dubner, 1957 (Leipzig). Translation: E.G. Clark (Liverpool, 1989).

———— *De Mysteriis* (*On the Mysteries*), ed. as *Les Mystères d'Égypte*, E. Des Places, 1966 (Paris). Translation: Clark, Dillon and Hershbell (2003).

———— *In Nicomachi Arithmeticam Instructionem Liber* (*Commentary on Nicomachus*), ed. H. Pistelli, 1894 (Leipzig).

———— *Protrepticus*, ed. as *Protreptique*, E. Des Places, 1989 (Paris).

———— *Theologoumena Arithmeticae* (*Theology of Arithmetic*), ed. V. de Falco, 1922 (Leipzig).

Irenaeus, *Adversus Haereses* (*Against Heresies*), edited with French translation (*Contre les Hérésies*), A. Roussell and L. Doutreleau, 10 vols, 1965-82 (Paris).

Justin Martyr, *Apologies*, ed. A. Wartelle, 1987 (Paris).

Longinus, *De Sublimitate*, ed. with fragments of rhetorical works, A.O. Prickard, 1906 (Oxford). See also the edition of the fragments by Brisson, 2001 (Paris).

Lydus, John, *De Mensibus* (*On Months*), ed. R. Wunsch, 1967 (Stuttgart), reprint of 1898 edn.

Marinus, *Proclus*, ed. H.-D. Saffrey, 2001 (Paris). Translation: Edwards (2000) below.

Maximus of Tyre, *Philosophoumena*, ed. H. Hobein, 1910 (Leipzig).

Macrobius, *Commentarii in Somnium Scipionis* (*Commentary on Dream of Scipio*), ed. J. Willies, 1963 (Leipzig).

Nag Hammadi Codices (including *Gospel of Thomas, Zostrianus, Allogenes, Apocryphon of John*), translation ed. J.M. Robinson, 1988 (Leiden).

Numenius, *Fragments*, ed. E. Des Places, 1973 (Paris).

Origen, *Commentary on John*, ed. as *Johanneskommentar*, E. Preuschen, 1903 (Leipzig).

———— *Commentary on Romans*, ed. as *Römerbriefkommentar*, C.P. Bammel, 3 vols, 1990-98 (Freiburg).

———— *Contra Celsum* (*Against Celsus*), ed. as *Gegen Celsus* with other works, P. Koetschau, 2 vols, 1899 (Leipzig). Translation: H. Chadwick, 1980 (Cambridge).

———— *De Oratione* (*On Prayer*) appears as *Die Schrift über Gebet* in above, vol. 2.

———— *De Principiis* (*First Principles*), ed. P. Koetschau, 1913 (Leipzig). Also ed. as *Traité des Principes*, H. Crouzel, 4 vols, 1976-80 (Paris). Translation: G.W. Butterworth, 1972 (Gloucester, Mass.).

———— *Homilia ad Canticum* (*Homilies on Song of Songs*), ed. as *Homilien zum Hohenlied* with other works, W. Baehrens, 1925 (Leipzig).

———— *Philokalia*, ed. J.A. Robinson, 1893 (Cambridge).

Philoponus, John, *De Aeternitate Mundi* (*On the Eternity of the World*), ed. H. Rabe, 1899 (Leipzig).

———— *In Aristotelis Physicorum Libros Commentaria* (*Commentary on Physics*), ed, H. Vitelli, 1887 (Berlin). Translation of Book 3: M.J. Edwards, 1994 (London).

Plotinus, *Enneads*, ed. E. Bréhier, 7 vols, 1924-8 (Paris).

———— ed. P. Henry and H.-R. Schwyzer, 3 vols, 1964 (Oxford).

———— ed. A.H. Armstrong, 7 vols, 1966-88 (New York/London). Translation: Armstrong (Loeb Classical Library).

Bibliography

Porphyry, *Ad Gaurum* (*To Gaurus*), ed. K. Kalbfleisch, *Abhandlungen der Königlichen Preussischen Akademie der Wissenschafte*, 1895 (Berlin), 33-62.
———— *Commentary on Parmenides*, in Hadot (1968), vol. 2.
———— *Contra Christianos* (*Against the Christians*), ed. as *Gegen die Christlicher* by A. Harnack, *Abhandlungen der Königlichen Preussischen Akademie der Wissenschafte*, 1916 (Berlin).
———— *Fragmenta*, ed. A. Smith, 1993 (Leipzig). Includes *De Statuis* (*On Statues*), *De Philosophia ex Oraculis Haurienda* (*Philosophy from Oracles*), *De Styge* (*On the Styx*), *Quaestiones Homericae* (*Homeric Questions*).
———— *In Platonis Timaeum Fragmenta* (*Timaeus Commentary*), ed. A. Sodano, 1964 (Naples). References in this volume, however, are to Proclus.
———— *In Ptolemaei Harmonica* (*On Ptolemy's Harmonics*), ed. I. Düring, 1932 (Göteborg).
———— *Isagoge* and *Commentary on Categories*, ed. A. Busse, 1887 (Berlin). Translations: *Isagoge*, Barnes (2003) below; *Commentary*, S. Strange, 1992 (London/Ithaca).
———— *Opuscula Selecta*, ed. A. Nauck, 1886 (Leipzig). Includes *Vita Pythagorae* (*Life of Pythagoras*), *De Abstinentia* (*On Abstinence*), *De Antro Nympharum* (*Cave of the Nymphs*), *Ad Marcellam* (*Letter to Marcella*). Translation of *On Abstinence*: E.G. Clark, 2000 (London/Ithaca).
———— *Sententiae* (*Aphorisms*), ed. E. Lamberz, 1975 (Leipzig).
———— *Symmikta Zetemata* (*Miscellaneous Questions*), ed. H. Dörrie, 1959 (Munich).
———— *Vita Plotini* (*On the Life of Plotinus and the Arrangement of his Works*), appears as introduction to all editions of Plotinus. Also edited separately by P. Kalligas, 1991 (Athens) and as *Vie de Plotin* by L. Brisson, 1992 (Paris) with a volume of *Études Préliminaires* (1982). Translation: Armstrong (above), Edwards (2000).
Proclus, *In Platonis Rem Publicam Commentarii* (*Commentary on Republic*), ed. W. Kroll, 2 vols, 1899-1901 (Leipzig).
———— *In Platonis Timaeum Commentaria*, ed. E. Diehl, 3 vols, 1903-6 (Leipzig).
Prolegomena to Plato, ed. G.L. Westerink, French trans. J. Trouillard, 1990 (Paris).
Psellus, M., cited from *Patrologia Graeca*, ed. J.-P. Migne, vol. 122.
Simplicius, *In Aristotelis Categorias Commentarium* (*Commentary on Categories*), ed. C. Kalbfleisch, 1907 (Berlin).
———— *In Aristotelis Physicorum libros Commentaria*, ed. H. Diels, 2 vols, 1882-95 (Berlin).
Stobaeus, *Anthologium, libri duo priores*, ed. C. Wachsmuth, 2 vols, 1884 (Berlin).
Suda, ed. A. Adler, 1935 (Leipzig).
Syrianus, *In Hermogenem commentaria*, vol. 2 (*Commentary on Hermogenes*), ed. H. Rabe, 1893 (Lepzig).
Tertullian, *De Anima* (*On the Soul*), ed. J. Waszink, 1959 (Amsterdam).
Theophrastus, *Metaphysica*, ed. as *Metafisici* by S. Romani (Milan).

Secondary sources

Alt, K. (1993), *Weltflucht und Weltbejahung. Zur Frage des Dualismus bei Plutarch, Numenios, Plotin* (Mainz).
Annas, J. (1981), *An Introduction to Plato's Republic* (Oxford).
Armstrong, A.H. (1936), 'Plotinus and India', *Classical Quarterly* 30, 22-8.

Bibliography

―――― (1955-6), 'Was Plotinus a Magician?', *Phronesis* 1, 73-9.

―――― (1960), 'The Origin of the Doctrine that the Intelligibles are not Outside the Intellect', Entretiens Hardt 5: *Les Sources de Plotin* (Geneva), 391-425.

Atkinson, M. (1980), *Plotinus: Enneads V.1* (Oxford).

Barnes, J. (1989), 'Antiochus of Ascalon', in M. Griffin and J. Barnes (eds), *Philosophia Togata. Essays on Roman Philosophy and Society* (Oxford), 81-96.

―――― (2003), *Porphyry, Introduction* (Oxford).

Baumgarten, A. (1981), *The Phoenician History of Philo of Byblos* (Leiden).

Beatrice, P.F. (1991), 'Le traité de Porphyre contre les chrétiens: l'état de la question', *Kernos* 4, 119-38.

Bechtle, G. (2000), 'The Question of Being and the Dating of the Anonymous *Parmenides* Commentary', *Ancient Philosophy* 20, 393-414.

Beierwaltes, W. (1999), '*Causa Sui*: Plotins Begriff des Einen als Ursprung des Gedankens der Selbtsursächlichkeit', in J. Cleary (ed.), *Traditions of Platonism* (Aldershot), 191-226.

Bidez, J. (1913), *Vie de Porphyre* (Ghent).

―――― (1919), 'Le philosophe Jamblique et son école', *Revue des Études Grecques* 27, 29-40.

Blois, L. de (1989), 'Plotinus and Gallienus', *Instrumenta Patristica* 19, 69-82.

Blumenthal, H.J. (1996), 'On Soul and Intellect', in Gerson, *Companion*, 82-104.

Böhm, T. (2002), 'Origenes – Theologe und (Neu-)Platonischer', *Adamantius* 8, 7-23.

Brisson, L. (1987), 'Amélius: sa vie, son oeuvre, sa doctrine', *Aufstieg und Niedergang der Römischen Welt* 2.36.2, 793-860.

―――― (1990), L'oracle d'Apollon dans la *Vie de Plotin* par Porphyre', *Kernos* 3, 77-88.

Brittain, C. (2001), *Philo of Larissa. The Last of the Academic Sceptics* (Oxford).

Burkert, W. (1972), *Lore and Science in Early Pythagoreanism* (Cambridge, Mass.).

Cameron, A. (1968), 'The Date of Iamblichus' Birth', *Hermes* 96. 374-6.

Chadwick, H. (1959), *The Sentences of Sextus* (Cambridge).

Cherniss, H. (1944), *Aristotle's Criticism of Plato and the Academy*, vol. 1 (Baltimore, sole volume).

―――― *The Riddle of the Academy* (Berkeley 1945).

Chroust, A. (1973), *Aristotle: Observations on Some of his Lost Works* (London).

Clark, E., Dillon, J., Hershbell, J. (2003), *Iamblichus: On the Mysteries* (Atlanta).

Copenhaver, B. (1992), *Hermetica* (Cambridge).

Corrigan, K. (1985), 'Body's Approach to Soul: an Examination of a Recurrent Theme in the *Enneads*', *Dionysius* 9, 37-52.

―――― (1986), 'Is there more than one Generation of Matter in the *Enneads*?', *Phronesis* 31, 167-81.

―――― (1987), 'Amelius, Plotinus and Porphyry on Beauty, Intellect and the One', *Aufstieg und Niedergang der Römischen Welt* 2.36.2, 975-93.

Courcelle, P. (1953), 'Les sages de Porphyre et les *viri novi* d'Arnobe', *Revue des Études Latines* 31, 257-71.

Cremer, H. (1969), *Die Chaldaïsche Orakel und Jamblich*, De Mysteriis (Meisenheim).

Crombie, I. (1963), *An Examination of Plato's Doctrines*, vol. 2 (London).

Cudworth, R. (1820), *True Intellectual System of the Universe*, vol. 3. Reprint of T. Birch's edition (1742) of the 1678 original (London).

Bibliography

Cumont, F. (1912), *Astrology and Magic among the Greeks and Romans*, trans. J. Baker (London).

——— (1919), 'Comment Plotin détourna Porphyre de suicide', *Revue des Études Grecques* 32, 113-20.

Dawson, D. (1992), *Allegorical Readers and Cultural Revision in Ancient Alexandria* (Berkeley).

Deck, A.N. (1967), *Nature, Contemplation and the One* (Toronto).

Deuse, W. (1983), *Untersuchungen zur mittelplatonischen und neuplatonischen Seelenlehre* (Wiesbaden).

Digeser, E.D. (2000), The *Making of a Christian Empire. Lactantius and Rome* (Ithaca, NY).

Dillon, J. (1969), 'A Date for the Death of Nicomachus of Gerasa?', *Classical Review* 19, 274-5.

——— (1972), 'Iamblichus and the Origin of the Doctrine of Henads', *Phronesis* 17, 102-6.

——— (1973), *Iamblichus, In Platonis Dialogos Fragmenta* (Leiden).

——— (1973a), 'The Concept of Two Intellects: a Footnote to the History of Platonism', *Phronesis* 18, 176-85.

——— (1977), *The Middle Platonists* (London).

——— (1983), 'What Happened to Plato's Garden?', *Hermathena* 133, 51-9.

——— (1993), *Alcinous. The Handbook of Platonism* (Oxford).

——— (2003), *The Heirs of Plato. A Study of the Old Academy (347-274 B.C.)* (Oxford).

——— (2005), 'Philosophy as a Profession in Late Antiquity', in A. Smith (ed.), *The Philosopher and Society in Late Antiquity* (Swansea), 1-18.

Dillon, J. and Morrow, G. (1970), *Proclus' Commentary on the Parmenides of Plato* (Ithaca, NY).

Dodds, E.R. (1928), 'The *Parmenides* of Plato and the Neoplatonic One', *Classical Quarterly* 22, 129-45.

——— (1960a), 'Numenius and Ammonius', Entretiens Hardt 5: *Les Sources de Plotin* (Geneva), 3-51.

——— (1960b), 'Tradition and Personal Achievement in Plotinus', *Journal of Roman Studies* 50, 1-7.

——— (1965), *Pagan and Christian in an Age of Anxiety* (Cambridge).

Dörrie, H. (1955), 'Ammonios, der Lehrer Plotins', *Hermes* 83, 439-77.

Edwards, M.J. (1988), 'Scenes from the Later Wanderings of Odysseus', *Classical Quarterly* 38, 509-21.

——— (1989), 'Numenius, Fr. 13: A Note on Interpretation', *Mnemosyne* 42, 478-83.

——— (1990a), 'Neglected Texts in the Study of Gnosticism', *Journal of Theological Studies* 41, 26-50.

——— (1990b), 'Numenius, Pherecydes and the *Cave of the Nymphs*', *Classical Quarterly* 40, 258-62.

——— (1990c), 'Porphyry and the Intelligible Triad', *Journal of Hellenic Studies* 110, 14-25.

——— (1990d), 'A Late Use of Empedocles: the *Oracle on Plotinus*', *Mnemosyne* 43, 151-5.

——— (1993a), 'Ammonius, Teacher of Origen', *Journal of Ecclesiastical History* 44, 1-13.

——— (1993b), 'A Portrait of Plotinus', *Classical Quarterly* 43, 480-90.

—— (1996), 'Porphyry's *Cave of the Nymphs* and the Gnostic Controversy', *Hermes* 124, 88-100.

—— (1999), 'Neoplatonism', in A. Fitzgerald (ed.), *Augustine through the Ages* (Grand Rapids), 588-91.

—— (2000a), *Neoplatonic Saints. The Lives of Plotinus and Proclus by their Pupils* (Liverpool).

—— (2000b), 'Birth, Death and Divinity in Porphyry's *Life of Plotinus*', in T. Hägg and P. Rousseau (eds), *Greek Biography and Panegyric in Late Antiquity* (Berkeley), 52-71.

—— (2007), 'Porphyry and the Christians', forthcoming in *Bulletin of the Institute of Classical Studies*.

Eitrem, S. (1942), 'La théurgie chez les néo-platoniciens et dans les papyrus magiques', *Symbolae Osloenses* 22, 48-79.

Elsas, G. (1975), *Neuplatonische und Gnostische Weltablehnung in der Schüle Plotins* (Amsterdam).

Festugière, A.-J. (1944), *La révélation d'Hermès Trismégiste, I: L'astrologie et les sciences occultes* (Paris).

—— (1954), *La révélation d'Hermès Trismégiste, III: Le Dieu inconnu et la gnose* (Paris).

Finamore, J. (1985), *Iamblichus and the Theory of the Vehicle of the Soul* (Chico, California).

Gerson, L. (1994), *Plotinus* (London).

——, ed. (1996), *The Cambridge Companion to Plotinus* (Cambridge).

—— (2003), *Aristotle and other Platonists* (Ithaca, NY).

Gleadow, R. (1968), *The Origin of the Zodiac* (London).

Glucker, J. (1978), *Antiochus of Ascalon and the Late Academy* (Göttingen).

Goulet, R. (1982), 'Variations romanesques sur la mélancolie de Porphyre', *Hermes* 110, 443-57.

Graham, D. (1987), *Aristotle's Two Systems* (Oxford).

Grmek, M.D. (1992), 'Les maladies et la mort de Plotin', in L. Brisson (ed.), *Vie de Plotin*, 335-54.

Gwyn Griffiths, J. (1996), *Triads and Trinity* (Cardiff).

Hadot, P. (1960), 'Être, vie, pensée chez Plotin et avant Plotin', Entretiens Hardt 5: *Les Sources de Plotin* (Geneva), 107-37.

—— (1961), 'Fragments d'un commentaire de Porphyre sur le *Parménide*', *Revue des Etudes Grecques* 74, 410-38.

—— (1967), 'La Métaphysique de Porphyre', Entretiens Hardt 12: *Porphyre* (Geneva), 123-62.

—— (1968), *Porphyre et Victorinus*, 2 vols (Paris)

—— (1990), 'The Harmony of Plato and Aristotle according to Porphyry', in R. Sorabji (ed.), *Aristotle Transformed* (London 1990), 125-40.

Hankins, J. (1990), *Plato in the Italian Renaissance* (Leiden).

Harder, R. (1960), 'Zur biographie Plotins', in *Kleine Schriften* (Munich), 277-82.

Heath, M. (1999), 'Longinus, On Sublimity', *Proceedings of the Cambridge Philological Society* 45, 43-74.

—— (2002), 'Porphyry's Rhetoric: Texts and Translation', *Leeds International Classical Studies* 1.5, 1-38.

—— (2003), 'Porphyry's Rhetoric', *Classical Quarterly* 53, 141-66.

Henry, P. (1934), *Plotin et l'occident* (Paris).

—— (1953), 'La dernière parole de Plotin', *Studi Classici Orientali* 2, 116-17.

Hijmans, B.J. (1987), 'Apuleius, Philosophus Platonicus', *Aufstieg und Niedergang der Römischen Welt* 2.36.1, 395-475.

Hirschle, M. (1979), *Sprachphilosophie und Namenmagie im Neuplatonismus* (Meisenheim).

Igal, J. (1982), 'The Gnostics and the Ancient Philosophy in Plotinus', in H.J. Blumenthal and R.A. Markus (eds), *Neoplatonism and Early Christian Thought* (London), 138-49.

—— (1982), *La Cronologia de la Vida de Plotino de Porfirio* (Deusto).

Inge, W.R. (1911-12), *The Philosophy of Plotinus*, 2 vols (London).

Jaeger, W. (1948), *Aristotle: Fundamentals of the History of his Development,* trans. R. Robinson (Oxford).

Johnston, S.I. (1990), *Hekate Soteira* (Atlanta).

Kahn, C. (1992), 'Aristotle on Thinking', in A.O. Rorty and M. Nussbaum (eds), *Essays on Aristotle's* De Anima (Oxford), 259-79.

Kalligas, P. (1997), 'Forms of Individuals in Plotinus: a Re-Examination', *Phronesis* 42, 206-27.

—— (2001), 'Traces of Longinus' Library in Eusebius' *Praeparatio Evangelica',* *Classical Quarterly* 51, 584-99.

Keaveney, A. and Madden, J.A. (1982), 'Phthiriasis and its Victims', *Symbolae Osoloenses* 57, 87-100.

Kelly, J.N.D. (1972), *Early Christian Creeds* (Oxford).

Kingsley, P. (1995), *Ancient Philosophy, Mystery and Magic* (Oxford).

Krämer, H.-J. (1990), *Plato and the Foundations of Metaphysics*, trans. J.R. Catan (Albany).

Kroll, W. (1892), 'Ein Neuplatonisches Parmenideskommentar in einem Turiner Palimpsest', *Rheinisches Museum* 47, 599-627.

Kruger, M. (1996), *Ichgeburt* (Hildesheim).

Lamberton, R. (1986), *Homer the Theologian* (Berkeley).

Lang, P. (1965), *De Speusippi Academici Scriptis*, reprint of 1911 edn (Frankfurt).

Langerbeck, H. (1957), 'The Philosophy of Ammonius Saccas', *Journal of Hellenic Studies* 77, 67-74.

Leroux, G. (1990), *Plotin: traité sur la liberté et la volonté de l'Un [Enneades VI.8 (39)]* (Paris).

Lloyd, A.C. (1987), 'Plotinus on the Genesis of Thought and Existence', *Oxford Studies in Ancient Philosophy* 5, 155-86.

L'Orange, P. (1951), 'The Portrait of Plotinus', *Cahiers Archéologiques* 5, 15-30.

Maier, P. (1992), *Plotinus on the One or the Good (Enneads VI.9)* (Amsterdam).

Majercik, R. (1992), 'The Existence-Life-Intellect Triad in Gnosticism and Neoplatonism', *Classical Quarterly* 42, 475-88.

—— (2005), 'Porphyry and Gnosticism', *Classical Quarterly* 55, 277-92.

Merlan, P. (1944), 'Plotinus and Magic', *Isis* 341-8.

Most, G. (2003), 'Plotinus' Last Words', *Classical Quarterly* 53, 376-87.

Murray, G. (1935), *Five Stages of Greek Religion* (London).

Nilsson, M. (1926), *History of Greek Religion* (London).

O'Brien, D. (1981), 'Plotinus on the Generation of Matter', in H.J. Blumenthal and R.A. Markus, *Neoplatonism and Early Christian Thought* (London), 108-23.

Olmstead, A.T. (1942), 'The Mid-Third Century of the Christian Era', *Classical Philology* 37, 241-62 and 398-420.

O'Meara, D.J. (1974), 'A propos d'un témoignage sur l'expérience mystique de Plotin', *Mnemosyne* 27, 238-44.

————— (1989), *Pythagoras Revived: Mathematics and Philosophy in Late Antiquity* (Oxford).

————— (1992), 'The Freedom of the One', *Phronesis* 37, 343-9.

————— (1993), 'Aspects of Political Philosophy in Iamblichus', in H.J. Blumenthal and E.G. Clark (eds), *The Divine Iamblichus* (London), 65-73.

————— (1999), 'Forms of Individuals in Plotinus: a Preface to the Question', in J. Cleary (ed.), *Traditions of Platonism* (Aldershot), 263-70.

————— (2003), *Platonopolis. Neoplatonic Political Theory in Late Antiquity* (Oxford).

O'Meara, J.J. (1959), *Porphyry's Philosophy from Oracles in Augustine* (Paris).

Parke, H.W. and Wormell, D.E.W. (1986), *The Delphic Oracle*, vol. 2: *The Oracular Responses* (Oxford).

Pépin, J. (1967), 'Porphyre, Exégète d'Homère', Entretiens Hardt 12: *Porphyre* (Geneva), 229-72.

Praechter, K. (1916), 'Zum Platoniker Gaios', *Hermes* 51, 510-29.

Reale, G. (1997), *Towards a New Interpretation of Plato*, tr. J.R. Catan and R. Davies (Washington DC).

Rich, A.M. (1954), 'The Platonic Ideas as Thoughts of God', *Mnemosyne* 7, 123-33.

Rist, J.M. (1961), 'Plotinus on Matter and Evil', *Phronesis* 6, 154-66.

————— (1962a), '*Theos* and the One in some Texts of Plotinus', *Medieval Studies* 24, 169-80.

————— (1962b), 'The Indefinite Dyad and Intelligible Matter in Plotinus', *Classical Quarterly* 12, 99-107.

————— (1963), 'Forms of Individuals in Plotinus', *Classical Quarterly* 13, 223-31.

————— (1967), *Plotinus. The Road to Reality* (Cambridge).

————— (1989), 'Back to the Mysticism of Plotinus', *Journal of the History of Philosophy* 27, 183-97.

Rives, J. (1999), 'The Decian Decree and the Religion of the Empire', *Journal of Roman Studies* 89, 239-54.

Rohde, E. (1871-2), 'Die Quelle des Iamblichus in seine Biographie des Pythagoras', *Rheinisches Museum* 26, 554-76 and 27, 23-61.

Rostovtzeff, M. (1926), *Social and Economic History of the Roman Empire*, 2 vols (Oxford)

Rutter, C. (1956), 'La doctrine des deux actes dans la philosophie de Plotin', *Revue Philosophique* 106, 100-6.

Saffrey, H.-D., (1971), 'Abamon, pseudonyme de Jamblique', in R.B. Palmer and K.G. Hammerton-Kelly (eds), *Philomathes. Studies and Essays in the Humanities in Memory of Philip Merlan* (The Hague), 227-39.

————— (1981), 'Les néoplatoniciens et les oracles chaldaïques', *Revue des Études Augustiniennes* 27, 209-25.

Schroeder, F.M. (1987), 'Ammonios Saccas', *Aufstieg und Niedergang der Römischen Welt* 2.36.1, 493-526.

————— (1996), 'Plotinus and Language', in Gerson, *Companion*, 336-55.

Schroeder, F.M. and R.D. Todd (1990), *Two Aristotelian Commentators on the Intellect* (Toronto).

Scott, W.B. (1936), *Hermetica IV* (Oxford).

Sedley, D. (1989), 'Philosophical Allegiance in the Roman World', in M. Griffin and J. Barnes (eds), *Philosophia Togata. Essays on Roman Philosophy and Society* (Oxford), 97-119.

Shaw, G. (1995), *Theurgy and the Soul* (University Park, Pennsylvania).

Smith, A. (1974), *Porphyry's Place in the Neoplatonic Tradition* (The Hague).

———— (1971), 'Did Porphyry Reject the Transmigration of Human Souls into Animals?', *Rheinisches Museum* 127, 276-84.

Simmons, M.B. (1995), *Arnobius of Sicca* (Oxford).

Snyder, H.G. (2000), *Teachers and Texts in the Ancient World* (London).

Sorabji, R. (1983), *Time, Creation and the Continuum* (London).

Strutwolf, H. (1999), *Die Trinitätstheologie und Christologie des Eusebs von Caesarea* (Göttingen).

Swain, S.C.R. and Edwards, M.J. (2004), *Approaching Late Antiquity* (Oxford).

Tarrant, H. (1993), *Thrasyllan Platonism* (Ithaca, NY).

Tester, J. (1987), *A History of Western Astrology* (Woodbridge, Suffolk).

Urbach, E.E. (1973), *The Sages*, trans. I Abraham (Cambridge, Mass.).

Vogel, C. de (1969), *Philosophia*, part 1 (Assen).

Walzer, R. (1949), *Galen on Jews and Christians* (Oxford).

Watson, G. (1988), *Phantasia in Classical Thought* (Galway).

Weiske, B. (1809), *Dionysii Longini De Sublimitate* (Leipzig).

Whittaker, J. (1969), 'Ammonius on the Delphic E', *Classical Quarterly* 19, 185-92.

———— (1973), 'Moses Atticizing', *Phoenix* 21, 196-201.

———— (1987), 'Platonic Philosophy in the Early Centuries of the Empire', *Aufstieg und Niedergang der Römischen Welt* 2.36.1, 87-123.

Zambon, M. (2002), *Porphyre et le moyen-platonisme* (Paris).

Zucker, F. (1950), 'Plotin und Lykopolis', *Sitzungsberichte der deutschen Akademie der Wissenschaften zu Berlin, Klasse für Sprache, Literatur und Kunst* (Berlin), 3-20.

Index